Praise for *Jungle Jean*

"*Jungle Jean* is the personal story of Jean Liedloff, the woman who wrote *The Continuum Concept,* a now-classic book about her adventures living with native rainforest tribes in the 1950s and '60s. These 'original people' reared their children to be linked, not ranked, and their human nature was untouched by oppressive patriarchal structures. Her book, plus this biography, shows how we can make the journey back to a society characterized by cooperation and joy."

—Gloria Steinem, *The Revolution Within*, and
Outrageous Acts and Everyday Rebellions

"Jean's legacy lives on in the lives of many families. The principles of intuitive parenting she witnessed in the Amazon rainforest and wrote about in *The Continuum Concept* are valued worldwide. The veracity of those principles is supported by decades of experience with Attachment Parenting, and now backed by modern science. In *Jungle Jean* her legacy continues. This riveting read gives parents tools to raise more competent and confident children, and to follow their 'mommy brain.'"

—William Sears, M.D, co-author of
The Attachment Parenting Book

"A refreshing view of human nature. *Jungle Jean* shows that we truly are designed to be happy."

—Marci Shimoff, *New York Times*
bestselling author of *Happy for No Reason*

"A unique and compelling story of explorer, author, and child-rearing maverick Jean Liedloff, told by her faithful friend Geralyn Gendreau. This biography is full of psychological drama, exotic locales, love lost and regained—all serving as a backdrop to deep insights into how early childhood experiences shape and mis-shape our adult lives. With access to Liedloff's private journals, boosted by meticulous research, Gendreau does an excellent job as biographer. She pulls no punches describing her subject's complex personality—a genius sabotaged by her own inner demons."

—Christian de Quincey, Ph.D.,
author of *Radical Knowing:*
Understanding Consciousness Through Relationship

"This compelling story takes you out of your living room and through the wildness of the jungle as you walk hand-in-hand through her personal struggles and profound discoveries. An inspiration to transcend your troubles and find the pattern that connects."

—Anodea Judith, Ph.D., author of *Eastern Body,*
Western Mind and *The Global Heart Awakens*

"Anyone concerned with healing childhood wounds will be deeply informed by the perspective offered in this book. Readers of personal growth books will be moved by powerful insights on how to create secure high-functioning relationships. We can learn a lot from observing the way of life of indigenous people."

—Susan Campbell, Ph.D., author of *Getting Real:*
Ten Truth Skills You Need to Live an Authentic Life

"A deeply moving story told by a master storyteller, this biography shows how our outlook on life impacts our LifeForce energy. *Jungle Jean* offers profound insights into the source of well-being; there are truths here that really can heal you and heal our world." —Deborah King, *New York Times* bestselling author of *Truth Heals*

"I especially enjoyed the interplay between the author and her mentor. Their shared passion for original ideas creates riveting conversations that make this biography unlike any I've read before." —Steve Sisgold, author of *Whole Body Intelligence*

"I picked up this book thinking I'd be reading a cool biography about an adventurous woman, which is true, but this book is so much more. My mind is blown with the revelations I've taken from the story. This is an important life-changing book, a juicy transformative biography of a pioneer and adventurer told by a fearless friend who reveals the shared wounds of the modern-day human condition. You may come for the storytelling, but you'll leave with compassionate understanding for yourself and others. Highly recommended."

—Arielle Ford, author of *The Soulmate Secret*

GERALYN GENDREAU

JUNGLE JEAN

The Life and Times of Jean Liedloff,
the Woman who Transformed Modern Parenting
with The Continuum Concept

PRECISION HOUSE PUBLISHING

Editor: Randy Peyser
Cover and Book Design: Susan Shankin
Precision House Publishing, Ventura, CA

First edition printed in the United States of America
ISBN: 978-1-7367914-1-7
Library of Congress Control Number: 2021908203

Author's Note

I have, in some instances, taken creative license for dramatic effect, most notably with the dialog in scenes Jean unfolded from memories of events that occurred decades earlier. This is a book of memory, and memory has its own story to tell. A few creative orchestrations of time, place, and circumstance were necessary to support the dramatic arc. On two occasions where the actual chronology of the events could not be determined, I've allowed the story to dictate placement. I have preserved the anonymity of those involved where I deemed it necessary. All of these minor adjustments were made in the spirit of sharing Jean Liedloff's deep insight into human nature and bringing her message home to the reader.

*To my mother, whose love and support
carried me through the rough patches
when I nearly lost faith in myself.*

Contents

Prologue   xv

PART ONE

1. Into the Jungle   3
2. The Glade   10
3. Sanema Territory   17
4. Maypole Dance   24
5. Hard to Hear But Good to Know   35
6. The Ile de France   56
7. The European Tour   63
8. Le Bal Oriental   74
9. "Stop the Train!"   86
10. Diamond Hunting   92

11. People of the Canoes   100

12. To Be Truly Seen   109

13. The Unlearning Continues   115

PART TWO

14. The Yequana Way   125

15. Jungle Captive   135

16. The Concrete Jungle   148

17. "Go Home and Be Free"   154

18. The Algorithm of Beauty   163

19. Diamonds Are NOT a Girl's Best Friend   171

20. Wild-eyed and Deeply Inspired   177

21. The Final Expedition   182

22. Questions Asked and Unasked Find Answers   192

23. Commissioned by the Cosmos   207

24. Allowing Human Nature to Work Successfully   214

25. Strong and Agile or Fearful and Fragile?   222

PART THREE

26. Where's Gloria?   235

27. The Push-away   244

28. Here We Go Again   249

29. Continuum Lessons   259

30. Our Secret   267

31. Triple Jeopardy   275

32. The Blind Spot   286

33. "You Be My Boswell"   306

34. The Bird Girl   315

Epilogue   329

Acknowledgments   335

About the Author   341

Prologue

In 1951, a young Manhattan socialite left her familiar life in New York and boarded a luxury liner bound for Europe. Once across the pond, she did a bit of modeling for *Vogue Paris* and took a few odd jobs as a translator, but spent the lion's share of her time sitting alone in cafés with her journal and sketch pad, or hobnobbing with artists, intellectuals, and high-society elites. One particular aristocrat, an Italian count with blonde hair and blue eyes, captured her attention—not for his good looks, but for his reputation as an explorer. When she learned of the count's plan to make another trip to the Venezuelan jungle, she convinced him to take her along. Thus did Jean Liedloff travel to the pristine regions of the Amazon rainforest on a diamond hunting expedition.

Two years later, on her second expedition to the jungle, Jean lost all interest in diamonds. The indigenous people of the Amazon had allowed her to see deeply into our ancestral past and into the heart of human nature. This was the real treasure.

Intrigued by the natural harmony among these forest dwelling people, Jean returned to their region on the far side of Le Gran Sabana[1] again and again. For months at a time, she lived among the Yequana,[2] a rainforest tribe that had successfully resisted contact with the civilized world. Far more sophisticated than we are on many levels, these supposedly "primitive" people lived in a state of blessed good cheer that was anything but savage.

After living for nearly three years with small hunter-gatherer tribes, Jean began to question our fundamental assumptions about what it means to be human. Her time with the Yequana had convinced her that, if we want to optimize for our essential nature, we'd best look at our instinctive way of life as dictated by seven million years of hominid evolution.

The truth she saw was explicit and palpable: the indigenous people were having an entirely different experience of human nature than we do in the Western world. Unlike us, the Yequana expected the inbuilt intelligence of our species to work perfectly—and it did, exquisitely so. The contrast was so stark, it shook her to the core.

Jean couldn't help but wonder why they were having such a good time with the very human nature that gives the rest of us so much trouble.

---

1 Known to the indigenous people of the Amazon as Wek-tá (the "place of mountains"), Le Gran Sabana is one of the most unusual landscapes on Earth. An area of 10,820 km2 (4,180 square miles), it features impenetrable jungles, savannas, countless rivers and waterfalls, deep gorges, vast valleys, and tabletop mesas called tepuis.

2 The tribal name Yequana is more commonly spelled Ye'kuana, but I have opted to use the same spellings of indigenous names and words that Liedloff used in her book.

1994, San Francisco Bay Area, California

I had just finished graduate school and left my job at Pomeroy House, a division of Women's Alcoholism Center (WAC). Pomeroy was a year-long residential treatment program for severe substance abusers. Most of the women were "hopeless cases" who would never have sought treatment if not for the fact that Child Protective Services had taken their kids away. Through WAC's family reunification program, mothers could regain custody of their children if they fulfilled two requirements: they had to remain clean and sober, and live at Pomeroy House with their children for a full year.

When I worked at WAC in the early 1990s, rock cocaine was the street drug of choice. Many of the kids living at Pomeroy were "crack babies." A few of them had fetal alcohol syndrome. Per the agency's Parenting Manual, moms were not permitted to breastfeed. They were forbidden to sleep with their children or lie down with them at all—even for a short nap. These women were taught, required in fact, to leave crying babies alone in their rooms when they wouldn't, or couldn't, go to sleep.

Although I wasn't a parent, these guidelines seemed downright wrong to me. I didn't know a better way; I only knew that my maternal instinct was hopping mad. After a year and a half, I simply could not enforce the rules any longer, so I quit.

While trying to figure out my next career move, I happened upon a book titled *The Chalice and the Blade*, by Riane Eisler. A study in the relational dynamics of societies based on partnership rather than domination, Eisler's book offered a deep dive into cultural evolution. The book explored the tens of thousands of years that humankind lived in a caring, sharing milieu. Her commentary on these peaceful societies activated something deep within me. I started wondering what mothers from an ancient society that worshiped a female deity would write in their Parenting Manual. While sitting with a friend who'd invited me over for afternoon tea, I joked, "If only I could pop into a time machine and revisit prehistoric cultures to find out."

She smiled, said, "You don't need a time machine," and walked across the room to her bookshelf. She returned with a dog-eared paperback and set it on the table. "Just read this."

"*The Continuum Concept*?"

"It's one of the most important books ever written."

I read it that very afternoon. The implications buckled my knees. I wept and wept and wept.

Liedloff's revolutionary concept grew out of informal observations while living among the Yequana, Sanema, and Tauripan tribes of South America in the 1950s, 60s, and early 70s. What she witnessed caused her to question our culture's view of human nature. In time, she arrived at a startling conclusion: that we are innately cooperative and designed to be happy. Furthermore, she cites our ignorance of this fact as the underlying cause of all our psychosocial ills.

Liedloff postulated that humans have a continuum of innate expectations derived from the broader continuum of evolution itself. In other words, we are born to *expect* certain very specific conditions—to experience the light, air, temperature, etc., to which our species adapted during the long, formative process of evolution. Similarly, we innately expect to experience the type of treatment (by parents especially) that allowed our antecedents to survive over hundreds of millennia.

Expectation is a key principle in Liedloff's concept. She argues that nature has endowed human infants with a sophisticated set of expectations as to how they will be treated. They are also equipped with an equally sophisticated set of signals to indicate when they are not getting the expected (i.e., "right") treatment, most notably, for contact with their mother's body during infancy. Moreover, the ramifications for infant nurture are just the beginning: Liedloff extrapolates the continuum concept to the whole human experience, across every stage of life.

Jean's book hit me like a bombshell and blasted my heart wide open. A powerful urge arose in me: I simply had to meet the woman.

According to the author bio on my copy of *The Continuum Concept* (an early edition), Jean Liedloff lived in London. There was no Google at the time, so I wrote a letter to her publisher. A few weeks later, I received a reply with surprising good news: Jean had moved to Sausalito and often gave public talks in San Francisco. She practically lived in my backyard. The letter also included a list of scheduled talks. She'd be giving a lecture in Pacific Heights later that month.

I sweet-talked my Swedish boyfriend, the father of a three-year old, into going with me to hear Jean speak. The venue for the event, a Victorian mansion in Pacific Heights, felt a bit pretentious upon entry. We were greeted warmly and led to a brightly lit front room where thirty people sat in rows. My eyes were drawn to a woman sitting quietly on the padded bench in the large bay window that looked out over Lafayette Park. I recognized her immediately as Jean.

After the host of the evening introduced her, Jean stood up and made her way to the front of the room. Her statuesque bearing broadcast her authority as she stepped up to the lectern.

"Hello, everyone. I'm delighted to see you. Thank you for coming out this evening."

Her accent, a peculiar blend of blue-blooded Manhattanite and British nobility, struck me as unnatural, almost forced; her warmhearted welcome clearly at odds with her stiff body language. But as she began to speak of the Yequana people, her manner softened. She unfolded her theory, taking care not to lose her audience. The tenderness with which she spoke of the tragic effects of what she called "missing experiences" touched a part of me that had been abandoned long ago. Every person in the room sat rapt as she spoke of our common suffering and the trouble we face as a society. Her insights into the root cause of alienation, the sense of separateness that creates so much tension within and between people, moved me to the edge of tears. She touched on difficult topics such as criminality, addiction, and what she termed *anti-self feelings* with that just-right touch of humor that makes it possible to hear painful truths. She even shared the pain of her own sense of loneliness. With gentle, soul-deep wit and playful panache, she called herself a "cat lady" and "spinster." Half an hour into the lecture, I felt so at ease and utterly enchanted, that long-since abandoned part of me wanted to crawl into her lap.

When she finished her talk, Jean stepped away from the lectern and said, "I'm happy to answer any questions."

My hand shot in the air. I don't recall the specifics of my question, only that her reply gave me goosebumps.

For the better part of an hour, Jean answered questions, fielded concerns, and swayed those who would oppose her ideas. Chief among the controversial childrearing practices she advanced were carrying babies in a sling throughout the entire day, and co-sleeping in a "family bed." The more she articulated the finer points of her theory, the more she moved the audience from perplexed into a state of pure awe. By the end of the evening, she had proven herself peerless.

I waited until most of the audience had left to approach her. After the initial niceties, I said, "When I finished graduate school, I found myself scratching my head and thinking: okay, now I know all about psychopathology and neurotic behavior, more than I ever wanted to know. What I really want to know is where are the truly happy, healthy human beings? And, more importantly, how did they get that way? Then I read your book and... "

"Yes," she said. "It's a tragedy that neurotic behavior is seen as normal in our eyes." She reached into her oversized handbag, pulled out a folder, and started flipping through some papers. "I don't seem to have a copy of the article I just wrote for *Mothering Magazine*," she said. "It's titled, 'Normal Neurotics Like Us.' I think you'll enjoy it."

As we spoke, I couldn't help but notice how much her demeanor had changed. She'd been so confident onstage. And now, out of the limelight, she seemed guarded, vigilant, almost afraid. She also had a barely perceptible tic. When asked a question, her head would jerk slightly and, for a millisecond, her face would do a little reverse-grimace.

Jean and I had been talking for a good ten minutes when my boyfriend stepped into view and gave me a look that said, "Can we please leave now?"

"I'm sorry, Jean. I could talk to you for hours. But my date is waiting, and I really must go."

She reached for my arm, saying, "Oh, but darling, I really want you to have a look at that article."

"What article?" I asked.

"*Normal Neurotics Like Us,*" she said. "Why don't you join me for lunch next week?"

Once again: goosebumps.

We met at the Depot Café and Bookstore in Mill Valley, just ten minutes north of San Francisco. Founded in 1896, over forty years before the construction of the Golden Gate Bridge, this idyllic little town sits in a redwood grove at the base of Mount Tamalpais. Named after its primary enterprise (a lumber mill), Mill Valley is home to famous rock-and-rollers, well-known authors, and big-name Hollywood escapees. In the heart of town sits a retired railroad station, the one-time transportation hub for freshly cut lumber destined for San Francisco. But these days, the place buzzes with shoppers milling through boutiques rather than the drone of a lumber saw. West of the former train station is the Depot Plaza, a charming village center that pulses with drum circles and musical laughter.

We sat on the outdoor patio at a table near the plaza. Jean ordered the turkey sandwich; I chose the salad Niçoise. She told me that she had moved to Marin because of its proximity to San Francisco, one of her favorite cities in the world. She'd bought a houseboat in Sausalito because it sounded romantic. Plus, the location bordered on the Golden Gate National Recreation Area—10,000 acres of undeveloped land known as the Marin Headlands.

We small-talked our way through lunch, then ordered tea.

"My big hero as a child was Tarzan," she told me. "But I didn't want to be Jane; I wanted to be a female Tarzan."

"I had a huge crush on Tarzan when I was a little girl," I replied. "I couldn't have been more than five years old. I used to dream of running through the jungle with Ron Ely."

She sat up in her chair and looked me straight in the eye—hard. "Yes, he made an appealing Tarzan, but we didn't have television when I was a child. I only knew Tarzan through books. Read every single one of those novels."

She went on to talk about another favorite book from her childhood: "I must've read *Green Mansions* half a dozen times. I loved Rima the bird girl with her dark hair and lovely chemise made of spider webs. I envied her ability to talk to the birds. To me, the jungle always felt like the original place— where nature has the upper hand, not man."

Then she launched into a series of questions that I later realized were designed to assess both my intelligence and my sensitivity. Twenty minutes later, I took the lead and started asking the questions. By the time we got up to leave, I knew a great deal about her life in New York before her first trip to South America.

I'd also seen a glimpse of a childhood that would make even the most robust among us guarded and vigilant. Rejected at birth by a mother who refused to embrace her newborn babe, Jean struggled with feeling unwelcome and unworthy throughout her life. Like many of us, she'd been wounded in the battle between human nature and Western culture. Like many of us, her chances of becoming a truly happy person were handicapped by a mother-infant bond that wasn't what nature intended.

During this and many more meetings to come, I would hear all about Jean's remarkable, paradoxical life. Over the years, I have grown ever more aware of the significance of her original insights and the power they hold to startle us back to the truth of who we are.

This is Jean's story.

PART ONE

1.

Into the Jungle

The French Archipelago, October 1951

By the time the plane landed at Guadeloupe in the Leeward Islands of the Caribbean, Jean had started to question her motives, and her sanity. It was the last stop before she and the other diamond hunters would fly to Venezuela. The leader of the expedition, Count Enrico Middleton, sensed her trepidation. For the fifth time in as many days, he leaned toward her and said, "There's no shame in changing your mind and turning back." But the prospect of looking for diamonds in the rivers and streams of the jungle held too much allure to abandon, especially having come this far. She was bound for Amazonia and nothing would get in her way. Once they boarded the Aeropostal Alas de Venezuela flight to Simón Bolívar Airport in Caracas, Enrico never again suggested that she change her mind and go home.

When Jean looked out the window of the Douglas DC-4 and first saw the jungle, it looked like a great green ocean that stretched to the horizon on every side. As the plane began its descent, she saw that this ocean was interlaced with waterways. Islands of green were raised high upon assertive mountains, then offered their beauty to the sky on the open hands of plateaus made of sandstone and Precambrian[3] quartz. She marveled at her surroundings as the vast, ever-changing, ever-intact, always perfect landscape awakened a feeling she hadn't felt since childhood.

They deplaned in Caracas under the assault of 80 percent humidity and a temperature of 98° Fahrenheit in the shade. The air was so thick with moisture that breathing became a strain.

They had to overcome many delays before the expedition could begin. Finally, all preparations were made. Enrico hired three men from the Tauripan tribe to be their guides and paddlers. Michu, the leader of the three, spoke Spanish. He pointed to the one-person bench at the front of the canoe, motioned to Jean to sit and said, *"Te sientas en frente."*

Once they pushed off into the river, she shifted in her seat and looked back at Enrico. Her eyes met his. She smiled and mouthed, "Thank you."

---

[3] In Earth's 4.5 billion year history, the Precambrian time is considered a "super eon" that lasted from 4 Billion years ago to approximately 540 million years ago. Life began in the ocean as single-celled bacteria during this era.

Enrico nodded, almost imperceptibly, and looked away.

They traveled up the Caroní River, a small, unexplored tributary of the Carcupi on the far side of the Gran Sabana. The Caroní wove gently, sometimes fiercely, through a vast expanse of jungle. Countless rivers and streams snaked through it.

The jungle reached out and over their canoes in a canopy of green. Climbing plants called *lianas* spiraled their way up the trees. *Cumares* palms ascended up through the forest, growing sixty feet tall. This totally alien world had the quality of a cathedral, a cathedral filled with music. Here, the river was the organ and the choir consisted of screeching macaws, hornbills, toucans, and parrots with their brilliant crimson and royal blue plumage. Jean opened her ears, hoping to fulfill her childhood dream of learning the language of the birds.

The Tauripan guides led the small party, paddling up the Caroní and into the endless forest. Hundreds of thousands of square miles stretched eastward to British Guiana. Their intended destination, a large village several weeks upriver.

"We will be entering Sanema territory," Enrico said. "They live in a very remote area of the jungle."

A Spaniard named Cardona, a descendant of famed explorers Nicholas de Cardona and his nephew Tomas de Cardona, had tramped through the region of the Sanema in the 1930s. The older Sanema remembered Cardona, but younger members of the tribe had never seen tall, fair-skinned people.

The Sanema were believed to be among the fiercest of the primitive tribes remaining in the world, but Jean did not know this. Enrico felt it unwise to tell her until this fact was demonstrated in their behavior. To forewarn her prematurely would unsettle her mind to no good advantage.

Jean stretched her neck and looked skyward. She could not see so much as a sliver of blue through 200-foot-tall trees. Weighed heavily with twisting vines, tangled and yet somehow coherent, the trees completely blocked out the sun.

When night began to fall, they beached their canoes on a riverbank. Their first night's dinner menu, carefully prepared by the Tauripan guides, consisted of freshly killed macaw and cassava, a nutty-flavored, starchy root vegetable, also called manioc. The tough, stringy meat of the macaw had a flavor that assaulted Jean's palate, so she only ate cassava. The next night, she felt so wild with hunger she would've eaten almost anything. When one of the guides handed her a plate of barbecued crocodile, she ate heartily of the rich, delicious flesh. In the weeks and months that followed, she found herself craving the tender, white, lobster-like meat of a young croc's tail.

The first two nights of the journey, the Tauripan were careful to strike camp near a majestic kapok tree[4]. The kapok has special buttress roots that keep it from tipping over in strong winds. Above ground, the roots can reach 15 feet tall and often form a teepee-like tent with enough space for three people to stand inside. It being Jean's first nights in the wild, the guides seemed to know that she would sleep better in her own private room. First, they cleared the ground inside her buttress-root tent, sweeping away termites, giant earthworms,

---

[4] Kapok or *Ceiba* (pronounced say-bah) trees were considered magical. They have umbrella-shaped crowns and branches extending in layers. The straight, branchless trunks, are ideal for making canoes big enough for 40 people. The seeds in their pods can be made into a silky fiber eight times lighter than cotton.

millipedes, and beetles. Then they carefully cleared a spot of ground and covered it with flat mats woven in intricate patterns.

Enrico and the other Italian, Beppi Orlando, financier of the expedition, received no such special treatment. They would have to make their own sleeping arrangements. Meanwhile, the guides strung up their hammocks. They took turns sitting watch throughout the night, protecting their small party from nocturnal creatures and the like.

But even in well-protected, private quarters, Jean could not sleep. The first layer of sound-assault came from the crickets; the second, from the bullfrogs; the third, from the all-night hunting parties of huge screech owls. She finally fell asleep an hour before dawn. She woke up drenched in sweat, having dreamed about a two-foot-wide spider that jumped like a flea. When she told Enrico about the dream he said, "That's the deadly *aranammono*. Don't worry. We'll get you a viper so you will be safe."

Jean thought he was teasing and half-smiled, half-scoffed, then turned and walked away.

"I mean it," he said, calling out. "They're quite handy to have around."

She shook her head and kept walking.

In time she would discover that Enrico wasn't kidding. The indigenous people did keep vipers as pets. The snakes fed on rats, iguanas, crickets, and spiders that would otherwise infest village huts.

A week went by. The Tauripan guides were experts at navigating the rapids. She marveled at their skillful avoidance of the whirlpools and small waterfalls that terrified the Italians out of fear they would capsize, lose all their supplies, and possibly even drown. They made their way steadily upriver despite many obstacles, primarily trees blocking their way. They frequently spent half a day hacking away with machetes and axes to cut a passage for the canoe.

One especially hot day, the guides decided to take the afternoon off and set up camp on a long sandy beach. Jean wandered away from the small party, far enough to feel alone but close enough to get back to camp straightaway. Once she found a nice spot to sit and relax, she fell into a jungle reverie.

She had no idea how long she'd been there when she turned her head with a start at the sound of a strange whistle. One of the Tauripan guides stood frozen in place, right in the middle of the river. *Odd,* she thought, following his gaze to the far shore. Her eyes settled on the two naked men at the edge of the riverbank; they were holding bent bows pointed straight at the Tauripan. Jean looked closer. These were not men, they were boys. The beauty of their skin, the softness of their facial features struck her. The taller of the two looked her in the eye and smiled a mischievous smile filled with so much intelligence it startled her.

She had heard that the Sanema dipped the tips of their arrows in poisonous tree sap that could kill an *acuri* (a rodent the size of a hare) with one tiny puncture. She wondered how many arrows it would take to kill a man. But the boys did not let their arrows fly. They stood there, motionless, a primeval tableau. After a few timeless moments, and much to her relief, they disappeared into the jungle without a sound.

Another two weeks of spending every day in a canoe, and the guides decided to take a full day off. They ate a hearty breakfast of crocodile, sugar cane, and sweet pineapple. Enrico and the guides went off to assess the geological features while Beppi relaxed in a hammock. Jean took one of the two paperback books she'd picked up at the airport and wandered up a small streamlet. She found a cozy spot where she could read, relax, and just be alone for awhile.

The river was indigo in color, shaded by mighty, majestic kapok trees whose crowns towered high above the jungle canopy. She opened her book and began to read. Looking up repeatedly, she caught sight of many a mynah bird and wild duck. She even spotted a couple of *guachama,* giant parrots with plumes of red, green, and yellow. She noted a new sense of comfort and felt grateful to have overcome the paralyzing fear that eyes were watching her from behind every tree.

She'd been reading along with normal attentiveness for nearly half an hour when she nodded off. A few moments later, her eyes shot open as a terrific force of realization struck her: "This is it! The Glade!"

2.

The Glade

Maine, 1936

The sensible voice in her head warned: You'll get lost. But a nudge from deep inside urged her to slow her pace even more. She could still hear the other girls screeching and giggling fifty, then a hundred yards ahead. She fell behind quite happily and felt relieved when she could no longer hear their voices. Her breathing changed as she fell into the silence. Spotting a deer trail to her right, she stepped off the main path, bent forward, and entered the woods.

Jean didn't fit in with the other young campers anyway. Never had. With her lean body and legs that were four inches longer than those of all her peers, she looked out of place, like a budding adolescent at ten years of age, an ingénue who'd taken a summer job that didn't fit her. But she loved the Maine woods. Every part of her, inside and out, smiled when she was in nature. That smile grew even wider this particular after-noon because she'd left her sister back at camp.

She felt the foreshock during their hot dog lunch. The moment Francie spilled mustard on her favorite raspberry colored T-shirt, a barely perceptible inner shudder signaled, "Brace yourself." When she saw her sister dip the corner of a clean washrag in a basin of greasy dishwater, she stood up and shouted, "Fran, no!" But the cacophony of pre-teen chatter drowned out the warning. Jean shook her head from side-to-side thinking: *Why not just walk to the far side of the kitchen area for clean running water, Fran?*

Her t-shirt now mustard-stained and greasy, Francie ran crying to their tent. Jean followed, walking with heavy sighs. She pulled up the tent flap. Her sister had plopped down on her sleeping bag and was sulking in a familiar play of helpless-ness smattered with sullen rage. Jean felt a pull to enter the tent and minister to her sister. She could, after all, skip the afternoon hike and stay in camp. Thinking ahead, she could see the rest of her day getting swallowed up by Fran's drama—yet again.

At home and at school, Jean was often her sister's refuge. Although the younger of the two, everyone thought of Jean as the big sister. Francie would throw a tantrum in the class-room or on the playground, race down the street and up the front steps of their grandmother's brownstone, then hide in their shared bedroom and sulk until sundown. While her sis-ter slaved under the weight of stormy emotions, Jean would wander the neighborhood or go roller-skating in Central

Park, knowing Fran would eventually wear herself out. That's when she could tiptoe into their room and soothe her sister, brushing the tangles out of her tear-drenched hair.

Not this time, Jean thought. She felt an odd combination of grief and relief as she walked away from the tent and left her sister to tantrum alone.

Five seconds later, she heard Francie scream, "Please don't leave me!"

Jean looked over at her favorite camp counselor and sighed. Nanette shook her head and nodded toward the woods. Jean followed, keeping her eyes on the path beneath her feet. Nanette glided past another camp counselor, saying, "Just leave Francie be. She'll come out of it on her own." She picked up her metal Girl Scout canteen with its red and yellow plaid cover and walked toward the trailhead. Jean trod along behind her; the other campers followed suit.

Once on the trail, Jean quickly took the lead. With each step away from camp, she felt the familiar cling of her sister loosen its grip. At times, Francie seemed to snuggle up on her shoulder like a koala bear. At others, she was more like an eagle sinking its talons into her neck. She'd become so accustomed to the whirlwinds of Fran's emotions she barely noticed how they pulled her off-center. All Jean wanted was to be free. She knew Fran wanted this as well. What she was too young to grasp intellectually, but understood at a deep level, was this: she would not be able to find her freedom as long as she remained tied-at-the-hip to her sister.

After half an hour of hiking with Nanette and the other campers, Jean felt a need for quiet. She could not stand another minute of the boy-talk, the chatter about clothes, the silent tooth-and-claw fight over who was most popular. She fell behind and watched the others grow smaller and smaller until they vanished among the trees and shrubs. Alone in the woods, her senses opened wide. Her hearing plumed, spreading out into the forest in every direction. She listened carefully, tuning into the natural world in stereo. She hadn't even heard the tweeting, twittering bird sounds until the gentle embrace of the woods wrapped itself around her. It was as if the birds lived in a separate dimension, and the doorway into that dimension was silence. She listened to the music of the leaves above and all around her. She smelled the dark musk of the ground beneath her feet.

Her breathing slowed as her thoughts seemed to grow more space between them. Then, through a break in the trees, she glimpsed a flash of the most luxurious shade of bright yellow-green she'd ever seen or imagined. Streaks of sunshine snuck between trees, tickling ferns and lighting tufts of grass. Jean parted the branches. No path. She stepped over a fallen log and felt her foot sink into soft, squishy earth. Another few steps and the forest floor no longer felt foreign. She kept walking, parting branches, looking overhead, finding a patch of sun and allowing it to warm her face. Even her eyelashes lit up in the noonday sun. She couldn't remember ever having seen her own eyelashes before. And yet, there they were, announcing themselves in her field of vision.

When she came upon a shaded hill, she tried to gauge the slope. But she lacked sufficient experience to draw on and decided to turn back. She'd taken three steps in what she hoped to be the right direction when a tiny stream of minty, acrid sweetness pulled first her head, then her body 90° to the left. Jean followed the scent, waving her way through a net of gnats. She stumbled over a moss-covered rock but took no notice of her skinned knee. She brushed off her dungarees, walked another five feet, and stumbled again. This time she stayed on her hands and knees, crawling through overhanging foliage that formed a tunnel on the forest floor. She pushed aside a clump of branches, blinked at the sunlight, and pulled up on her knees as if in prayer. Her eyes grew wide as they took in the source of the scent. A glorious glade spread out before her, a meadow rimmed with wild flowers in shades of pink, purple, yellow, red, and blue. She stayed there, letting the colors, the smells, the sounds wash over and through her for what could have been moments or hours.

When she stood up and walked into the meadow, a lush fir tree at the far side of the glade came into view. It seemed to be spreading its branches like a gigantic pair of wings. Right in the center of the glade was a knoll covered in luminous green moss. It looked like an altar. Against a backdrop of the black-green pine forest, rays of the sun cast horizontal lines that seemed to caress the earth. The perfectly blue sky made for a magical all-there quality of such density, such perfection, that she could do nothing but stand there, motionless, in awe of this holy place.

She walked toward the knoll taking great care with each step to leave the peace and sacred feeling of the place unruffled. She reached the center altar and lay down on the knoll, resting the side of her face on a soft pillow of fresh moss. At last, here in the glade, things were exactly as they ought to be. Everything fit. Everything was perfectly placed. And everything would remain so in autumn and even under the winter snow.

Jean felt she had discovered the missing center that held everything together in perfect balance. She'd been handed the key to rightness itself. She had stepped through that door and lay down in its perfection. She thought to take an amulet of moss with her, but her gut said, "Don't." Then, she stumbled into a rather grown-up idea: taking even one small souvenir from that perfect place would violate an unwritten code that had come into being long before the alphabet. She embraced this insight, sensing that to steal a bit of treasure would, in time, leave her with nothing but a clump of dead flora.

She left empty-handed, vowing to return to the Glade every night in her imagination. She promised herself that when camp ended and she had to go back to the city, she would do whatever it took to stay in touch with the Glade's stabilizing power. She knew all too well what going home to New York held in store. Once again, she'd be tangled up in other people's values, with no choice but to submit to the expectations of nannies, teachers, absentee parents, and even other children. She could almost see the terrain ahead: a thicket of moral codes, attractions, aversions, unmet needs, and wants. If she could focus on the Glade every night before she went to sleep, then she would always know the way back to her center.

That night, when she crawled into her sleeping bag, she wasn't in the least bit bothered by the hot, itchy mosquito bites that spotted her long legs. She wasn't plagued by the anxiety that so often kept her awake at night. She felt more gratitude than she had ever known. Drunk on that intoxicating brew

Thoreau called, "the tonic of wildness," she strolled through the Glade in her mind's eye. Approaching the knoll, she laid her head on her moss pillow and fell asleep.

Fifteen years later, deep in the South American jungle, Jean drank that intoxicating brew of wildness once again. And once again, she fell into a state of motionless awe. Her heart melted into the vast completeness. She felt the utter rightness at the core of all things. All of her senses opened up as she merged with the sublime order of it all. The world of duality vanished into the timeless where birth, death, growth, and decay were part of a magnificent, beautiful whole. At last, she was home, fully embraced exactly as she was, in the heartbeat of the jungle.

Before curling up for the night, she pulled out her journal and wrote: "All the excitement of the little girl's insight came back. I had lost it. And now, in a grown-up glade, the biggest jungle on Earth, I feel at home, just as I felt that day so long ago at summer camp in Maine."

The sense of belonging and acceptance, of being in her just-right place—nothing could compare. This was the real treasure, the promise she'd sensed the jungle might hold, more valuable than any cache of diamonds. She felt as though she'd lived in the jungle all her life and would remain there forever.

As she drifted off to sleep, the sound of crickets chirping, bullfrogs croaking, and even the high-pitched screech of owls on the hunt, blended together in perfect harmony.

3.

Sanema Territory

The next morning, Jean was full of energy. A marvelous feeling of freedom tickled her every thought. As they continued their journey, she sat forward in the canoe enjoying another unexpected pleasure: her body was bursting with vigor.

But after two more grueling weeks traveling upriver, she began to grow impatient. The feeling of freedom had dissipated; the exhilaration of being in the jungle had faded. She felt weary. She wanted a nice cold glass of iced tea.

One day, without warning, the river halved in volume. They were surrounded by a dense growth of asparagus, fichus, and philodendron, as well as a few *Titan arum,* the world's largest tropical flower.[5] Enrico recognized this passage; he had

---

[5] Titan arum is often called the "corpse flower" because it can smell an awful lot like rotting flesh.

traversed it before, and he began to describe the challenge that lay ahead in detail.

"We'll have to climb over the steep granite wall next to Arepuchi Falls," he said.

"How steep?" Jean asked.

"Quite," Enrico replied, avoiding her eyes.

"This is the passage you told me about," Beppi frowned nervously.

"Yes," he replied. Then, with a single slow nod of his head, "This is the one." Still avoiding Jean's gaze, he went on, "They place logs across the path of the canoe and haul it, inch by inch. The sun is merciless; you could easily get heatstroke." He described the pain he'd experienced, time and again, when the canoe would slip into a crevice between boulders and pivot out of control, scraping his shins and ankles against the granite. Jean's face remained stoic; Beppi looked horrified. Fearing what lay ahead, the three of them spent several days bracing themselves for the hard work and pain that was sure to follow. They arrived at the waterfall full of dread and primed to suffer, already hating every moment of the portage.

They started off, grim-faced, dragging the canoe up the rocky slope. When the canoe swung sideways, the sheer weight of it would pin a member of the work party to a burning rock while the others scrambled to move it off. A quarter of the way up, all ankles were bleeding. By way of begging off for a bit, Jean jumped ahead to photograph the scene. She climbed up ten yards and perched high on a rock. From that vantage point at a distance from the action, she noticed a curious fact.

There, before her, was a group of men engaged in a single shared task. Two of them were tense, frowning, losing their tempers at everything and everyone, cursing in the distinctive way of Tuscan men. The Tauripan guides, on the other hand, were having a fine time of it. They were laughing at the unwieldy canoe and making a game of the battle with gravity and rock. Between pushes, they showed off their scrapes and bruises. When, once again, the canoe would wobble forward, pin one, then another of them underneath it, they responded with amusement rather than upset. The fellow who was held barebacked against the scorching granite invariably laughed the loudest—once he could breathe again.

All the men were doing the same work. All were experiencing strain and pain. All were sweating in the blazing hot sun. There was no difference in their situations except one— Jean and the Italians had been conditioned by their culture to believe that such a combination of circumstances was at the very bottom of the scale of wellbeing. What's more, they were quite unaware they had a choice, any other option, as to how they could experience that situation.

The guides were equally unaware of their choice. These supposedly primitive people had also been conditioned to deal with their circumstances in a particular way. They knew what lay ahead but hadn't spent the days before the trek wallowing in dread—quite the contrary. They approached the portage in a perfectly merry mood. They seemed to revel in the camaraderie. Each forward move of the canoe was viewed as a victory, a cause for celebration.

Jean finished photographing the scene and rejoined the team, opting out of the civilized choice and enjoying, quite genuinely, the rest of the uphill climb. The cuts and bruises she sustained were reduced to nothing more significant than what they actually were: small hurts that would soon heal. Her injuries required neither an unpleasant emotional reaction, such as anger or self-pity, nor any anxiety over how much more pain she would have to endure before the end of the long haul. On the contrary, she found herself appreciating the excellent design of her body, which would patch itself up with no instructions from her whatsoever. So pure was the sweet freedom she experienced that afternoon, she vowed to live that liberation ever after. But within a few days, the sweetness gave way to the tyranny of habit, to the great pull of conditioning that only sustained conscious effort can countermand. She was unable to conjure the devotion required to sustain the marvelous sense of freedom she'd discovered that day. Not having made the necessary effort, she came away from the experience without much profit. Still, the realization never left her.

Once at the top of Arepuchi Falls, the Tauripan were on high alert. They had entered Sanema territory without permission. Late each afternoon, as evening came on, their guides started calling into the darkening forest, shouting, *"Shamantari!"* But the Sanema never showed up.

Keenly aware of the apprehension in their shouts, Jean prodded Enrico to explain. He refused. Then, hours before dawn on a moonless night when they were both unable to sleep, he finally gave in and told her what he had heretofore withheld.

"The Sanema were at war with other clans for centuries." He was still in his makeshift bed, seven feet away from her.

Barely able to see him in the darkness, Jean rolled over to get closer.

Enrico continued, "They've long since stopped roasting and eating their enemies but are still thought of as cannibals because they still eat their own after they die."

"Oh my," Jean said with a look of disgust. An image of a circle of people feasting on a roasted body popped into her mind. This was no joke. Her thoughts raced: *Those flesh-eating cannibals could be surrounding us this very moment.* She shuddered.

"With great reverence, they burn the corpse to a crisp," he said.

She grimaced. "Ghastly!" she exclaimed, the tone in her voice belying her horror and bone-shaking fear.

"Then they take the ashes and mix them with plantains." Enrico's matter-of-fact description of the Sanema's shameless anthropophagy triggered Jean's failsafe defense mechanism— an irreverent sense of humor—as he continued: "The dead person's relatives take in the person's essence."

"Not to mention a boost of calcium," Jean said from her mattress of leaves.

Enrico chastised her with a look and raised his voice a notch as if scolding a naughty child. "These savages believe that when they eat the remains of someone who has died, that person's power is preserved and increases the strength of the tribe."

"They should try your mother's roasted garlic tortellini," Jean said.

Enrico sat up, shook his head with disdain, snorted, and rolled over.

Unable to resist noodling him further, she deadpanned, "I suppose it's their version of *you are what you eat.*"

When they arrived at the Sanema village two days later, they were greeted with suspicion. The Taurpin guides set up camp fifty yards down river and waited to see if the Sanema would warm to their presence. Every day for two weeks, a member of the tribe would sit in the forest not far from their small encampment and watch the tall, odd-looking white people. This pattern changed the day the chief joined one of the watchmen and sat watching for a time. The following day, one of the Sanema men they'd seen sitting in the forest several days in a row walked into their camp. He greeted the Tauripan with two words and what appeared to be a friendly gesture.

"He's the chief's sheriff," Enrico said. Then, in a firm tone, he warned: "Do not look him in the eye unless he speaks to you directly."

It would be another week before the foreigners were allowed to go near the village. Initially, they were only allowed on the periphery. A few more days passed. On the fourth night, two women approached, making eye contact with Jean, but not with Enrico or Beppi. With outstretched arms, they presented two large bowls of freshly caught fish wrapped in banana leaves sitting atop a mixture of vegetables and herbs from the forest floor. This was the cue the Tauripan guides had been waiting for. It signaled that they had fulfilled their duty and earned their considerable fee. Assured their charges would be safe among the Sanema, they could return home to their village.

The women's visit rocked through Jean's body in waves, shaking loose a cornerstone of her faulty foundation. When they walked into the stranger's camp and made eye contact with her, but not with any of the men, she felt surprised at how perfectly natural it seemed. Clearly, the women were unafraid and offering friendship. And, most powerful and far-reaching for Jean, their demeanor conveyed wholehearted welcome.

4.

Maypole Dance

New York City, 1937

April wrapped up its foolishness and surrendered to May. Eight months had passed since her transcendent experience in the Glade. Jean and Francie were flitting around Central Park amidst the birds and the bees. An adult pair of eyes would have noticed the human mating dance going on all around them: couples strolling along, making out beneath blooming dogwood trees, or rolling around on the grass while their picnics were sacrificed to flies. But the girls took no notice, their estrogen levels still skimpy, their breasts yet to fill their training bras.

"Come 'ere!" Francie yelped, uncharacteristically taking the lead. She waved at Jean. The frenzy in her gesture signaled she'd seen something big. As was their habit, they'd stayed off the main path, hunting for nothing in particular.

"Look!" Francie said.

Jean took four steps toward Fran and followed her pointing finger. She smiled when she saw what had caught her sister's attention. A large tree with its trunk wrapped up in a braid of bright, colored ribbons stood proudly on the far side of the clearing.

"That's a Maypole," Jean trilled. Realizing Fran had never seen one before, she explained, "They must have had a May Day festival. People dance around the pole to celebrate the first day in May." Knowing Fran to be in one of her daddy-pleasing Christian phases, Jean didn't mention that the Maypole Dance was a pagan ritual.

It was one of the downsides to the special bond Francie shared with their religious fanatic of a father. At regular intervals (and generally after a stiff martini), the big man, "Pop," would lean over Francie and threaten her with damnation if she did not worship the Lord. Unable to grasp his grinding, oppressive Bible teaching, little Francie would stand there, bewildered. Jean could almost see the shame stirring up in her sister's shrinking heart as she tried to understand her father's Jesus.

Decades later, Jean would say, "For some reason, I was not subject to *that* particular torture," emphasizing "that" to highlight the fact that she was plenty tortured nonetheless. "Perhaps I was not worthy of being spared damnation."

Francie and her father had an unspoken pact that every member of the family, immediate and extended, could see. It showed in the way they looked at each other, in the way Pop would look straight through anyone in the room at Francie. In the way he would turn 45 degrees away from Jean whenever Fran was present. He always called Francie his "Princess."

Every time Jean heard him say the word, she would feel a painful icy burn on her ears, the same kind of pain she'd felt one December day when she walked through Central Park without her winter hat.

Pop's obvious affection for his elder daughter and the way he constantly indulged the girl, made Francie all but impossible to manage when he was away from New York for a week, sometimes two. Upon his return, he'd sit the girls down, lift his Princess onto his lap, open his leather man-purse, and pull out "treasures for my girls." It must have taken supreme effort to treat the girls as though he loved them equally at these welcome home parties. And yet his favors and affection remained with Francie. Nothing Jean did turned his eyes into the bright stars they became when Francie would talk about nothing in particular.

Jean knew the risks of demonstrating the Maypole Dance for Francie. What if Pop found out? But today she didn't care.

"C'mon, I'll show you," she said.

Jean took Francie by the hand and stepped into the clearing. The grass shone bright green in the late afternoon sun.

"I smell peanuts," Francie said.

Jean let go of her sister's hand and pointed at a tall tree on the far side of the clearing where greenish-yellow blossoms blanketed the ground beneath it. "That smell comes from that tree over there. It's called the Tree of Heaven," she said. "And that," she said, pointing at the tree wrapped in colorful ribbon, "is a Canadian Hemlock."

"How do you know what kinds of trees they are?" Francie asked.

"I read a book about Central Park," Jean replied. "Look. That one over there is an American Oak."

Francie looked at her sister and nodded, a smile of admiration wisped over her face.

Taking Francie by the hand again, Jean walked toward the tree wrapped in ribbon. Doing her best to explain how the trunk got dressed up that way, she skipped around the tree. "Over, under, over, under," she said, alternately lifting up an imaginary ribbon and then ducking under the ribbon held by the imaginary person skipping toward her. "They keep going round and round, moving closer and closer to the tree until they run out of ribbon."

Jean's memory kicked up the sound of the drummers surrounding the circle, keeping a steady rhythm. Her imagination played with a full palette of colors as her mind's eye conjured up women wearing flowered tiaras.

"I watched it once," Jean said. Then, by way of explanation, she continued, "Remember last spring when I went up to Vermont with Aunt Mouse? I went off by myself one afternoon and wandered into a wooded area at the edge of town. That's when I saw a group of people dancing the Maypole."

"I wanna do it!" Francie said. She grabbed an imaginary ribbon and skipped around the tree behind her sister. After a few minutes, they fell giggling to the ground.

When Jean saw a man step into the clearing, she got up immediately and said, "Let's go home." She grabbed her sister's hand and headed toward Central Park West. Her ears had screened out the traffic noise while they were in the park, but now the sound grew louder and louder. Rather than take their usual route home, Jean detoured down a narrow path. When the path spilled out onto a hidden patch of bright green grass, she stopped abruptly. Perhaps it was the light that caused her to stop so suddenly, or the flurry of a small flock of starlings taking flight. The sound of traffic faded once again, and she entered a comforting silence. She stood frozen in place, completely still. There, before her, was a brilliant meadow. She was immediately transported back to the Glade. A sharp pain of grief shot through her body as she suddenly realized that the magical power of the Glade had dimmed to almost nothing.

In the months since her mystical encounter in the woods, Jean's world had expanded in direct proportion to her shrinking ability to recapture the perfection and salvation of the Glade. Good girl, bad girl, beautiful girl, gawky girl—she lived in a muddle of family values. The priorities that defined New York City's cultured class during the 1940s were their own kind of prison. She was bombarded by Puritan and Victorian values marbled with her mother's liberal talk. The tug-o-war between these various forces ripped apart the inner peace she'd discovered in the Glade, leaving her innermost self in tatters.

These days she rarely thought about the Glade. With effort, she could call up a vision of the perfect woodland scene, but it had lost its stabilizing force. It was as if an omnipotent square-dance caller had commanded her to stumble. She always felt off-balance, and often in the midst of a fall. The centripetal force of the Glade, which had kept her close to her true center of gravity, was replaced by an overpowering centrifugal force. That force was her mother Helen, who was so self-involved she hardly noticed Jean.

Reflecting back, Jean said: "I don't think she even noticed that I was a person who had feelings—that I could hurt. I was an object, a funny or tedious little animal." In fact, Jean often felt herself no more than an annoying creature who constantly got in her mother's way.

A woman brimming with pride, Helen took an uppity, rebel stance at every opportunity. This was compounded by a mean streak of which she was totally unaware. She wanted to show everyone, especially her parents, that she would not, in any way whatsoever, conform to conventional expectations. She declared with absolute certainty that she would never become the attentive, obliging mother her mother had been. No, she would go her own way, snubbing the conventional and throwing out the natural along with it. Her anger and hatred overrode all good sense. She knew better than everyone else, was superior in her judgment, and stood firm against all of her family's values.

Two months before she was to graduate, Helen left high school seemingly determined to upset everyone by dropping out. Her sister Mouse, whose diminutive stature had inspired her unusual nickname, was already in college when Helen asserted herself against her parents and the entire sector of New York high society her family inhabited. But Helen's ever-placating mother—Jean's grandmother, affectionately known by all as "Darling"—wanted desperately to please her rebellious daughter. When Helen refused to return to school and insisted she be allowed to study sculpture and painting at the Art Students League, Darling willingly obliged. A few months later, Helen completed her renunciation of family values when, at the age of 17, she eloped with 24-year old James E. Liedloff.

A poor, anti-social artist of humble Minnesota origins, James Liedloff was a sculptor. He was tall, blond, and handsome. His dark eyebrows highlighted a sulking disposition that, apparently, made him quite attractive to his female classmates. But James was unmoved by their adoring looks and coy attempts to gain his attention. It was Helen who had captured his eye. Her long, perfectly sculpted nose, penetrating brown eyes and unflinching gaze put him under her spell. He openly admired her high cheekbones and "regal" profile, referring to her bone structure as her "armature." Eventually, he dared to ask if he could sketch her. After many such sketches, he dared again and asked Helen to be his "model." Helen knew what it meant to be an artist's model and gleefully went to his room on lower Broadway to pose for him in the nude.

Helen was the most beautiful creature James Liedloff had ever seen. Tall, slender, and athletic, Helen's body bore witness to her daily habit of swimming at the public baths, and her refusal to take a subway across town. She preferred to walk, regardless of the weather.

Making long strokes with his charcoal, James glanced back and forth from his sketchpad to her graceful arms, then her legs. He outlined the bones of her hips, the gentle curve of her shoulders, the waves of her hair. It mattered not that he wasn't nearly as talented and certainly not as self-possessed as she; James Liedloff was over the moon for Helen. Her attraction to him was less ardent, but she found his similarly self-righteous disposition appealing. Likewise, his personal philosophy—which was as opposed to convention as hers. Naturally, they eloped.

Darling had a weeklong panic attack before the private investigator found her ungrateful daughter in Minneapolis. Helen was stuck in a cheap motel, surfing her own waves of panic while James looked for work. What had she done? Had her quest for freedom landed her in a different sort of prison? To marry without her parents knowing had seemed a grand adventure, but there was nothing grand or adventurous about her circumstance at that moment. Sobered by what she'd done and repelled by her new husband's short temper and sullen attitude about getting a job, she was inwardly relieved when the private investigator found them.

The newlyweds were shuttled back to New York that very day and sent to separate rooms in Darling's house. Ever the *enfant terrible* (an attribution she would one day level against her own daughters), Helen feigned fury and refused to speak to her parents. The following day, James left without his bride; he'd been forbidden to see her until proper arrangements were made. There must be a wedding. He must have a job. And if he didn't have a job, Darling would give him a position at The Fan Company. The family would set them up in a little apartment and pay their rent for six months. Helen felt trapped. In attempting to break free of her parent's influence, she had locked herself into a marriage she wasn't sure she wanted.

Thus did the two smart-alecks get married and set up house on the West Side. Whether or not they had planned to have children was unclear. After the girls were born, they were at their wits end to provide the nurturance little ones need.

Decades later, Jean reflected, "It was entirely clear that they felt overburdened by the mandate to keep us alive—just."

Fed up with each other, the two loveless birds would break up (many times over) with Helen storming out the door howling like a caged animal, "Damn it! I never wanted to be a mother."

After the final breakup that eventually led to divorce, Helen bundled Jean and Fran up, brought them to their grandmother's house on Central Park West and unloaded them on Darling's household. With genuine joy and no small amount of relief, Darling received the girls with willing arms. Helen escaped all family obligations and moved into her own studio on West 56th where she could devote herself to art. Knowing she always had an open invitation to dinner at Darling's, Helen would turn up late, as per her usual. And Darling, as per her usual, would excuse her daughter's bad behavior saying, "It's because she's an artist."

Even as a young girl, Jean wondered why her grandmother never suggested that Helen might wear a watch. Perhaps it never occurred to her. Or perhaps her grandmother knew that to offer any such guidance, no matter how gentle and respectful, would be piddling.

The girls remained at Darling's throughout their growing up years. "Pop would take us on Sunday outings when it pleased him," Jean would say, her nose flaring. Whether she ever felt affection for her father or not, she could not recall. But she could recall with great clarity that two-year stint when Helen made a "heroically half-hearted effort" to rejoin with her daughters.

"She would attempt to make a home for us—her way," Jean explained. "We lived in a tiny apartment on 4th Street in the Village. It barely had a kitchen, but we stayed for nearly a year. Then we moved to an apartment on Central Park West that had a real kitchen. Mother tried cooking, chops or chicken. One day she tried to cook a turkey but didn't know how to do it. The bird kept spurting blood so she pulled it out to cool off then put it back in the oven. The turkey was a complete failure. She took this as proof she could never be a conventional mother. But she stuck it out for a year and a half before giving us up to Darling again. "

Through it all, Jean and Fran never questioned what they felt and understood: that they simply did not merit their mother's attention. She merely tolerated them, and not willingly.

Jean turned away from the meadow as the sound of traffic on Central Park West once again filled her ears. She suddenly remembered what her grandmother had told her earlier that day: "Your mother has invited guests over this evening. You girls will have dinner in the kitchen. Be home by 5:30."

Jean grabbed Francie's hand and said, "Mother will be angry if we're not home when they arrive." Still ten blocks away, they had to hurry. As the sun dipped below the rooftops of the Upper West Side, they raced from the Tavern on the Green at 62nd Street toward the Hudson River, zigzagging through the crowded sidewalks.

Breathless when they reached the landing in front of Darling's building, they scrambled up the stairs and slipped through the door of the apartment, trying to shrink themselves down to an unnoticeable size.

Helen was sitting in the formal living room with a man in a green beret. Seated next to him was a large-breasted woman in a low-cut dress; her bedraggled red hair tumbled toward her cleavage. The three of them were laughing and drinking martinis. Helen paid no notice to the arrival of her daughters.

The nanny motioned the girls into the kitchen, gave them each a plate of potatoes and corned beef, and pointed to the banquette near the window. As soon as they finished their dinner, she shooed them upstairs.

Still full of energy from their adventure in the park, the girls crawled into bed. The rule "children are to be seen and not heard" was strictly enforced when Helen was entertaining. But Jean and Francie could not contain their laughter. They would shush each other, only to succumb to a giggle or two, and then infect each other with muffled laughter. This went on for fifteen minutes until the waves of laughter reached a crescendo of guffaws. The girls knew better, but their funny bones didn't care.

With a bump and squeak that seemed to scrape the floor even though the door hung several inches above it, their mother appeared. The girls were unhinged by the scowl on her face. She said not a word, just looked at them with utter disdain. Seeing that look, and the hatred behind it, Jean broke out in a cold sweat. Reflecting back on it many years later, she said, "I would much rather have been spanked or beaten. Anything but that look."

5.

Hard to Hear
but Good to Know

Jean left Manhattan at age fourteen to attend Oakwood Boarding School, near Vassar in Poughkeepsie, NY. There, she demonstrated a bit of literary promise— prowess, actually. But her obvious talent caused a ruckus when the headmaster balked at an English project she submitted.

Per the assignment, each student had to write a short story, compose a poem, or make a Shakespearean stage set— anything literary. Jean had put it off for weeks. It was now Friday and the assignment was due on Monday. She reasoned the shortest thing to create would be a poem, so she decided to write a verse called, "The Year." It would have a quatrain for each month. She finished the poem late Sunday night and handed it in the next morning.

A few days later, she was summoned to the headmaster's office. Ushered in by his secretary who pointed at the floor to indicate exactly where she should stand in front of his desk, Jean stared at the headmaster's back while he finished feeding his goldfish. He turned to face her and, with eyes of stone, looked down at his massive desk. There it was: her English assignment. All three pages of it. As if in slow motion, he reached forward, placed five fingers steeple-like over "The Year," and pushed the assignment across the desk in her direction.

"We don't believe you wrote this poem," he said.

She looked down at the paper, still impaled by his fingers.

"Not only that, we don't think you could even understand it at such a young age. Do you have any other examples of your poetry?"

Prior to the assignment, Jean had written only one other poem in her entire life. The poem had spilled out of her onto the page the night before her 13th birthday. It consisted of two stanzas:

The sound of a trumpet dies in the darkness,
I am alone.
I kneel in the ashes of my life
But cannot weep,
For tears have in them hope,
And hope is gone.

I searched. I found the world was not my world.
Its gods and temples woke in me no faith.
My love, that is, my life,
Unable to exist alone,
Destroyed itself.
And me.

The poem was so personal she had never shown it to anyone. She wasn't about to offer it as proof of her ability and expose herself to further suspicion. She shook her head.

The headmaster said, "Write me one now."

She replied, "One can't write poetry under pressure."

"In that case, your teacher and I will have to discuss your grade. This will not go unnoticed."

When graduation day for the seniors came along (Jean was only a junior), she had not yet received a grade for the assignment. She resented that the issue had not been resolved. Her honor was important to her; she wanted closure, finality.

She sulked as she watched parents arrive, so proud that their girls were graduating from such a prestigious school. The graduates were all lined up wearing caps and gowns. As they walked across the stage, Mrs. Stanley, the Academic Chair, handed out diplomas. The headmaster stood next to her, shaking students' hands, patting their backs, and looking head masterly.

After the ceremony, once most of the graduates and parents had gone, Jean approached the headmaster. He told her that they had looked in the Poughkeepsie library to see what books she'd taken out. Only a rhyming dictionary, only that one book. They called in a poetry expert who said it looked like Shelley. Jean challenged him to look at the complete works of Shelley, saying, "They're not a secret. Just go and look. Is it there or isn't it there? Do you believe me, or don't you believe me?"

The headmaster gave no answer. In the end, she was given a B minus for the assignment. To her small cadre of confidantes—her best friend at Oakwood, sister Fran, and grandmother Darling—Jean was vehement. "So that's the grade they give Shelley, a B minus? That's preposterous!" All three agreed. But she had no choice other than to accept the grade.

Summer found Jean deeply troubled at the thought of dealing with a headmaster who thought of her as a dishonorable person. She could not abide attending a school where she was regarded as a liar. She couldn't tolerate being under the aegis of people who thought her dishonest when, in truth, she'd been falsely accused. They didn't trust her, and she could not remain at Oakwood under those circumstances. The only way she would go back was if they gave her a clean slate, but she saw no path to that end. There was only one solution: she simply had to change schools for her senior year.

To gain entrance to Drew School for Girls, she needed a statement from Oakwood explaining why she left the school. The statement consisted of four words: "She was a cheat." She applied to Drew anyway. With the help of a family connection, she managed to get an interview with the headmaster. Mr. Philip Sydney Waters was a kind man. He agreed that she'd been treated badly and accepted her application.

The assumption among the faculty at Drew was that all graduates would go on to college. That meant all students were required to take certain prerequisites. Jean had nearly failed algebra; it was the only D grade she'd received while at Oakwood. Now in her senior year, she was required to take geometry. She thought, *Oh God, more mathematics*. But she found geometry interesting, even enchanting. She instinctively understood what is known as the *kissing number problem,* citing its name as the "main attraction." When called to the front of the class to demonstrate the proof, she walked up to the chalkboard, drew a single circle, and said: "Consider a circle with center C that is touched by circles with centers C_1, C_2, C_3, and so on." She drew a total of six non-overlapping circles around the central circle and explained: "Each of the six rays emanate from the same center C, which makes the sum of angles between them 360°."

Jean got along with geometry so beautifully she felt redeemed, no longer inferior to those with a mathematical mind. Reflecting back on the incident many years later, she said, "I came to the conclusion that I was a visual learner, which was why I did so well with geometry. The conceptual side of mathematics did not interest me. Needless to say, I did not choose trigonometry as one of my electives."

After graduating from Drew, Jean moved back to New York and into her grandmother's apartment. Darling was thrilled to have her home, and Aunt Mouse squealed with delight when her beloved niece returned to the Big Apple. Mouse tapped her high-society connections, flashing the news to potential suitors, always referring to Jean as "my gorgeous niece." But Jean thought herself rather plain looking and dismissed her aunt's compliment as no more than "honeyed words." It mattered not that everyone in town regarded Mouse as an authority on attractiveness.

By then a fashion leader in New York, Mouse was not good looking, had none of her sister Helen's extraordinary beauty, but made up for it in style. Unlike Helen, who'd dropped out of high school, Mouse was well educated. She had a dynamic career, was a literary success, a sought-after freelance writer, and an editor for *Vanity Fair*. Despite her small stature and rather homely visage, she had a stellar reputation in the fashion world. But none of these facts gave credence to her "honeyed words." In Jean's mind, the only authority was her mother.

Decades later, she traced her poor self-image back to what happened when she was six years old: "My mother's exhibit, *Hands of Famous Persons*,[6] was featured at the Art Center in New York. The afternoon of her big opening, I sat on the bed while she dressed. I remember watching her stand in front of the mirror, looking over her shoulder at herself, posing her legs, admiring her own figure. I felt entirely invisible. Then she turned to me and said: 'How can you bear to be so ugly?' For some mysterious reason, I internalized her view of me. I still feel invisible much of the time. And nothing could convince me I was attractive, not even those silly modeling assignments I reluctantly agreed to in my 20s."

Regardless of feeling invisible, the statuesque 18-year old Jean became highly visible, receiving invitations to one party or benefit after the other. She declined most of the invitations but accepted one offered by Count Friedrich Ledebur of Austria. The party turned out to be a reception for the Maharaja of Kutch, an Indian state near the border with Pakistan. An assemblage of cover girls, would-be film starlets, and New

---

[6] Helen Liedloff's sculpture exhibit featured the hands of Amelia Erhart, Lily Pons, Albert Einstein, Elaeanor Smith and Captain Bob Bartlett. A New York Times art critic wrote, "Miss Liedloff's technique seldom ventures beyond literal realism, and her use of all-too-obvious symbols (Bobby Jones grasping a truncated golf club, Vincent Richrads with the handle of a tennis racket, Sergei Rachmaninoff skimming a segment of a piano keyboard) is not always happy."

York debutante types were served up to His Highness on a shiny hardwood floor of a platter. Jean wrote in her journal: "By the time I realized that I was on the à la carte menu, I had already been chosen the favorite, the winner—or, in my estimation, the loser."

The maharaja asked her out. She accepted the invitation (her station required her to do so), however, she found him altogether uninteresting as a person, albeit temporarily amusing as an exotic. At the end of the evening, he told her he would take her to Cartier the next day to choose a diamond. She danced around his offer of marriage, shrouded as it was, saying, "It is not correct to offer diamonds to girls of good family."

He asked her, "Then tell me: what is your favorite stone?"

Diamonds were, in fact her favorite stone, emeralds her second-favorite. But she knew better than to encourage the maharaja. To allow him to buy her an emerald ring would only serve to spur him on as a suitor.

Side-stepping his second advance, she said, "Amethyst."

He scolded her: "That is a SEMI-precious stone."

He then went on to tell her that he owned the world's greatest ruby collection. "On my birthday, a national holiday of course, I ride one of my elephants through the streets of Bhuj wearing a ruby ring with a stone so big I cannot put my fingers together." He held his arm out in front of him. With a nod, he gestured to her to visualize the ruby on his hand and showed her how far apart his fingers would be if he were actually wearing the ring.

A smile of admiration lit up Jean's face as she pretended to moon over the imaginary ring. Satisfied that he had impressed her, the maharaja grunted softly and nodded his royal head.

Little did he know that Jean's admiration wasn't directed at his ring, rather, at the marvel of her deft deflection of his veiled proposal. Her smile grew even brighter as she reflected, thinking *Darling would be proud*.

Unable to conceive the possibility that a woman might not feel attracted to him, the maharaja invited Jean to travel to his country for a visit. She could do social work for his people if she wanted. She was welcome to bring her grandmother along, as well as Rina, their maid.

"I only desire to be able to look at you," he promised.

She declined his invitation on the grounds that she would be entering Cornell University in the fall.

When His Highness returned to New York three months later, he asked Jean out again. Grandmother Darling said, "You ought, at least, to invite him to dinner, since you have not answered any of his letters."

Darling would never have ignored the letters of a maharaja, but she did not scold Jean or criticize her failure to reply. Rather, she offered a remedy, and offered it with such equanimity, Jean agreed to think it over.

Unlike Helen, who disapproved of nearly everything Jean did, Grandmother Darling always accepted her.

"Darling did not dote on Francie and me," she would later recall. "She always remained more or less neutral—polite, accessible, generous, but unenthusiastic. I think she feared my mother would criticize her for spoiling us if she showed too much affection."

In Jean's mind, Darling wasn't sure how to behave around her incredibly talented daughter. "Imagine," she would say, "she was afraid of rejection from her own offspring! That's how much power my mother had over people. She could intimidate anyone. She always spoke as though she were the ultimate authority. And the manner in which she stated her opinion, so sure she was right . . . the way she would use her beauty to get under a person's skin . . . people wouldn't dare contradict or challenge her. Most people, anyway. They knew better than to oppose her and risk incurring her disdain."

Jean's grandmother, on the other hand, never showed disdain for anyone in her expansive sphere of influence. With regard to her granddaughters, Darling's very constitution made it impossible for her to disapprove, much less disdain the girls. Jean could not remember a single time when her grandmother pressed her to do something she did not come by naturally. She didn't criticize either—even when Jean would stay up all night reading *Time Magazine* and *The New Yorker* in the bathtub. After spending hours in the tub, Jean would fall into bed, sleep until the late afternoon, wake up irritable, guilty, useless. Darling did not judge. On occasion, she'd suggest Jean might like to do some charity work but, rather than say, "It would be good for you," and imply that Jean wasn't able to choose her own path, she simply offered the suggestion. But Jean wasn't interested. She preferred to stay out late, spend her evenings at the Stork Club or the El Morocco, and wallow in her uselessness. She continued going out at night, dancing, and doing nothing particularly useful, nor evil. Not overtly evil at least, mostly the sin of waste.

Jean forced herself to overcome her own dislike of New York society, embracing it as a way to rally against her mother's reverse-snobbery. To that end, she began to associate with society types. On Tuesday evenings, she and Darling held a weekly open house for people with names or titles, distinguished writers, and foreigners. She craved acceptability, respect, and belonging. And she was accepted; at least, everyone accepted her invitations. She made them feel welcome, just as she had in childhood when serving endless soda pop and popcorn to every child for miles around.

Over a decade earlier, after Jean and Francie were finally handed off to Darling for the last time, Jean asked for a Ping-Pong[7] table. A tournament-size Ping-Pong table. When she requisitioned the dining room and turned it into a Ping-Pong room, Darling voiced no objection. Thereafter, the family took their meals at the end of the unusually broad hallway next to a little conservatory at the south end of the apartment.

Jean remembered Sunday brunches there—the soda biscuits, fried chicken and fresh squeezed orange juice. And there was her cousin Timmy who would come up from his home two floors below for a second breakfast. Somehow, Jean knew that Timmy was loved, wanted, even spoiled in his home. Timmy's parents, Unk and Mouse, allowed him to waste paper by penciling a single line at the bottom of a page of blank paper. He would display them as drawings of snakes at his "snake shows," which included live snakes that his adoring parents permitted him to keep as pets.

---

[7] Invented in the 1880s, table tennis made it possible for fans of lawn tennis to play inside during the colder months. It quickly became popular, spawning many variations marketed under names such as Gossima, Whiff Waff, Pom-Pom, and Pim-Pam. Although "Ping-Pong" is a registered trademark, the name quickly became the generic term just as was the case with Aspirin, Dry Ice, and Cellophane.

Throughout her childhood, and even into adulthood, Jean envied the welcoming atmosphere in which her cousin grew up. In her later years, she noted that the assumption she made as a child—that Timmy was worthy of love and that she and Francie were not—held sway in her psyche regardless of how much therapy and self-reflection she did. So tenacious was this particular fixation and the unbelievable sadness it wrought, Jean eventually accepted it as a permanent feature of her psychology.

It mattered not that Darling always welcomed Jean and her sister. Darling was easy. Moving into her home seemed natural. And yet somehow, Darling's slightly detached, but consistent, approval did not mitigate Jean's feelings of unworthiness. Years later, she would write in a journal:

> Darling did not judge, and therefore, perhaps, was no judge. I <u>expected</u> [triple underline] to be excluded. I suppose because that was my base, my origin, my real place—that Dark Place from which I was rescued without deserving or earning it. Once we moved to Grandmother's house for good, I wondered what I had done to be so incredibly lucky. To be taken to the beautiful, elegant, bright, welcoming place where Darling and Grandpa lived. I can remember the first amazed sight of my new home and the feeling I had . . . that some happy mistake had been made, admitting me to this wondrous setting . . . and my joy, mixed with continuing disbelief, that I would get to stay there for as long as I liked.

Jean was never truly convinced that she would not be returned to the dreadful Dark Place, that apartment somewhere in

Manhattan where she'd spent an eternity with her mother before the notion of the passage of time entered her mental development. To her child's mind, it was just "The Way Things Are For Me."

Later, as an adult who'd become an expert in mother-infant bonding, she would often reflect on the fact that she felt "unworthy and unwelcome." That feeling had been instilled in her by her mother's first dictum when Jean was presented to her in the delivery room. In another journal entry, she wrote:

After my struggle toward the light, my birth, my severance from her body, my being mishandled and cleaned up by strangers in preparation for the momentous presentation, Mother turned from me in disgust and bid the servile nurse: *'Tolgo il disturbo'*—an Italian expression that meant: 'remove the disturbance.' As was ordained, I was immediately removed from her sovereign presence and taken to a place where I would not offend anyone, i.e.: isolation—a room, I think, where there were instruments and tables, but no people. Empty. Silent. But I did not willingly retire. I cried. I screamed. I wanted. I could not give up. It seemed life or death to me: the silent abyss, the shock and trauma that branded a template—'unwelcome'—into my unformed mind. And every succeeding moment of my life was lived in reference to my mother's offhanded pronouncement. How to escape it? What do I have to do to bluff my way a little longer? How could Mommy be made all right so that she could, maybe later, somehow be fulfilled, made happy? If only she would dress better, be nice to Darling; be 'in' not 'out,' of what

> I wasn't even sure. All I knew is that my mother mocked
> me for wishing to be one of those confident girls in
> parades who march to the drumbeat strutting in white
> uniforms with gold braids and buttons. It was clear to me
> those girls had something...

And there Jean's writing trailed off, as if she was unable to finish the thought.

At every moment, Jean had to make an effort to prove she was blameless, to make excuses for her presence, to win games, show valor, merit, wit, strength, humor, virtue—fairy tale values. Not so much to gain recognition as to evade being recognized as an imposter in a world full of the right people. Never, of course, did she put any of this into words and form a clear thought about it as a youngster. She was only able to do so in retrospect when, as an adult, she remembered the constant anxiety in which she had lived as a child—so tense and apprehensive, she could hardly swallow the excellent food that was served her thrice a day and always available in the icebox and pantry.

True to her station, Darling received a telephone call from the butcher, Mr. Schiffer, twice a week. He would ask her for her order—some combination of Porterhouse steak, filet mignon, three-rib roast of beef, rump of veal, leg of lamb, loin chops. These were some of the phrases Jean heard Darling speak into the phone. But she never knew about these things. She just plopped down at the table to be served by the housekeeper, Mae, whom everyone except for Jean and Francie called "the maid."

The summer Jean was five, Mae lived with the family in their country house. "I'll never forget the look on Mae's face when I walked through the swinging screen door into the kitchen with a jar full of spiders," Jean said, reflecting. "I sure gave her a fright!"

Best remembered by Jean was Celia Gull, aka "Pussy." She was Polish, by way of Wilkes-Barre, Pennsylvania. She always welcomed Jean and Francie in the kitchen. Jean spent a lot of time enjoying Pussy's peasantry coziness, the polite talking and teasing. She had no cause to feel inferior to her, so she was able to enjoy herself in Pussy's company without anxiety or fear of judgment. Pussy was simple; she was merry. But feeling accepted, even loved by her, did nothing for Jean's view of herself. Pussy was the maid.

Darling never forced anything on Jean and Francie when they were children in her household. She was gentle, accepting of her daughter and her two granddaughters. She hired nannies for the girls, never made them eat or wear anything they did not like, and trusted them with charge accounts everywhere. The girls never abused the privilege, nor violated their grandmother's trust. They charged reasonable amounts of sundaes and sodas at the drugstore, and reasonable goodies at the grocery store. Their charges were never discussed nor questioned.

Later, as teenagers, when they could jump on buses, they charged their clothes in the department stores on 5th Avenue. Darling had charge accounts at Bloomingdales, Lord & Taylor, Saks Fifth Avenue, and many of the specialty boutiques. They might have asked permission before making a big purchase—Jean couldn't remember—but there was no strain, no conflict. They always had whatever they needed or wanted, including the expensive beaver coat Fran fell in love with, and the muskrat coat and new boots Jean bought when she began her studies at Cornell.

But none of this—not the clothes, the comforts, the marvelous food served by excellent cooks, or the sense of being "upper class" coupled with a complete lack of restrictions on the friends they chose—did anything to increase Jean's feeling of her own respectability. And, more importantly, her likeability, an asset she considered far beyond her reach.

Paradoxically, the fear of being unlikeable led to a certain kinship with people she found it difficult to like. People like His Highness, the maharaja.

Jean had to admit that Darling's argument about hosting him was sound. She really ought to invite him to dinner. It was the right thing to do. She swept her dislike under the sheepskin and penned an invitation.

Her next challenge was to think up a menu that would please a fellow who was entertained as frequently and lavishly as His Highness. She decided on roast beef. When Darling reminded her that one of the maharaja's titles was "Protector of Cows and Beggars," she pivoted and asked Rina, who hailed from the South of France, to make a nice *poulet sous cloche* out of non-sacred pig and chicken. After dinner, Jean told His Highness of her near-blunder in etiquette, saying, "Darling stepped in to save my karma." She then asked what he would have thought if she'd served him beef. He replied: "I should have been shocked!"

Fall arrived and Jean began her studies at Cornell as planned, but she did not fare well in college. For one thing, she couldn't get up in the morning and was often late for class. This annoyed her professors to no end. When she tried to explain that she felt physically weak, they sent her to the Cornell Clinic where she was given vitamin shots. Jean would later recall: "Even I, an amateur, knew that if someone couldn't get up, you immediately take their blood pressure. But I had to convince the creeps at the clinic. It turned out I was right. I had low blood pressure."

When she went to her professors to explain her frequent absences, they told her she hadn't been in class enough to get a passing grade. She flunked—ironically, both Psychology 101 and a creative writing class. But Jean didn't care all that much. She decided to move to Florida and attend what she described as "a flea-bitten, junk college, the kind that took people who'd flunked out of better schools." She reasoned that even though Florida Southern was a third-rate college, she could, at least, be nice and warm there. She enrolled in their New School for Social Research, but dropped out after her first semester.

From Jean's point of view, dropping out of college marked "the end of the interference." She believed she'd been fortunate not to have her learning constrained by an education that interfered with original thinking. Throughout her adult life, she disdained education and often reiterated her firm belief that, had her perception (and thus her thinking) been narrowed by academic concepts, she would have been blind to what she was able to perceive while living among the people of the jungle.

With a second college fiasco under her belt, Jean went back to New York and took up with a man named Carlos Salamanca. He was Bolivian, and one of the great loves of her life.

Salamanca was an ambassador to the United Nations. Among other diplomatic duties, he was a trustee of a group of islands in the Pacific. One of his friends, a fellow trustee, was Sir Andrew Cohen of England, the former governor of Uganda. Cohen was a big, almost blimp-sized, ambassador. He and Jean became great friends.

She and Carlos would often dine with Sir Andrew and his wife, Lady Cohen, who referred to Carlos as "a magnificent piece of horseflesh." Jean and Lady Cohen didn't have much in common; they never formed a bond. But she and Andrew did. The foursome would go to dinner and then to the Roseland ballroom. After dancing, they'd have a few drinks (Jean had been a teetotaler until then), and she would smoke a cigar with Andrew—a big fat stogie. At that point, Lady Cohen would excuse herself and go home, but not before looking down her nose at Jean.

She'd met Carlos at a charity benefit. He was standing in the middle of the room in a stance that broadcast, in her words: "I am a lover, irresistible to all female traffic." Jean surveyed him: slicked back black hair ("probably Brill Cream"), decided she was definitely above all that, admonished herself ("for God's sakes"), and swept aside her attraction to this "Latin lover prototype."

He walked near her, keeping a too-little distance for a man to whom she had not been formally introduced. She felt the magnetism between them and realized it was strong, really strong—stronger than her intellect. She was drawn to him, to the merciless, purely magnetic force. That's how it started, with this thing she came to call the *Tercera Fuerza,* the "Third Force" that drew her helplessly into his arms, moved against her will, time after time. It went on to become a love affair governed by this irresistible force. She was enthralled, unable to resist. But he annoyed her almost as mercilessly as he seduced her. He was always late for appointments and often disrespectful when they were in public. This ate away at the Third Force.

"His behavior was quite ridiculous," she would say when looking back on the affair. "The epitome of the machismo stereotype."

Jean was astonished when the Tercera Fuerza continued to rule her for months, despite her better judgment. Then, one afternoon, it snapped like a twig. One too many times, Carlos showed up hours late for a tryst. She walked across the room and slapped his face. Instant liberation.

No sooner had she been freed did her lower back go out, the physical pain serving to spare her the nigh-unbearable emotional pain of the end of their affair. She never for a moment missed him. Even seeing his once irresistible, six-foot four-inch figure at UN parties did not stir her in the least.

She would later recall: "It was not unlike my physiological reaction to losing Darling. I simply never felt it, her death. I guess I still cannot. I never mourned and, at the time, couldn't even say the words, 'My grandmother died,' much less accept her demise. I'd always avoided the fact that it would happen one day. When it did, I was living alone with her, but it was my sister who found her. Francie stopped by on a rare morning visit and found Darling dead in her bed. I never even saw her corpse."

While Mouse saw to the funeral arrangements, Jean took sedatives to get through the first few days after her grandmother died. "I did not go to the funeral," she confessed. "It wasn't that I couldn't bear it, I just didn't feel a thing."

In a heartbeat, Jean's tone changed. She gave me a hard look and said, "That's enough," brushing the air as if she could whisk away any hint of vulnerability. "I'm done telling stories about the distant past."

We'd been sitting on the patio at the Depot Café for three hours, and had long since finished lunch, plus cappuccinos and peach pie. As the sun went down behind Mt. Tam, a chill breeze sashayed into town from the ocean.

Unable to ignore the vulnerable territory she'd just exposed, I fell into therapist mode: "It seems as though you've always had difficulty forming emotional bonds."

"Yeaaahhhh . . ." she said, drawing out the y-sound and putting a long tail on the *-eaaahhh*.

Her breath whistled quietly as she took in my observation. She pondered, straightened her chair and said, "Hard to hear, but good to know."

We collected our things to leave. Jean cursed the word processor that had been sitting idle all afternoon and stuffed it into her oversized, overflowing handbag. I felt a pang of concern. Had my bold statement about her relationships crossed a line? I didn't say a word, just walked into the square to watch a group of people practicing martial arts. When I heard her say "Adios!" to the busboys with her usual gusto, my fear of a reprimand dissipated.

She waved at me from the far end of the patio. When within earshot, she said, "Darling, we really need to get started on the childrearing book." Grateful for the change of subject, I replied, "I'd be happy to help. In fact, it would be an honor."

"I'll tell you how you can help: I need a contract and an advance from a publisher. That's the only way I'll get over my writer's block. Once I put my signature on the line, I have to make good on my word." She stopped and faced me. "Do you think you could help me write a proposal? Maybe you can help me find an agent . . . "

"Sure," I said. I had no idea what I was getting into. I was simply relying on the advice my father had given me time and again: "Say yes to any opportunity, even if you don't have the foggiest idea how to approach it, you'll learn by doing."

I walked Jean to her car. As she drove away, I felt a wave of melancholy. It was clear to me this remarkable woman felt somehow unfulfilled in her life. It was more than the fact that she'd never married, that she'd lost her fiancée to a brain tumor. It wasn't even the fact that she'd never had children— an issue with which she'd made her peace. No, this lack of fulfillment was more fundamental. There was something very tender at the core of her that even her book and worldwide following couldn't touch.

Looking back now, I realize that Jean had shared her tender, vulnerable side early on in our friendship. It came in the form of a self-revelatory remark and what seemed a trivial request. There was no way I could have understood the import of this request at the time, nor could I have foreseen how it would shape our friendship.

We'd met at the Depot at what was to become our regular weekly lunch meeting place. I showed up in my favorite summer sundress; she wore a pair of linen slacks, a navy blue shell, and a lightweight blazer with an emblem on the pocket. Around her neck, she wore her signature Hermes scarf in white, blue and gold. We finished our lunch and ordered cappuccinos. Then she leaned toward me and said in a low voice, "Darling, there's something I want you to know."

"What's that?" I said, meeting her serious tone with a cheerful one.

"I have this strange habit of pushing people away," she said. "I don't know how I do it, but it keeps happening. I even did it with Gloria Steinem. We were friends for a while, but then I offended her somehow. She stopped returning my calls. I don't understand what I do that makes people go away. Promise me you won't go away, pussycat. Please, just tell me when I do whatever it is that I do. Don't let me push you away."

"Of course," I promised. I reached across the table and put my hand on hers. I nodded and held her gaze for a long moment, completely oblivious to the full measure of the promise I'd just made.

Over the next several weeks and months, my role in Jean's life morphed into a combination of personal assistant, administrative secretary, and cheerleader. Although I had plenty of experience cheerleading, I had very little in the way of organizational skills. I could run her errands, stop at the post box, answer letters to members of The Continuum Concept Network, and help her pull together the occasional newsletter. But getting her organized proved impossible. And we never got around to writing that book proposal. Nonetheless, between chatty lunches at the Depot and long talks in her living room, I learned a great deal about the choices she'd made that shaped her worldview.

6.

The Ile de France

fter dropping out of college in 1951, Jean decided higher education was not for her. "None of the paths my family expected me to follow held any life," she recalled. "Writing for fashion magazines sounded boring, a career as a model even more so. The Fan Company was an option; I could, after all, step into my grandmother's shoes. I'd always admired Darling's business savvy, but the idea of taking on that role held no allure at all. But what else could I do?"

After several days of high anxiety, Jean decided it would be prudent to at least consider taking over the family business. Her great grandfather founded The Fan Company in the 1870s after a trip to the Orient. In those days, there was no such thing as air conditioning and people sought relief from the heat by fanning themselves. The Japanese fans he brought back from his trip quickly became popular among the well-to-do. In time, he began to import all manner of Oriental art:

prints, scrolls, screens, as well as calligraphy, ivories, and, of course, kimonos. The company offices and warehouse were located on lower Broadway, with a satellite office in Tokyo and representatives in Peking, Hong Kong, and Shanghai. Every year, Jean's great grandfather would travel by steamer to Japan and China. He often took his wife and young children along. Thus, did Darling experience international travel and gain knowledge of cultures quite different from that of New York.

Along with her cousins and siblings, Darling had an unusually exotic upbringing. Their playthings included Kabuki masks, ornamental swords, Chinese dolls, kimonos, and fireworks like none that could be found in America. Jean believed that her own wanderlust and desire to visit exotic places was part of her grandmother's legacy. Inspired by Darling's knowledge of the world, Jean dreamed of acquiring that type of knowledge for herself.

When Darling's father died, she and her husband took over The Fan Company. When her husband died, Darling became the sole captain of the ship. After she passed, Jean discovered the enterprise that had supported the family for the better part of 80 years, the business Darling had worked ten hours a day to keep afloat was, in fact, sinking. Darling— ever the "handler" who fixed whatever needed to be fixed, the ever-pleasant, ever-calm, always gracious matriarch—had, in effect, sunk the ship. Determined not to bother anyone with her troubles, she had stayed at the helm and taken full responsibility, bailing as fast as she could to keep The Fan Company afloat. The disaster she left behind became obvious to Jean when she met with the company controller and reviewed the books. There was nothing to do but sell what remained.

The sale happened in a matter of weeks. Jean received her share of the proceeds, but having her own money did nothing to clear her muddled thoughts about what to do next. All she knew for certain was that turning to her mother for advice was a bad idea. Such conversations always ended in anger and hurt.

"I had to get on my own two feet, even if it took a gigantic effort," she said.

In March 1951, two months after Darling's funeral, she purchased a one-way tourist class transatlantic ticket for $125. When Mouse learned of her niece's pending departure, she introduced Jean to Iva Patcevitch, the president of Condé Nast. He promised to contact Michel de Brunhoff, the Editor-in-Chief of *Vogue Paris,* and let him know that Jean was on her way to Europe and he should give her modeling jobs.

"Iva will be expecting you," her aunt had told her. "Ring him up when you arrive."

But Jean had only a few half-conceived plans and even fewer expectations. She saw no point in making specific arrangements, wanted only to feed her hunger for adventure.

As her taxi approached the New York Harbor, Jean could see the *SS Ile de France* moored at the pier. She was startled by the sheer presence of the mammoth ocean liner. The first major vessel built after the end of World War I, *Ile de France* was neither the fastest nor the largest ship of her kind. At the time, passenger ships featured the traditional aristocratic décor seen in the manors and chateaus of Europe. Not so, the *Ile de France* with her colorful Art Deco design. Within months of her maiden voyage in 1927, she was the preferred ocean liner for Atlantic crossings among wealthy Americans, especially the young, the stylish, and the famous.

With huge ornate public rooms, a foyer that rose four decks high, a dining room with a grand staircase at its entrance, a massive sundeck, a chapel in neo-gothic style, beds in the cabins instead of bunks, a shooting gallery, an elaborate gymnasium, and even a merry-go-round to entertain the children, the *Ile de France* was an entirely new breed of luxury liner.

It was a near perfect sunny day in New York, but Jean did not so much as glance back toward the city. *This is the beginning of a new life,* she thought. With each step up the ramp, she felt something calling her. She knew not what, nor how she would get there. She only knew that to stay in New York meant to accept a solemn fate, to ignore the prophetic prompting of destiny. She had no choice but to trust her heart.

Jean kept her eyes straight ahead as she walked up the long ramp toward the ship. Head-turning gorgeous, she barely noticed that every man looked at her with admiration. She had long since become accustomed to such attention, although just what her admirers saw remained a mystery.

When she reached the top of the ramp, a tuxedoed man offered her a glass of champagne. She accepted. Her warm smile and direct eye contact startled the waiter—a butler, really—who was accustomed to being invisible to passengers.

Jean stepped onto the main deck. All around her, she saw her fellow passengers surrounded by friends and family members they'd invited aboard for a Bon Voyage party. The guests brought flowers, gifts, champagne; the wealthier the passenger, the more guests in their entourage. She hadn't even thought to invite her sister and felt no regret that her mother was not there to bid her farewell. She moved toward the massive sundeck that wrapped around the bow of the ship, hoping to escape the dense crowd. An attractive young couple stood near the shiny brass railing that rimmed the deck. With the city's skyline behind them, a photographer captured the innocent joy of newlyweds. Jean recognized a few faces, then realized she was standing among the couple's wedding party. She smiled her best high-society smile, and wove her way through the crowd without stopping to speak with anyone. Amid all the hugging and laughing, she could not, would not, allow herself to feel the undertow of loneliness that threatened to drag her out to sea, beyond the reach of other human beings, where she might very well drown in her misery.

Jean made her way to her private cabin, lay down on the bed and began to weep. Filled with fear, she wondered: *Why walk away from all that is familiar in the vague hope of finding something I cannot name?* She felt frightened by her own boldness. Self-condemning thoughts assaulted her, one after the other, demanding that she change her mind and abandon ship before it was too late. But Jean refused to soften her resolve. She would not remit. She stood up in her tiny berth, nearly bumping the ceiling. Catching a glimpse of her reddened face in the mirror, she wiped away the tears, squared off in front of her own reflection, and said, "You will not hide away in this little room." She lifted one foot and stomped the floor. Looking herself in the eye, she growled, "Go out and explore the ship." Then she slowly turned the nob, opened the cabin door, and stepped out.

The following day, she ran into the man who had welcomed her aboard with a glass of champagne. He was working behind a small bar on one of the ship's many sundecks. She lingered for quite a while, enjoying the waiter's knowledge of the ship's history.

"When World War II broke out," he told her, "the *Ile de France* was the last ship to leave France, just hours before the September 3, 1939 Declaration of War on Germany. She was carrying 400 passengers over capacity!"

The famous ocean liner had been overrun with American tourists desperate to get out of Europe. The voyage was a treacherous one; overcrowding was the least of the worries facing the ship's captain. In order to avoid becoming a casualty of war, he zigzagged the ship across the Atlantic at an average speed of 26 knots. He insisted on keeping the running lights extinguished. Thus did the *Ile de France* avoid Germany's U-boats and arrive safely in the New York harbor on September 9th.

The waiter spoke of the crossing as though he himself had been on board. "Over the course of those six days, German military submarines sank sixteen vessels on the high seas. Sixteen!"

He continued with the attention to detail typical of a docent: "Once she berthed in New York, her career as a passenger ship was suspended. In March 1940, after her troopship conversion, she was loaded up with 12,000 tons of material, including submarine oil, tanks, shells, and several uncrated bombers that were stowed on open decks. Over the next six years, she carried the stuff of war, including the 814th

Tank Destroyer Battalion, across the ocean to Europe. She even served as a floating POW camp for a time. In August 1942, while moored at Port Elizabeth, she was gutted. Hundreds of square feet of rare and beautiful paneling were ripped out. Furniture, ornate chandeliers, carpets, paintings, and fixtures were thrown on the dock to rot. After five years of military service, she returned to the builder's yard. Restoration took two years. She made her first postwar crossing in July 1949 and immediately became just as popular as she was before the war."

By the time they docked in Paris, Jean not only knew all about the ship's history, she also knew the waiter intimately. Years later, she would remember him fondly: "He was very intelligent and so much more interesting than the passengers lying around, waving for another drink, and trying to impress anyone within earshot."

But despite the fact that she enjoyed the waiter and found in him a wonderful lover, when he asked if he could see her sometime in the future, she declined. It wasn't in her nature to hold onto someone, to expect anything of a man beyond what was happening in the moment.

7.

The European Tour

The minute she stepped on European soil, Jean knew she'd made the right decision. She had in her possession letters of introduction that afforded her a comfortable place among the European upper class. In New York, she had crossed Central Park often enough to feel at home among the American royals of the Upper East Side. These family connections assured her a French bank account and a place to stay in Paris.

Upon arrival, she went to the Hotel Matignon on the Champs-Élysées. They allowed her to rent one of their compact rooms reserved for girls from blue-blooded families. The room was surprisingly inexpensive. Jean wandered around Paris, walking aimlessly through neighborhoods, exploring town squares and verdant parks, or passing the time in some patisserie where she would sit alone writing poetry, sketching buildings, and chit-chatting with passersby. She frequented

Café Les Deux Magots[8] and Café Flore where she sat and wrote in her diary. She loved Les Deux Magots and would often sit up on its second floor, enjoying the view of the Eiffel Tower. Startled by the decidedly non-American beauty of her surroundings, she often found herself people-watching for hours. The French had such strong, remarkable features. She found the women more sensual and natural than any of the New York women whose tireless concern for their appearance was so tedious. In Paris, Jean felt more at home than she'd ever felt in Manhattan.

After she'd been in Paris for six weeks, Jean called Iva Patcevitch at *Vogue Paris*.

"Where have you been?" he said. "I've been waiting for you."

The following day, he called her with a modeling assignment. She would be working with a famous French photographer; the setting: a boat in the Seine.

Shortly thereafter, Jean decided to sign with a modeling agency. She was offered a steady job as a model for Dior but turned it down. Uncomfortable with obligations, she only accepted occasional assignments that involved no commitment. This allowed her to make some money and not be trapped. If the agency rang her up, she could always say, "I'm busy, but please call me next time."

Decades later, she would look down her nose, assume an above-it-all posture, and say, "It wasn't wonderfully amusing."

---

[8] The famous café in the Saint-Germain-des-Prés area of Paris pulsed with the avant-garde, a meeting place for intellectuals, artists and literary figures, including: Simone de Beauvoir, Albert Camus, Pablo Picasso, James Joyce, Julia Child, and Ernest Hemingway.

Then, in a supercilious tone, she'd add, "You don't get proud of yourself for being a model."

She found it far more interesting to work as an interpreter. Somehow, in a matter of weeks, she had learned to speak fluent French and Spanish with no formal language studies. Once again, she signed with an agency. They would hire her for the day and sometimes just for an hour or two.

After several months of traveling around Europe, attending the "right" parties, and meeting all the "right" people, Jean boarded a train to Venice. She wanted to add Italian to the list of languages she spoke. Once there, she found a comfortable pensione,[9] settled in, and vowed to speak only Italian until she became fluent.

She'd only been in Venice a week when she was introduced to a fellow named Manfredo Camperio, an aristocratic landowner. He invited her to visit his family's estate in the Province of Monza and Brianza in northern Italy. Actually, in order to be "correct" and adhere to the expectations of his position, Manfredo had his mother invite her.

Jean was not oblivious to Manfredo's interest in her. But she was skilled at ignoring or deflecting men's advances and felt comfortable accepting the invitation. Once she arrived, she discovered that Manfredo was rather unlike other Italians. Years later, she would remember him as quite the marvel: "Imagine! A shy Italian man." Although gregarious in large groups, Manfredo became tongue-tied when he had occasion to speak with Jean alone. "By and large, he was an extrovert,"

---

[9] Pronounced *pen-see-oh-nay*, an Italian pensione is like a boarding house or long-stay hotel, similar to a youth hostel.

she said. "But alone, he turned into a very different animal. It was actually quite endearing."

Approximately 14 kilometers from Milan in the northwest of Lombardy, Brianza sits at the foot of the Alps. Both culturally and historically significant, the area is a favorite summer resort for residents of Milan. During the Middle Ages, the towns of Brianza saw the rise and fall of several religious movements, including the Cathars[10] and the Humiliati.[11] In the eleventh century, the area had been home to the Pataria, a movement that sought to reform the ecclesiastic government by supporting papal sanctions against marriage among the clergy, as well as simony, the practice of selling church offices and roles.

Jean wasn't interested in the area's religious history so much as its cultural significance. She was particularly fascinated with the life of a one-time resident of Brianza, the Italian poet and sociologist, Filippo Turati, who had died two decades earlier. One of the most important artists of his day, Turati participated in the *Scapigliatura*[12] movement, which consisted of an odd mix of poets, writers, musicians, painters and sculptors. Turati's *Inno dei Lavoratori,* the "Workman's Hymn," became the most popular song of the Italian labor movement.

Jean very much enjoyed her time at the Compario family estate and would have stayed on through the summer had

---

[10] Catharism was a Gnostic movement that flourished in northern Italy and southern France in the 1300s.

[11] Formed in the 12th century, Humiliati was an Italian religious order of men.

[12] The word *scapigliatura* is the Italian equivalent of the French *bohème,* i.e., bohemian.

she not received an invitation to visit another big estate in Tuscany. Once owned by an aristocratic family, the Tuscan estate had become a sort of private retreat. More than half of the guests were high-born Italians who were in dire straits; others were there to wait it out while some predicament or another passed. It was there that she was introduced to Pierro Stucchi, an actor whose family was considered pioneers of Chianti. He was on holiday and clearly enjoyed the colorful crew. Upon request, Stucchi agreed to drive Jean to Florence where he handed her over to a woman named Livia, who happened to be of the Medici family. Thus did Jean become friends with Livia Malvezzi Dei Medici, and later with Livia's sister, Mina.

"Livia had a little Topolino, a Mickey Mouse car really," Jean would later recall. Livia wanted to introduce her guest to the men of the town. It didn't matter how wrong they were for Jean, or how unattractive, they were wealthy and from the right families. Livia arranged to meet two such men in a café in Florence.

They set out in the tiny Topolino. If anybody dared tailgate Livia or do something to annoy her, she would swear at them, *"Stupido idiota!"* While on their way to the café, Livia talked and talked about a count who lived in the vicinity. It was the first time Jean heard the name Enrico Middleton Ventivoldo.

Speaking loud so Jean could hear over the whining of the sports car's overworked engine, Livia gossiped, "His great grandfather, Henry, was governor of South Carolina after the American Civil War. But Enrico was not recognized as a member of the family; he was a love child, the bastard son of Hermes Middleton, favorite son of Henry."

Jean's mind conjured up a scene from *Gone with the Wind*. "Frankly, my dear, I don't give a damn if he's a bastard," she quipped in her best Clark Gable voice.

Livia caught the reference and joined in the improvisation as Butterfly McQueen's character, Prissy. "Miss Scarlett! Miss Scarlett! I don't know nothin' about Italian men!"

They burst into laughter and continued the preposterous parody for a while, until Jean remembered she was actually curious about Enrico. "So how did he become an Italian nobleman?"

Livia's smile began to fade as she picked up the story. "Enrico's mother died in childbirth so his father adopted him, but the poor little boy was always treated as an orphan in the Middleton household."

Jean noticed an uncharacteristic, and yet quite genuine, sadness in this report on Enrico's misfortune. But she did not let on that she'd seen Livia's softer side.

"Slavery had been abolished, but the segregation that took its place still oppressed Blacks and gave them little in the way of freedom," Livia explained. "No gentleman, and certainly no landowner, could yet prosper in America without slaves. Enrico found the situation untenable, so he left America for his dead mother's home country. She had emigrated from Italy in 1918. Once here, he used his natural charm and intelligence to get himself knighted by Italy's King Victor Emmanuel III. And he fulfilled his dream of living among the landed gentry when he married Countess Bentivoglio. At last, he received the coveted title Count he felt he deserved. When the countess died two years later, he inherited her full estate."

Knowing how the story goes, Jean said, "So he was suddenly a bachelor. A bachelor with a title."

Livia pulled her sunglasses down just far enough to look over them and said, "A tall, blond, blue-eyed, handsome bachelor." Her eyes now off the road altogether, Livia leaned toward Jean and lowered her voice as if she were sharing some big secret. "All the American girls in Europe are throwing themselves at his feet, hoping to get the title of Countess if they play their cards right."

I'm not about to join the ranks of those American girls, no matter how beautiful his blond hair and blue eyes, Jean thought.

"Livia! Watch out!" she snapped, pointing at the lipstick-red Mercedes Benz coupe headed their way. Livia had inched into the oncoming lane right in its path. Jean reached for the wheel. Livia's left arm shot out, blocking Jean's reach. She let out a devil-may-care screech of laughter as she drove the sports car off the road. Jean's hands flew to her face, covering her eyes. A long moment and half a spin later, the car stopped in the dirt, twenty yards from the road. The wrong side of the road. Livia laughed and laughed as if she'd planned the whole thing. Jean was not amused.

When Jean met Enrico Middleton a few days later, she did not find him particularly attractive. She was, however, immensely curious about one bit of gossip Livia had shared with her: Enrico had supposedly brought a liter-size olive jar full of diamonds back from an expedition to South America the year before. According to rumor, he had taken the raw diamonds to America, sold them in New York City's highly competitive diamond district, and made a small fortune.

Jean continued to travel around Italy, and eventually to Rome. Her letters of introduction allowed her to avoid the trouble of finding accommodations; instead, she was the guest of aristocrats. She did not, however, feel a part of Western Europe's privileged class and found the aristocracy narrow and boring. Always a perfect guest in their overly spacious homes, she privately disdained what she viewed as the "highbrow attitude" and "lack of true curiosity" characteristic of the privileged. "I was basically a snob about snobs," she would say.

In late March of 1951, she traveled to the South of France and fell in love with the beaches and bays of the Mediterranean Sea. Through a Condé Nast connection, she was introduced to Philippe de Croisset. He, in turn, introduced her to Panchito Iturbi, and expressly instructed him to take care of Jean and, "Make sure she's okay." Jean registered the twinkle in Philippe's eye and knew immediately that this assignment was, in part, a joke. But Panchito had no sense of humor and took it seriously.

"It was the only way he could take anything," Jean wrote in her diary. His interpretation of "take care of Jean" was: *We are putting you in charge of making sure she meets the right people.*

One afternoon, Jean and Panchito were at the hotel pool where a large crowd lazed around, enjoying their cocktails. A group of young men who were more boisterous than the rest of the guests, wanted to meet her. Years later she would remember: "They were good clean American boys, washed behind the ears, the kind I'd have liked to meet. One in particular caught my eye. Tall and handsome. But the young men didn't have titles, and Panchito would only introduce me to men with titles. Even if they had paunches and double chins. People like Count Deronbet, a really unbeautiful, titled Frenchman."

Frustrated with Panchito's surveillance, Jean escaped early one afternoon and went swimming in the Mediterranean Sea. She swam out to where a number of yachts were anchored in the bay. Not a particularly strong swimmer, she got over-tired, and grabbed onto the nearest anchor chain to rest. The people on board were English. When they saw her holding onto the chain, they invited her aboard, dragged her on deck, dried her off and introduced her around. There was Michael Tree, son of Berbold Tree, a well-known actor. Plus Elizabeth Cavendish and Doone Plunkett. She was introduced to Duke Charlie Rutland, a well-known peer of the realm, and to his brother, Lord John Manors. Also aboard were Lucien Freud, the famous painter and grandson of Sigmund, and Lucien's wife, Lady Caroline Blackwood.

Duke Rutland quickly decided Jean was his date. In the fol-lowing weeks, he took her out to lunch at the home of Gianni Agnelli, "the head pussycat of Fiat." Johnny, as he was called, lived with his mistress Pamela Churchill,[13] the ex-wife of Ran-dolph Churchill, son of Winston. Pamela had a son by Ran-dolph and took up with Johnny after her divorce because, as she was wont to say, "He spent his money so well." They had a big, expensive villa where she lived with Johnny and his brother.

Pamela and Johnny were usually generous hosts. Several nights a week, they would invite all of their guests to join

---

[13] In a 1996 Irish Times article titled "Affairs of state aplenty for the century's great-est courtesan," we learn that it was her "unhappy marriage to British Prime Minister Winston Churchill's hard drinking, womanizing, gambling son, Randolph, [that] brought Pamela to No 10 Downing Street during the second World War."

them at a restaurant, order extravagantly, insist on picking up the bill, then invite everyone back to the villa to continue the party. Johnny and Pamela's place became Jean's home base.

"Unfortunately," she said, remembering, "It also became Duke Rutland's. He took to courting me, but I could not abide his advances and uncouth ways. At one point, I wanted to take a bath, but had run out of soap. Rutland suggested I go up to his room where I would find a fresh bar. I didn't take it to mean anything more than that, but the scoundrel saw an opportunity."

Half a minute later, the Duke climbed the stairs, walked down the hall to his room and stood at the door. There stood Jean, alone in his room, holding his bar of soap in her hand while he looked her up and down. "I pushed past him and headed for the bathroom, sans soap bar. When I saw him downstairs an hour later, I gave him the evil eye. Apparently, he didn't get the message because he made an even more outrageous advance a few days later."

Telling the story more than half a century later, she was still wide-eyed with disbelief. "A few of us went down to a private beach for the afternoon. We'd been there for a couple hours when I went out for a swim. Meanwhile, some starlet became overwrought about who-knows-what, so everybody packed up and left. The Duke volunteered to stay back and walk me home. You can imagine my surprise when I walked out of the water and found myself alone with him on the beach. He decided it was a fine time to go skinny dipping and dropped his drawers. Somehow the man had deluded himself into thinking that, by now, I must see him as a worthy suitor. Never mind I ignored him completely every time he spoke of divorcing Duchess Rutland. And whenever he hinted that he might propose, I either changed the subject or simply walked away. I felt so deeply offended by his behavior on the beach, I lost all decorum and told him directly, 'I have no feelings for you whatsoever.' Then, to make sure he felt unequivocally rejected, I added, 'No, that's not quite true. Due to your behavior here today, I feel nothing but contempt for you.'"

The situation with Rutland had been bad enough, but this incident made her horribly uncomfortable at the otherwise delightful Agnelli Villa. She left immediately when a letter from Panchito arrived later that week. For the first time in days, Jean could take a full deep breath. Panchito would put her up at the Grand Hotel in Venice, and that was the end of the non-affair with Rutland.

Upon her arrival in Venice, Panchito invited her to what he called, "my cousin's party."

"Your cousin?" she asked.

"Carlos de Beistegui," he replied.

Jean concealed her surprise. Well aware that everyone who was anyone had been vying for an invitation to what would surely be the event of the year, she smiled inside. *A masquerade ball hosted by Carlos de Beistegui at his palace on the Grand Canal,* she thought. *This should be entertaining.*

Tilting up her head, she sighed and asked, "What party?"

"Le Bal Oriental," Panchito replied. "At the Palazzo Labia."

8.

Le Bal Oriental

He was one of the most flamboyant characters of the 1900s. Art collector. Interior designer. Heir to a huge Mexican fortune. His friends always called him Charlie, but the world knew him as the mysterious bachelor, Don Carlos de Beistegui.

In the 1930s, Don Carlos decided to build a penthouse on the Champs-Élysées. Designed by Le Corbusier, the penthouse was alive with the eccentric and eclectic. Don Carlos commisioned Salvador Dalí to design his rooftop terrace, and engaged an expert craftsman to build him a moveable, electronically operated hedge that, once opened, afforded him a view of the Arc de Triomphe.

Telephones had gone from the wall to the desktop. The gossip bench became an important piece of furniture in the home simply because people needed a comfortable place to sit and confabulate on the phone. But discussions about the eccentric millionaire were anything but idle chit chat. He was, after all, the trendsetting icon of the day. Known far and wide as a connoisseur of the finest in all things, he objected to only one detail of the public's perception of him: he was often referred to as The Count of Monte Cristo. It was a poor and inaccurate comparison. Don Carlos had never been to prison. Not that he didn't push the limits of the law; he did. Especially in the upper echelons of the art world.

His wealth, and the power it bestowed on him, placed Don Carlos a notch above the law. He once commissioned a copy (some would say a forgery) of Hans Holbein's portrait of Henry VII, and then insisted his painting was the original and the portrait owned by the British Royal Family was a fake. An admirer of Far Eastern art, he owned giant jars made of tin that looked so much like authentic Chinese vases, even elite collectors were fooled. Don Carlos prized intricate tapestries of historical events in the style of Goya, a 17th century painter whose designs were woven by the Royal Tapestry Factory. Naturally, he commissioned Spanish weavers to create tapestries in the Goya style for his homes.

He also owned a huge collection of authentic art. One of his many prized possessions was a Louis XVI desk. Made of ebony and bronze, the desk had once been owned by Ignacy Jan Paderewski—the composer famous for the Minuet in G major—who became the Prime Minister of Poland in the early 20th century.

Don Carlos' taste in art impressed even his uncle and namesake, who owned a priceless collection of paintings from the 18th and 19th centuries that he donated to the Louvre near the end of his life.

Born to parents of Basque origin, his ancestors migrated to Mexico in the 1700s. There, his family made a fortune in real estate, agriculture, and silver. After the Mexican emperor was executed in 1867, the family left Mexico and returned to Europe. Don Carlos was born in France and spent most of his childhood in Paris. He also lived in England and Spain for periods of time—often with members of his extended family who were diplomats to Spain, Russia, and the United Kingdom.

As a young man, Don Carlos attended Eton, a boy's boarding school in Berkshire, England. He fell in love with language, even writing a volume of poetry that he illustrated himself. When his Cambridge matriculation plans were thwarted by the outbreak of World War I, he moved to his parent's mansion on the esplanade of Les Invalides in Paris. During the Roaring 20s, his renown on the Parisienne social scene reached far beyond France, inspiring him to sumptuous grandiosity in the style of the Decadent Movement of the late 19th century.

In 1939, Don Carlos acquired the Château de Groussay[14] at Montfort-l'Amaury, in the Yvelines west of Paris. An aesthete who lived by the maxim "art for art's sake," he embodied the idea that art is a rarified, sensuous pleasure, rather than a medium to convey moral and socio-political agendas. His plans to remodel the Château were waylaid by World War II, but in the 1950s, he commissioned Emilio Terry to collaborate with him on the interior design. They uprooted

---

[14] Built in 1815 by the Duchesse de Charest, daughter of Louise Elisabeth de Croÿ-Havré, marquise de Tourzel, who was the governess of the royal *enfants de France* of Louis XVI and Marie Antoinette.

and redesigned the grounds, designed a new park à l'anglaise (English landscape garden), and added 18th-century-style follies to the grounds. The enchanted gardens and landscape architecture of Château de Groussay were so close to perfection, the French government listed it among the Remarkable Gardens of France. Cecil Beaton, the renowned photographer and set designer, was so moved by the beauty of this remarkable pièce de résistance, he immortalized the house by using it as a model for the set of Henry Higgins' library in the movie *My Fair Lady*.

In 1948, Don Carlos purchased one of the last remaining palaces in all of Italy: the Tiepolo-adorned Palazzo Labia on the Grand Canal in Venice. Once again, he undertook a major remodel and renovation. His new home became yet another gallery for his growing art collection, including frescoes by Raphael and Guido Reni. He brought in exquisite tapestries and treasured antiques. So opulent, even excessive, was his taste in art that aficionados of the day began to refer to his style as "le gout Beistegui."

To show off the restoration of his palace, Don Carlos decided to host a masquerade ball. Everyone took notice: high-society Paris, New York, London. The intellectual elite. Famed artists and composers. Movie stars, authors, Pulitzer and Nobel Prize winners. Diplomats, counts and countesses. Princes from faraway lands. Haut monde around the globe began scrambling for invitations to Le Bal Oriental, which would one day become known as "The Party of the Century." Invitations to his inaugural "Fête des Fêtes" went out six months in advance. Guests began madly preparing for the grand affair, designing elaborate costumes that had to be custom made. As the day drew near, the pressure mounted. Everyone felt the need to make a dramatic, luxuriant entrée into the ball. In the weeks before the ball, the competition to be seen as the winner of an undeclared competition for "best costume" crossed the line into the absurd.

It was 1951, solidly into the post-war years. There was full employment in Western Europe. Italy had formed a fragile new democracy. Bankrolled by the Marshall Plan, the country was enjoying what soon became known as the "Italian Economic Miracle." Gas was still being rationed, but that did not dissuade the partygoers. Traveling by whatever means available, they set off for Venice.

At 10:30 in the evening on September 5th, 1951, a frivolous night of festivities that would metamorphose into myth began. Le Bal Oriental would mark the re-emergence of Venice as the pleasure capital of Europe. It was an ephemeral night, reminiscent of the opulent pre-war stunt parties hosted by gossip columnist Elsa Maxwell.

At the behest of Don Carlos, the ball was presided over by Anthony and Cleopatra. He asked the English beauty, Lady Diana Cooper, wife of the former British ambassador to France, to play the role of Cleopatra. His choice to play Anthony was Baron Alfred de Cabrol.[15] The pair dressed in elaborate costumes based on the Tiepolo fresco of Anthony and Cleopatra that hung in the grand entryway of the palace.

---

[15] Born in 1918, Baron Alfred de Cabrol came of age in the 1930s, a period characterized by the conflict between Marxist Socialism, Capitalist Democracy, and totalitarianism. Among his other influences was Surrealism, the avant-guard movement in art an literature that sought to release the creative potential of the unconscious mind.

An hour before the party was to begin, the canal to the palace was a bottleneck of launches and gondolas as guests from around the world made their way along the Grand Canal. Renowned art collector Arturo Lopez-Willshaw, dressed as the Emperor of China, pulled up in front of the palace in a Chinese junk. Attended by a retinue of Mandarins, he and his wife were carried into the party in a litter. Barbara Hutton, the Woolworth heiress, arrived dressed as Mozart. Princess Radzi-will disembarked on the arm of the Aga Khan disguised as an Eastern potentate. Jacques Fath came down the canal standing upright in his gondola, dressed as Louis XIV, the Sun King. His costume was so stiff, so tightly fitted, so weighted with embroi-dery, he could not sit down. Christian Dior, accompanied by a host of carnival giants, wore a costume created by Salvador Dalí. Half an hour later, Dalí himself arrived, in a costume designed by Dior. More than thirty guests wore costumes by a newcomer to the world of high fashion: Pierre Cardin.

The canal teemed with ladies and gentlemen flawlessly costumed, ready for a night of uncorked revelry. Crowds gathered to watch the spectacle, erupting in cheers at the sight of magnificent costumes, classic headpieces, elaborate wigs, and massive crinoline petticoats. Reporters paid own-ers of neighboring palazzos up to 80,000 liras to be allowed to photograph the parade from their second- and third-story windows.

Guests disembarked, bowing to one another. The curved staircase leading up to the palace was lined with footmen dressed in liveries that had been worn at Duchess Richmond's reception on the eve of Waterloo. The sound of a live orchestra lilted through the air as they ascended the stairs.

Towering over his guests in 16-inch platforms, Don Carlos greeted each one at the entrance to the grand hall. He wore a floor-length scarlet robe with an ascot made of the finest lace obtainable—presumably to hide his abnormally large Adam's apple. An 18th century sausage-curl wig cascaded over his shoulders and flowed down onto his robe.

Jean and Panchito arrived just before 11:00 pm. She looked beautiful and stately in her ruby-red gown. Her youthful pheromones spritzed the air as she ascended the stairs. Panchito noticed his uncle's eyes following Jean and immediately approached him to properly introduce her. "Uncle Charlie," he said with a slight bow, "I'd like you to meet my friend from America. Jean, this is my cousin, Don Carlos de Beistegui."

Jean extended a bejeweled hand. Don Carlos dipped his head, bent forward, reached down from his platforms and took her hand. But his shoes made him too tall to draw her hand to his lips, so he simply pet it and held her gaze.

At midnight, the 1,500 guests were summoned to the Great Hall by the sound of trumpets. Don Carlos welcomed everyone with a troupe of acrobats and announced that the festivities would continue through dawn the next morning. The entertainment included ballets, more acrobats, sambas, a room dedicated solely to the Charleston, and—of course— bountiful champagne.

At two o'clock in the morning, Jean stood alone on the bottom step of a stairway that led to the second floor, smiling as she watched society's upper crust go wild. Don Carlos stepped up behind her (by that time, he had taken off his platform shoes), and took her by the arm. He gently steered her across the room toward the only party guest not in costume. Jean recognized the man as Orson Welles. The woman on his arm was dressed as a classical Indian Bharatanatyam dancer. Introductions were made; bows and curtsies were pantomimed. A twelve-piece orchestra began to play. Welles' companion tapped his arm. As they swirled away in a waltz, he looked back at Jean with exasperation on his face. She was puzzled at first, but immediately understood when she saw Welles attempt a waltz.

Don Carlos nodded in the direction of a hearty looking chap wearing a midnight blue Renaissance shirt with lace-up neck. If Jean had seen the man-to-man signal that passed between the two, she would've declined the handsome chap's invitation to dance. But she did not see the unspoken communication Don Carlos flashed his friend. The man swept off his feathered Tudor cap and took a deep bow. Jean curtsied, dipped her chin, and gave him a coy smile. With the grace of a prince, he returned his cap to his head and extended an arm. Jean openly admired the gold satin that peeked through the slashes in his sleeves. Still playing coy, she giggled and took the man's outstretched hand. Don Carlos, ever the elegant host, turned and gave his full attention to the Duchess of Devonshire.

Waltzing away in another direction, Jean looked over her dance partner's shoulder and noticed a dark-skinned man with a star in his eye. He was tracking her from the far side of the dance floor. Dressed as a Jungle King, he moved with a regal grace that seemed to undulate off his body. Distracted and self-conscious, Jean had to force herself to focus on the next 1-2-3, 1-2-3. The dark skinned man continued to follow her with his gaze. When the waltz brought him close, she felt a warm sensation in her lower belly. She chatted with her dance partner in a failed attempt to ignore the Jungle King. Each time he came within her visual field, his beauty and grace penetrated her more deeply. The magnetic pull between them was undeniable, relentless. She felt helpless and whispered to herself: *Not The Third Force!* Pulled between two strong urges, she wondered if she should run from his gaze or surrender to its power.

"Do you know him?" asked the man holding her at the waist.

Jean shook her head. She was slightly embarrassed, had hoped her silent exchange with the dark-skinned man would go unnoticed. She missed a step but caught the waltz on the next beat.

"That is Aga Khan the Third's nephew," her dance partner said.

An hour later, Jean sat on a settee, a heavy crystal wine glass in her hand, chatting and laughing with another man who had no name. He told story after story, intermittently howling. *He sounds like a horny hyena,* Jean thought. But she quite liked the man, so she attributed his outbursts to the champagne.

Quite the storyteller, the man meadered from one tall tale to the next until Jean interrupted him saying, "Isn't that the famous painter? What's his name? Fabrizio . . . ?"

"Clerici," her new friend said, sitting upright on the settee, "Yes. That is Fabrizio Clerici." He then cocked his head slightly to the left, started to laugh, and touched Jean's hand as he directed her gaze toward a woman who had just entered the Grand Ballroom. Dressed as a standard poodle, the woman pranced through the parade of wild costumes.

When the still anonymous man asked if she'd like to go upstairs, Jean said, "Yes, I'd like that. But first I'd like to know your name."

"I'm Henry," he said, taking her hand for a kiss. She allowed her hand to glide up to his mouth. "And you are?" he asked.

"My name is Jean," she said. "A pleasure to meet you, Henry." She still had no idea who he was.

Henry took her arm in his and the two walked up the stairs, stopping here and there to greet friends and introduce themselves to strangers.

A woman Jean had never met came up behind her and whispered in her ear, "I hear his marriage is almost over. He loves younger women, you know." Before Jean could respond, the woman continued, "Will you introduce us? I loved his latest book."

Jean turned her head toward the woman, but not far enough to see her face. "What book?" she asked below her breath.

"Why, *Sexus,*" the woman said, "Have you read it?"

Jean swallowed, hard. She smiled, said, "I never read," and turned her head back around to her companion who was talking and laughing with a handsome couple wearing white masks.

Henry guided Jean upstairs and they wandered through various rooms. He hesitated at the door of a dark, smoky room, leaned toward her and said, "We may want to go down that way," attempting to steer her away from the door and into a hallway that led to the East Wing.

Jean caught the mischievous look in Henry's eye, said, "Nonsense," and skirted around him into the room.

There, on the bed, were three naked bodies in the midst of a ménage à trois. Jean did her best to conceal her startle at the scene that lay before her: a pair of legs with garter belt and seamed stockings making a "V" in the air while the man between her legs titillated the buxom blond standing on the bed before him.

She whispered to Henry, "Isn't that?—"

He interrupted her with a nudge and, having noted her absorption in the scene, redirected her eyes to the far corner of the room. An attractive couple lay draped across a red velvet chaise lounge, fondling each other while watching the writhing threesome on the bed. Jean covered her eyes with a mock-modest smile, muffled a girlish laugh, and peeked through her fingers.

Hours later, as first light began to inch its way up the sky, Jean spotted Christian Dior and Salvador Dalí, still in their costumes and deep in conversation. They were walking toward the canal and an awaiting gondola. Despite the fact that she hadn't been properly introduced to the two icons, she stepped into their path and proffered one of her signature puns: "Come now, you mustn't dilly-Dalí, Salvador." Then turning toward his companion, she said, "I just a-Dior the morning light, don't you, Christian?"

The two men smiled, nodded, and continued their conversation.

Jean turned back toward the palace, and strolled up the curved staircase and along the wrap-around walkway. She sat on a bench among a cluster of exhausted party-goers, most of whom had lost or been stripped of superfluous accessories, wigs, ruffles and all manner of boots and booties. Her own costume, a regal silk gown, was falling from her shoulders.

Her long, braided hairpiece was still perfectly draped over her breast.

From where she sat, Jean saw a tall, blond man walk out of the Grand Hall. He turned his face toward the early morning light and tried to conceal a yawn. She admired him for just a moment, then recognized him as Count Enrico Middleton. Shifting her gaze, Jean's eyes landed on the Jungle King as he stepped out of the hall. She recognized him instantly. *The nephew!* She wondered what sort of, or sordid, escapades had kept him occupied since their encounter on the dance floor. He stretched his arms toward the sky, expanding his chest as he yawned, then practically leapt down a flight of cement stairs and headed for the massive fountain in front of the palace. When Jean noticed Enrico walking in her direction, she skirted behind a statue to avoid him. The Count's pursuits had begun in earnest at their first meeting in Florence, but rapidly became tiresome. She found him no more regal than an imitation leopard print rug. But Enrico had caught a glimpse of her before she slipped out of view and began a not-so discreet vigil, waiting for the right moment to approach her.

Jean escaped down the stairs to the front entryway. She made a tremendous effort not to stare at the Jungle King as he lifted his beautiful body out of the fountain. His sculpted chest wet and shining, he wore nothing but a loincloth tied around his hips. Jean turned away, trying to hide her pleasure. A moment later, she looked up and smiled as their eyes met.

Watching from the walkway above, Enrico turned and walked away.

9.

"Stop the Train!"

Two weeks after Le Bal Oriental, Jean ran into Count Enrico in Milan. She didn't know it at the time, but he was there to meet Beppi Orlando, a man of means who had convinced the Count to make another expedition to South America. Beppi's father was an industrialist who made torpedoes, bombs, and submarines. Enrico only agreed to the expedition because Beppi offered to pay all of the expenses. In order to avoid pressure from others who would want to join them on the trip, they maintained complete secrecy about their plans.

During the early planning stages, the two men had fallen into a daily routine of meeting at a certain café at precisely 5:30 pm. By strange coincidence, Jean showed up at that very café late one afternoon. Enrico invited her over to their table, insisting she join them for dinner. While enjoying their meal, the two men spoke of their plan to take the train from

Florence to Paris for a meeting with a diamond merchant the following day. Enrico flirted with Jean throughout the meal. She would have excused herself had Beppi Orlando not been such a gracious host. Enrico, on the other hand, kept looking at her in an almost lascivious way. He was impervious to her polite deflections and, as the evening wore on, outright rejections. He persisted so ardently, she wasn't surprised when he invited her to join them on the trip to Paris.

"I was a very prissy girl," Jean would later recall. "Mother used to complain that I was too prudish. Anyway, I'd already been to Paris and didn't have any reason to go back. And if I did, it wouldn't have been with Enrico."

She loved to play a little game with herself, to see what happened when she was short with people, especially arrogant people. And Enrico was one of the most arrogant men she'd ever met. Careful not to be rude, she simply declined his Paris invitation, saying, "I'd prefer not," and left it at that.

But the Count was relentless. They were about to leave the restaurant when Enrico, emboldened by her rejection and more sure of himself than ever, said: "If you change your mind and want to go with us to Paris, I will be sitting at the Excelsior Hotel tomorrow. I will stay there all morning so my friends can come and say good-bye."

She wondered why his friends would want to say good-bye. A trip to Paris was de rigueur.

The following morning, she got dressed and went down to the nearby cheese shop where she typically ate her favorite breakfast: a thick slab of bread and a hunk of stinky cheese. She greeted Antonio, the owner of the shop, saying, "*Buongiorno Amico*." He walked across the hardwood floor with its familiar pattern of creaky boards and set a plate in front of her. She looked down at the food; her appetite suddenly vanished. She had no interest whatsoever in breakfast, which was usually her favorite meal. Out of nowhere, a powerful nudge from a place below conscious awareness pushed her up and out of her chair. "I'm afraid I'm just not hungry this morning," she said, handing Antonio 50 liras. "*Bel giorno.*"

The Excelsior Hotel was only three blocks away. A few minutes later, she was sitting at a window table in the hotel's café with her sketchpad. Enrico sat at a table on the other side of the room. When the stream of well-wishers slowed to a trickle, he stood up from his chair, took ten paces in her direction, and sat down at Jean's table. Moving his chair right next to hers, he said, "One day I would like to show you London."

She looked at him, expressionless. "I've been to London."

"Well, then. Will you allow me to take you to Rome when I get back from the jungle?"

"The jungle?" Now she understood the reason for all the good-byes. He was going back to South America, likely leaving straightaway.

"Yes. When we finish our business in Paris we will fly to New York then on to Caracas. Would you like to come with us?" he asked. It was clear to her he was teasing.

Jean's rational mind shorted out. "I certainly would," she said.

Enrico's smile said, "Surely, you're joking."

"I really would."

"That's a big responsibility, taking a white girl to the jungle," he said.

"No, no," she insisted. "The responsibility would be mine. I really do want to go."

Enrico smiled again. This time his smile said, "You can't be serious."

Jean pressed on. "When do you depart?"

"Beppe will be here soon," he said. "The train to Paris leaves at noon."

"That's in half an hour," she said.

Enrico smiled. "Yes." The creases around his eyes showed confusion, but his tone of voice offered a challenge.

"I'm coming," she said. It was a fearless, seemingly irrational, utterly instinctive decision. "Don't leave without me."

Jean pushed through the crowded foyer of the Excelsior Hotel. Count Enrico's words, "The train for Paris leaves at noon," echoed in her ears. She barely knew the count and had only met his plump little financier, Beppi, the day before. But that didn't matter; she would go to the jungle with anybody.

She stepped into the late morning sun and looked at her watch. Eleven thirty. *I can make it in 30 minutes,* she thought.

Her pensione was three blocks away—three blocks in the opposite direction from the Milano Centrale Railway Station. She turned east and started down the sidewalk, noting that her stride was longer than that of any other pedestrian on the street. For the first time in her life, she felt grateful for her long, skinny legs.

Half a foot taller than the average American woman, Jean saw herself as awkward, too thin. Decades later, she would reflect on her younger self: "Unlike my sister, I was just a skinny bag of bones. Fran had a beautiful body like our mother. She was certainly sexier than me. I had no boobs, no bottom. Later on, I learned that it wasn't about the boobs and the bottom. It wasn't the shape of the body; it was the way of carrying it around. Apparently, that's what made me more attractive to men than my sister, although I couldn't see it."

Jean ran up the stairs of the pensione where she'd been living and grabbed the phone on the second- floor landing. The pensione owner picked up her call; she asked him to prepare her bill right away. "E mi chiami un taxi." She flew down the hall to her room, pleased that she'd never fully unpacked.

Once in the cab, Jean had a moment to think. Never had she acted with such certainty before. She sensed there were unimaginable dangers ahead, but she refused to think about that now. In fact, she refused to think about anything at all. Her body began to shake with excitement.

The cab pulled up to the curb in front of the station. She handed the driver ten thousand lira and jumped out, suitcase in hand. A train whistle ripped through the air. The train conductor's voice boomed: *"Tous à bord!"* No time to buy a ticket. She ran into the station house and headed straight for the platform, pushing through the heavy doors just as the conductor stepped onto the metal stair of the second car and held up his arm to signal departure.

"Stop!" she shouted. The wheels of the train began to screech on the rails. She ran, her suitcase bouncing off her legs. The straight-backed conductor glanced her way and shook his head. She shouted, "Stop the train!" with an authority she did not actually possess, compelling the conductor to reach out his hand. A quick moment later, she was standing next to him on the moving train.

Had she taken the time to evaluate the pros and cons of embarking on such an adventure, she might have passed up the opportunity. As it was, only after she had settled into the train compartment, did she take account of what had just happened. *I am on my way to a genuine jungle,* she thought. The implications were incalculable—and rather frightening. She looked at all the suitcases piled high in the corner and felt doubtful, but only for a moment. After all, digging for diamonds in riverbeds deep in the forest sounded far more interesting than modeling, or any other occupation she could imagine.

Whenever she said the word, *jungle,* whether within her own mind or aloud, that feeling of rightness she'd experienced as a child in the woods of Maine swarmed her awareness. Sitting there on the train, she once again felt that delicious wholeness in every part of her body. It even seemed to increase the amount of oxygen in the air. In that moment, any doubts she had about tagging along with Enrico flew out the dusty train window.

10.

Diamond Hunting

Amazonia, 1951

In order to leave the Sanema village and set out on their diamond hunt, Enrico, Beppi and the rest of their small party would need at least two men to be their guides. It was a long trek from the village to the remote region of the jungle where Enrico found diamonds on his previous expedition. He would have to ask the Sanema chief to let two of his men leave the village for weeks. That would require offering something of value in trade. He would have to wait for the right moment. In the meantime, he did his best to prepare Jean and Beppi for what lay ahead.

"Diamond hunters are a rough, international group," he explained. "They live alone or in pairs deep in the bush for months at a time, and only come out when they run out of provisions or have a booty of diamonds to sell. Once they get their money, they often go on drunken sprees and spend all of it in a matter of days. They set aside only as much as they need to equip themselves for the next expedition. Many of them never return to civilization. Whether they die in the jungle or decide to make their home there is usually unknown."

They sound like the most foolish daredevils in the world, Jean thought. *And yet I completely understand their fascination with the jungle.*

Enrico continued: "The diamonds are formed deep in the mountains over thousands of years. They get washed out as gravel from mountain erosion and come down into countless streams."

He described the diamond hunting method in detail. "You will be given a three-screened pan to sift through the dirt and mud," he said.

She nodded, giving Enrico her full attention while Beppi listened, rapt.

"Instead of walking through the woods looking at the ground for something that sparkles," he said, "we go to the edge of a stream where the land starts to dip down. Then you start digging and keep on digging until you get to a layer that's a slightly different color than the top layer of soil. Fill your bucket, then grab a handful of the dirt at a time and place it in the saruca. Shake and twist it. Shake, one-quarter turn; shake, one-quarter turn; shake, one-quarter turn." He demonstrated the movement, then went on: "Shake for a bit then rinse in the stream. Repeat this sequence and keep rinsing until all the muck is gone."

"Sounds like we should have brought my hairdresser," Jean quipped, mocking the female stereotype contradicted by her presence in the jungle.

Enrico shook his head, missing only the slightest beat, then went on: "The top layer of a saruca has the largest holes, so stones fall through to the medium-screened layer and finally into the finest screen. Then it's time to find a spot, hopefully in the sun, and dump the contents of the smallest screen in a pile in the dirt. Keep doing this until the bucket is empty. By then, the first piles you made will be dry. The diamonds will be on top of the pile where you'll see them gleaming in the sun."

"If the reflections from Beppi's bald spot don't blind me first," she said, poker-faced.

"*Sei impossibile!*" Enrico said and turned away.

After nearly a month of listening to Beppi complain, Enrico finally approached the chief and asked him to allow two of his men to be their guides. The chief refused his request. A week later, the chief sent his sheriff to negotiate a deal. All of the tribespeople—men, women, and children—had become fascinated with a pair of scissors the foreigners had in their possession. The chief would accept this as a gift in exchange for two guides.

When Enrico told Jean, "We're leaving tomorrow," and pointed to a well-provisioned canoe, she felt awash with mixed emotions. Life in the village suited her. She had just settled into a comfortable routine and made friends with a few of the women. What would a diamond hunt—with all that digging, sifting, and muck—have in store?

I guess I'll find out, she thought.

Two days upriver, they set up a base camp on the riverbank. The guides went off to hunt, taking their bows and arrows as well as a couple of machetes. They came back with a roebuck and roasted it over an open fire. In the morning, Jean ate sweet pineapple for breakfast and packed up some food while Enrico and Beppi collected their gear. When they left the base camp, Enrico walked ahead of Jean. Two hundred yards into the forest, he turned around and repeated what he had said a number of times before, "You must never forget that the jungle is dangerous. It is incredibly easy to get lost." That was obvious, of course. Nonetheless, she thanked him with genuine appreciation for his concern.

A ceiling made of interlacing treetops made it nearly impossible to see the sky. The green walls echoed with incessant birdsong, deadening all other sound. She had barely begun to develop that special awareness essential for survival in the jungle, a second sense that neither exaggerates nor underestimates potential dangers. Half an hour later, she turned around a bend in the path and came face-to-face with a 12-foot brown and orange bushmaster snake, coiled and ready to strike. She froze. The Sanema guide who had been walking a couple of yards behind her was suddenly facing her, standing behind the snake. She watched as he swung his machete to the ground and whacked off the snake's head. How had he moved from behind to facing her in a split second without making a sound? Jean's respect for these people immediately increased in direct proportion to the gratitude she felt for this man who had just saved her life.

From that point on, Jean never felt endangered by the Sanema. Clearly, they respected women. In the months and years that followed, almost every man in the tribes she visited propositioned her. Even ten-year old boys and old men proposed marriage.

"It was all very friendly," she recalled. "They would smile and nod, make graphic signals. The adolescents would even make sexual gestures to show me what was in store should I choose them as my mate. It wasn't offensive to me because they did it with the utmost respect. I only had to smile and shake my head no. They never got angry or took it personally."

What a prize she would be, this tall light-haired woman with the gangly legs. Yes, she was ugly by their standards, but to have her would considerably increase a man's status.

After several hours of scrambling through the forest, Jean's feet hurt so much that she reached for Enrico and took his arm. He startled, snapped his arm away, and said, "I like to walk free." In time she discovered that Enrico didn't want to have any feelings. *Odd for an Italian,* she thought. *The English are terrified of feelings, but an Italian?* It was highly unusual.

They found no diamonds on this first trek into the jungle. But Enrico was happy and quite satisfied that he'd successfully trained two novices how to hunt for diamonds. When the small party arrived back at the village, they were given a warm welcome. In their absence, the Sanema had moved all of their guest's belongings to a small area they had cleared inside the village perimeter. They had also constructed a small hut for Jean.

She stayed close to "home" for the next two weeks. Content to stay in the village, she excused herself when Enrico and Beppi went on walkabouts in the forest. She came to understand why diamond hunters were so fascinated with the jungle. She wrote in her journal: "The mysteries of life in the rainforest, the ways of the animals and plants, the dramatic storms and sunsets, the snakes, the orchids, the virginity, the burden of making one's way in it, and the generosity of its beauty all make it profoundly right."

The time approached to make another trek into the jungle. Five days upriver they reached the delta and set up their base camp. The next day, the diamond hunt began in earnest. The first step involved a daunting construction project, made far more difficult by the fact of having only meager tools and human labor. If only they had a single mule, the procedure could have been completed in half the time. They had to divert the stream, break up the uppermost crust of the diamond formation, and shovel the gravel away to get to the deeper stratum that, hopefully, held the prized stones. This preparatory operation would require two days of backbreaking work from dawn to dusk.

Jean was assigned the perplexing task of sifting each shovel of gravel through a saruca. She wondered: *Why sift all that gravel if the diamonds are in the deeper stratum?* For two days straight she sieved and sieved and sieved until her fingers and the palms of her hands were covered with blisters. But she didn't find a single diamond, only a few flecks of gold.

On the third day, they slept late and ate a hearty breakfast of grilled woodcock before getting to work. Spirits were high. It wasn't long before Beppi found the first diamond. *"Trionfo!"* he shouted, his voice echoing through the surrounding jungle. Enrico congratulated him with a manly hug.

Late that afternoon, as dusk spread its golden hues through the forest, Jean saw a gleam in the second screen of her saruca. The pain in her back and hands vanished the moment she held the glittering stone to the sky. Here was a crystal formation formed one hundred miles below the surface of the Earth, a very long time ago in the history of our planet. Brought to the upper mantle of Earth's surface by violent volcanic eruptions, each diamond comprised carbon atoms subjected to extreme pressures and temperatures—conditions that forced the atoms to bond, locking into a precise and perfectly organized crystalline structure. She was hooked.

Two weeks later, Enrico and Beppi had harvested a handful each of uncut diamonds; Enrico guessed their quarry to be thirty karats. Jean only found four small diamonds, but she returned to the Sanema village with something else altogether. The jungle had tested her courage, and she had won. She was changed. And that was a treasure all the diamonds in the world could not buy. In her journal, she wrote:

> I have come to the end of my search. My goal has been achieved. The four diamonds represent the clear view of things at their undiluted best. Here is the rightness I longed for through the bafflements of my childhood. It's what I was seeking throughout my adolescent years in all those talks, discussions, and arguments—often pursued until dawn in the hope of getting a glimpse of it. Here it is, The Glade: lost, found, and now recognized, this time forever. Around me, overhead, underfoot, everything is right, being born, living, dying, being replaced without a break in the order of it all.

At the end of the successful expedition, they went back to the little outpost of Los Caribes for supplies. Jean saw herself in the mirror and was startled; she'd gained about fifteen pounds. For the first time in her life, she was slender, not skinny. She felt stronger, more able, and less afraid than ever before. She was thriving in her beloved jungle and began to think seriously about staying behind when Enrico went back to Europe. But she need not settle that question just yet. She still had six months to think about it. They had only been back in the village two days when an owl monkey decided Jean was his mother. "The cute little critter started following me around. Finally, I adopted him as my pet. Everyone in the village smiled with approval. They were happy for both of us."

By the time another six months passed, Jean was ready to go home. She'd suffered a horrible case of malaria. Her health was at an all-time low. Thinner than ever, she suffered a painful hunger for meat and vegetables, and would have parted with one of her hard-won diamonds for a glass of orange juice.

11.

People of the Canoes

In 1953, a year after returning from the jungle, Jean embarked on her second expedition to Venezuela. The leader of the trip, an Italian professor, firmly believed girls had no business in the jungle. But Enrico insisted, "An experienced female jungle explorer with journalistic skills would make an excellent photographer to record our journey." The professor begrudgingly agreed. Soon Jean would enter the Stone Age world of the Yequana, a tribe whose way of life had been protected by the impenetrable rainforest of the upper Cauran River basin for centuries.

Among South Americans, the Yequana are viewed as *finished*. Quite the opposite of "doomed," the word "finished" in this context means highly evolved and complete, a culturally advanced society consisting of uniformly kind, intelligent people. Once Jean got to know them, she was amazed at the strong personalities and distinct individuality of the Yequana people. "They had never even seen a white man," she told me. "So they didn't have that defensive blank-face-for-strangers I saw on the faces of Tauripans who were accustomed to dealing with outsiders."

The first historical reference to the Yequana dates back to 1744 when Manuel Román, a Jesuit priest, recorded their existence. In the late 1700s, the Spaniards and Portuguese had encountered the Yequana. The Europeans attempted to convert the indigenous people and "save their savage souls" but were unsuccessful. The Yequana rebelled and outsmarted the white man's attempts to exploit them, maintaining only the most stealthy, sporadic contact with the strangers.

The Yequana inhabit a region north of the upper Orinoco River in the Guiana Highlands of Venezuela. Crisscrossed by the major tributaries of the Orinoco—the Cunucunuma, Iguapo, Padamo, upper Ventuari, and upper Caura, as well as countless minor tributaries and meandering streams—their habitat is primarily thick rainforest. In the early 1950s, when Jean traveled into Yequana territory, the area was completely inaccessible to any but the most fearless explorers and fiercest exploiters.

Caribbean languages are spoken throughout northernmost South America, from the mouth of the Amazon in northern Brazil to the Andes Mountains in Columbia. There are fifteen to twenty Caribbean dialects,[16] all closely related; most were still spoken in the early 1950s. The Yequana

---

[16] A unique feature of one Cariban dialect, Hixkaryana, makes it fascinating to linguists: a rare reversal in word-order wherein the object comes before the verb and the subject, for example: "Bananas ate Mother," or "Huts build people" or "Tobacco smokes Father."

speak a unique dialect of this indigenous tongue. Rare were the indigenous people who had learned any Spanish, but some Spanish-speakers learned enough Cariban to serve as translators.

The Yequana call themselves *So'to,* which translates as "the people." The word "Yequana" means "canoe people" or "people of the branch in the river," a reference to the placement of their villages in close proximity to the river. Canoes are their only means of transportation other than on foot. They make canoes by burning out the center of large trees. They also make bongos, hammocks, and crude pottery. Men and women alike wear jewelry made of seeds, animal teeth, claws, and beads carved from deer hoofs. They make their eating utensils out of smoothed and polished calabash gourds that have a water resistant coating inside. Yequana women weave wuwas, bell-shaped baskets that mimic the female form. They decorate the baskets with intricate designs using natural dyes. The baskets are eminently practical, made to fit into the small of a woman's back so she can easily carry a load.

The Yequana also make weapons: blowguns, hand-carved clubs, and slingshots. Decorated with ornate, intricate carvings that tell the story of their tribe, these weapons carry great symbolic weight among the people. The Yequana are not strictly hunter-gatherers, however, for theirs is also an agrarian society. Their staple crop is bitter manioc. They also grow bananas, maize, sweet potato, peppers, and tobacco. They live in close harmony with the earth and rely on that relationship to provide for them and preserve their way of life.

Among the Yequana, each important life-passage or initiatory rite is honored and celebrated by an exchange of baskets between families, and between the sexes. Before they can marry, Yequana men are required to demonstrate their basket-making prowess to the proposed wife's family. Especially valued are flat serving baskets that are believed to be cosmograms of the universe. These baskets feature complex designs that represent the dome of the heavens and circular fields filled with elaborate drawings depicting atmospheric patterns and the "Overseers"—power animals that protect the tribe and their world.

The complex cosmology of the Yequana views the Universe as multidimensional, consisting of three levels—heaven, earth, and the underworld—with eight strata that connect Heaven to the Earth. Each heavenly stratum is a cosmological station, the highest of which is home to their celestial protector and hero, Wanadi. The son of the sun, Wanadi resides in the celestial realms along with his family and an elite group of ancestors. Only the shamans have contact with Wanadi, who bestows on them their healing powers. Yequana regard sickness as indicative of an intrusion by unwanted spirits. Shamans chant, rattle, smudge with tobacco, use celestial crystals, blow and suck out illnesses. The Yequana believe that if an individual falls ill due to a transgression of tribal custom, his soul becomes fragmented. The shaman can heal him by performing a soul-retrieval.

According to one Yequana legend, a group of tribesmen stole a treasured box from a vicious forest monkey. When they looked inside the box, they found depictions of protective animal spirits that are used to this day in their art.

Communal living is a way of life among these forest-dwellers. A Yequana village is built around a large communal roundhouse.

Inside the house there is a central room reserved for rituals and ceremonies. This room is primarily for the men—they sit, they eat, they carve, they weave. Women do not enter except to serve meals or clean the space. If a shaman decides to perform a séance or do ritual magic to expel a harmful spirit, he sits near the center pole on a bench specially carved for this purpose. A shaman's bench is carved in the shape of a stylized jaguar, always from a single piece of wood.

The communal roundhouse also serves as sleeping quarters for unmarried men who have been initiated into manhood but have not yet taken a bride. A wall consisting of palm fronds, barks, wattle and daub separates the inner room from concentric living spaces that house the young men. Each has a small space of his own, sectioned-off by bark panels with a door into the central room.

The houses in the village, called atta or ëttë, are circular in shape with a conical palm-leaf roof that reaches to the sky. The cone-shaped roof is both symbolic and practical. When tribesmen and women come together to build an atta, they are recreating the cosmic home of Wanadi, the Great One, their creator. Likewise, the architecture of the communal living space is believed to replicate an original tiered-design provided by Wanadi.

Labor among the Yequana is divided along traditional lines. The women cultivate and harvest the garden but spend most of their working hours processing manioc and preparing food. The women are especially adept at collecting earthworms, leafcutter ants, palm-borer larvae, turtle eggs, frogs, and wild fruits, all of which generate a flurry of excitement when brought back to the kitchen. The men hunt tapir, deer, peccaries, anteaters, male alligators,[17] armadillos, and turtles, either by tracking or communal hunting drives. Fishing is generally viewed as a job for the women, although men occasionally join in for sport, showing off for one another by spearing fish with harpoons. Rather than fish with spears, the women use barbasco, a poison made by pulping leaves from a combination of plants. They place the mixture in baskets that are made from leaves gathered near their fishing spot. When the basket is placed in the water, it releases a poison that extracts the oxygen from the water. Stunned, the fish float to the surface, and the women hit them over the head with a stick and throw them into a collecting basket on the riverbank.

Jean found great satisfaction in participating in the weekly fishing trip. "The method is really quite elegant," she wrote in her journal, "and far more efficient than spearfishing."

Both men and women wear loincloths, and both sexes wear wristlets and bands around the upper arm and ankle. They often tie these bands so tight at the arm and below the knee that their biceps and calf muscles grow huge. Men pierce their ears with pieces of arrow reed decorated with colorful bird feathers. All members of the tribe wear a short bowl-shaped haircut and frequently paint themselves with dark blue and red body paint.

One of their most unattractive habits (in Jean's estimation) is sucking on a wad of tobacco or coca leaves. Even children walk around with a wad of leaves between their gums and teeth. This gives them a bizarre black smile that makes them

---

[17] They knew better than to destroy the mothers of the prized reptiles.

look like zombies. For them, the habit is as common—and as stimulating—as our habit of reaching for a cup of coffee.

Enrico, along with the Italian professor and the two diamond hunters who'd joined them in Caracas, tramped off into the bush, intending to be gone for two or three days. Jean was content to stay behind with the Yequana. After a week passed, she began to feel concerned. When the men returned three weeks later, they reported having been detained by a large band of pygmies who kept them as pets.

During those weeks of living alone with the Yequana, Jean had many a startling awakening that began to unravel her beliefs about human nature.

The unlearning process began in earnest as she witnessed the Yequana going about their day-to-day lives. Jean fell in love with the women's routine; she took great pleasure in their bathing and swimming rituals, which she participated in daily. She enjoyed the sound of their musical chatter as they hiked along the bank of the river to a deep swimming hole. The flat rocks around the edges made it a perfect spot to languish in the shade while the children splashed and played in the cool water. To her, they appeared not all that different from American families at the community pool, although none of the mothers showed the least bit of concern for her child's safety.

In the flow of daily life, she took note of the contrast between Yequana infants and infants in the modern world. Yequana babies were soft and easy to handle. They didn't arch their backs, kick their little legs, or wave their chubby little arms in distress. In contrast, infants in the "civilized" world wriggle and strain in their cribs, then continue to do so when they are picked up, which makes tending to a baby more of a chore than a pleasure. Yequana infants are carried about in any position that makes it easy for the mother to do what needs to be done. They have no tension in their bodies whatsoever. In the entire three weeks she lived alone with the Yequana, she never once heard a baby cry.

This, and countless other observations, caused Jean to question the assumption that civilized people are more advanced, more sophisticated, and more intelligent and evolved, than these so-called "savages."

One example of the Yequana way, piqued her interest early on: these tribal people never displayed even a smidgen of boredom. Unquestioned by them and yet notable to Jean, she reflected on this, comparing it to the tendency of civilized culture to rob people of well-being by assigning them repetitive tasks, thus depriving them of a variety of stimuli. For example, factory workers must ignore the discomfort of boredom and quash their natural urge to alter their focus if they want to keep their job.

In contrast, the Yequana respect the limits of their attention and answer the signal to "do something else" long before boredom disturbs their state of well-being. Jobs that we would consider humdrum—such as making a manioc grater by hammering rows of sharp metal bits onto a board—are turned into an art project. Instead of a monotonous pattern of row after horizontal row, the women begin with a diamond pattern then work inward, filling in the diamond until the pattern disappears.

Likewise, a long day of roof building—which involves lashing palm leaves to a framework with a woody vine called a liana—is transformed from a dull, tedious task into a party. The men inch along a makeshift scaffold carrying piles of leaves. For hours, they lash the cumbersome palm leaves to the framework one by one without getting the least bit bored. Often they invite men from a neighboring village to help and serve a special drink made of fermented manioc that keeps everyone a wee bit tipsy.

Throughout the workday, the staccato beat of a drum sets the pace for the workers who, in preparation for the task ahead, have painted their faces and dressed in festive attire. Men and boys work together, laughing and joking, trading off tasks whenever they feel like making a change. If a member of the crew is not in the mood to work, no one judges his choice to sit it out. Even at night, when everyone (including the children) start drinking and the men get completely drunk, there is never a disagreement or harsh exchange of words.

The Yequana take it for granted that life is a celebration. Whereas we feel lucky when our pursuit of happiness pays off, Yequana people live in a state of blessed good cheer that is anything but savage.

12.

To Be Truly Seen

When the expedition was over, Jean returned to Paris with a cache of diamonds worth seven thousand dollars. She took an apartment in Belleville-Menilmontant, the quartier Edith Piaf called home. Like all Parisian neighborhoods, the area was infused with a rich history and yet was compelled to constantly reinvent itself. She chose her small studio on a charming corner, the Parc de Belleville, because of its panoramic views.

After two trips to South America with Enrico and his compadres, she'd had enough of the Italians. But she'd not had enough of the jungle. She wanted to spend more time with the Yequana and began making plans to lead an expedition herself. She had not yet formed a conscious intention to study their ways; she simply felt more at home in her own skin among the Yequana than she felt among New Yorkers or Europeans.

She was almost as much an anomaly at soirées in Paris as she'd been among the tribal people. In the jungle, Jean was given respect. In Europe, she was a curiosity, the focus of gossip. People would whisper: "That's the woman who went to the jungle and lived with those savages." The more people took an interest in her, the less interest Jean took in them—with a few rare and wonderful exceptions.

In Venice, there is an art exhibit every two years called *La Biennale*. The event features the best painters, both recognized and unrecognized. People come from all over Europe, America, Australia. The daughter of two artists, Jean thought nothing of it when she painted, quite skillfully, a few of the people she'd seen in the jungle. She'd captured one in a portrait, another carrying a canoe overhead. She was surprised and delighted when she was asked to exhibit the two pieces in a small gallery as part of La Biennale in 1955.

In the spring of that year, she spent an entire week in Venice. One day, while she stood viewing a rather puzzling painting in the latest modernist style, a man stepped up beside her. She couldn't remember who spoke first, but she suspected it had been her because she always loved talking to strangers.

The man turned out to be Serge Lifar, the great Russian dancer who'd become the head of the Paris Opera Ballet. The two of them pirouetted into a conversation, and then a romance. For the next four days, they danced through the bridges and palaces, through shadows, through architecture, through history and culture.

Serge was by her side the day she met art historian Renaldo Dubois, who taught at École des Beaux-Arts. He approached her at a sidewalk café. *"Excusez moi,"* he said, *"Mademoiselle Liedloff?"*

Serge stood up and extended his hand, "*Monsieur DuBois. Serge Lifar. Au plaisir de vous revoir.*"

M. DuBois replied in English, "Yes, yes. Pleasure to see you as well, Lifar. I look forward to your spring performance."

Serge nodded. "Have you met, *Mademoiselle?*"

"I have not," he said. He turned to Jean, extended his right hand, palm up. She lifted hers for the customary kiss. "I have seen your paintings at La Biennale. Remarkable work."

"Thank you, sir."

"Where did you study?"

"Oh goodness," she said, looking down and pretending to be embarrassed before looking him in the eye. "I haven't studied painting."

"Excellent," he said. "You should never go to art school."

For Jean, those four days in Venice were exquisite, la crème de la crème. They were perfect in themselves, of a quality that was neither defined nor limited by space and time. It was very beautiful. Her love affair with Serge started itself and finished itself. And to be truly seen by Monsieur DuBois . . . well . . .

She felt similarly seen by Leo Longanesi to whom she was introduced while in Milan. A political activist (some would say anarchist), Longanesi was a philosopher, writer, and director of ten distinguished newspapers including *L'italiano, Omnibus,* and *Il Borghese.* According to the intellectuals of the day, he was the most intelligent person in Italy. But Jean described him as "an anti-intellectual intellectual—like me."

She and Longanesi struck up a friendship and spent quite a bit of time together in the years between her second and third expedition. She had a special affection for him and often spoke fondly of their relationship: "Once, we were in a taxi headed to some event in Rome and he quoted Socrates, saying, 'The unexamined life isn't worth living.' When I disagreed, he bristled then slapped my face, which was odd because he wasn't a slapper. I was, but he wasn't. He must've felt justified. How dare I disagree with Socrates? I pressed the point, saying, 'A fisherman goes out and catches fish day after day. He sells fish, makes money to provide for his family, and is respected. He might not be worthy of being called a philosopher. He has no reason to examine his life. He is a fisherman. Is his life not worth living?'"

Jean and Longanesi had discussions of this sort everywhere they went. "People were dying of curiosity to know what we were talking about," she would say. "He was a figure, the head of *Il Borghese*. He was also a painter, an arbiter of taste in furniture, art. Italy in general looked to him for what was good, bad, beautiful, or ugly." To his public, Longanesi was 'the one who knows' and the informal head of a political party: the monarchist fascists.[18] When he exhibited his paintings, Umberto II, the last King of Italy, was the first to buy one. Leo took me to meet the exiled king where he was living in Cascais on the Portuguese Riviera."[19]

---

[18] Known as Partito Nazionale Monarchico the monarchist fascists sought to unite conservatives, liberals, and nationalists. Especially strong in Southern Italy, the party was a right-wing competitor to Christian Democracy.

[19] Jean was especially moved when, over dinner, the king shared the details of his decision to leave Italy, rather than start a civil war after losing the 1946 Italian institutional referendum, which put an end to the monarchy. Umberto had reigned for only 34 days when Italy became a republic.

Jean would become particularly animated when she quoted Longanesi as having said to her: "You're the only person more intelligent than I am." In her journal she wrote:

> His respect for my intelligence and seeming lack of interest in my physical beauty was quite unusual. I'd even say uplifting. He would take my opinion into account, even change his point of view at times. He told me how much he appreciated having a sounding board. He cared about our relationship as much for that as anything.

Whenever Jean spoke of Longanesi, she did so with great affection: "For all his stature, Leo was a short man. He had strong, handsome features, and took great care in his manner of dress. That made him quite appealing to women. He would walk down the sidewalks of great Italian cities like he was one of Italy's greatest minds, which he was."

Jean noted that he had such a charming smile and manner one could only love him. "At times his nihilistic cynicism was a bit much, but that was somehow counter-balanced by his remarkable psychological strength. More than anyone I've ever known, Longanesi had the courage to face his own nemesis—himself."

Her tone would shift as she continued her story about Longanesi: "I did not know how much he loved me until after he died. I loved him, too, but never in a romantic way. I really wasn't aware of his feelings for me until he wrote me a letter accusing me of sleeping with some film director. I wanted to respond but was unsure what to say."

Jean was shocked when she learned that Longanesi had died. A week later, while in the midst of dinner at an Italian restaurant, she overheard the people at the next table talking about Leo. One said to the other, "The director of *Il Borghese* has died, heart attack I hear. But there's a rumor he was heartbroken over that beautiful American girl he ran around with all the time." Jean sighed, shook her head and rolled her eyes, thinking; *People simply could not pigeonhole our relationship in some familiar category so they make up silly gossip to satisfy their curiosity. Ridiculous.*

Some years later, she attended a dinner party at the home of the cultural attaché for the Italian embassy. A man she didn't know walked up to her and said, "You know Longanesi smoked and drank himself to death because of you. A man like that doesn't drop dead for no reason."

Reflecting back, Jean's eyes became wet as she said, "It wasn't a conversation I wanted to have with a stranger so I ignored him and walked away. But it ruined my evening. I kept hearing the words 'drop dead' in my head and couldn't stop thinking: *maybe it's true.* I've never been able to make peace with that one."

13.

The Unlearning Continues

Intent on returning to the jungle, this time without Count Enrico, Jean went back to the States. Her Aunt Mouse arranged for her to meet with a wealthy man by the name of Jack Roache, who had been her grandmother's dear friend. Roache could not understand Jean's fascination with the jungle, but he admired her courage and agreed to fund her next expedition. She began preparations in earnest.

When they arrived in Venezuela, Jean and her small party stayed with a Tauripan tribe for two weeks. Their relatively large, well-established village overlooked the Caroní not far from Arepuchi Falls. The view from the guest huts was breathtaking—a magnificent white beach bordering a lagoon in a crescent of rocks. The place was so relaxing, the people so welcoming, that Jean found it difficult to rally the momentum needed to make the trip upriver.

It was during those two weeks that she met Pepe and Cesar. Jean was quite intrigued by the way in which these two men's families had come to live together.

Cesar was Tauripan, but he'd lived most of his younger years in a small Venezuelan town. He went to school, learned to read and write, and was brought up by a family who essentially adopted him. Once he was grown, he went to the Upper Caroní to go diamond hunting with a group of men from the town. One day he crossed paths with the chief of the Tauripans at Guayparu. The chief recognized him straightaway.

"You are Tauripan," the chief told him. "You must return to your people."

Cesar gave this considerable thought and decided he would fare better living with his own tribe than with the Venezuelans. He headed back with the chief to Arecupuchi, and that is where he met Pepe.

Over the next five years, Cesar lived with Pepe and his family. He married a pretty Tauripan woman and they had a daughter. But Cesar did not like to work, which was uncharacteristic of native Tauripan. Pepe did not object; he simply shared the food he grew on his plantation with Cesar's family. They never discussed the matter; Pepe simply understood and accepted that Cesar had a strong aversion to work.

Cesar's wife helped the women prepare cassava, but all Cesar did to contribute to the food supply was hunt tapir and other game. The arrangement suited everyone.

A few years passed and Cesar began to enjoy fishing, so he added his catch to that of Pepe and his two sons. In time Cesar decided to clear a garden of his own. Pepe helped with every detail. He helped Cesar choose the site and sent his boys to help fell and burn trees. He also gave Cesar seeds and cuttings to populate his new garden. Cesar was delighted with every stage of garden building. He laughed and joked with Pepe the whole time.

When Pepe told Jean this story, he laughed and laughed, saying: "Cesar did not know that planting a garden would make him happy!"

Jean would retell this story many years later, reflecting on the powerful lesson Pepe had taught her: "Cesar didn't know he wanted to grow his own food, you see. He didn't realize it was in his nature to work."

Jean always pointed out the real beauty of this story, highlighting one of the remarkable differences between indigenous ways and the ways of her people. "Pepe never pressured Cesar," she would say. "Neither Pepe nor the other tribesmen condemned him, judged him as lazy, or pushed him into the project. In his own time and by his own volition, Cesar discovered that he enjoyed work. He felt much happier and relaxed after that. No longer irritable, he stopped sitting around with a look of discontent on his face. Everyone from the village felt happy for him."

The concept of work was likewise foreign to the Yequana; they had no word for it in their native tongue. Among all the words she learned from the Yequana, the only Spanish derivative was *trabaho,* which is very close to *trabajo,* the conquistador's word for "job." The Yequana had plenty of words for specific tasks but no general term for work. Later, Jean would recall: "They did not make a distinction between the many chores, tasks, even laborious projects like building a hut, and the other ways they spent their time."

Another lesson, similar to the one she'd learned from Pepe and Cesar, was brought home to her when she witnessed six Yequana men, each carrying a 75-pound load on his back, walk across a narrow bridge made of a single felled log. During the crossing, one of them would stop mid-log, causing a pile-up while he told his companions a joke or story, and then continue across the log. Far from complaining about this distraction—what we would view as an interruption, inconvenience, or annoyance—the Yequana men simply laughed in their usual musical way and carried on. "Their merriment had a strange, zany quality about it," Jean recalled many years later.

As the unlearning continued, her appetite for new ideas grew. Assumptions that had been closed and treated as facts were blasted open. She no longer accepted the supposedly obvious truth of beliefs such as: "Progress is good," and "Leisure is preferable to work." Also confronted was the American notion that a man's emotions are a sign of weakness that ought to be hidden, lest the feeling man lose the esteem of his peers. A boy in the civilized world will be taught this lesson in a myriad of ways long before he approaches manhood. But no such lesson or expectation is foisted upon a Yequana boy. Repressing emotions does not become a cornerstone of his identity as a man.

One day a Yequana boy of ten years old came to see her, screaming loud enough for the entire village to hear. Jean knew the boy. She had observed him playing with the other boys for weeks. She thought of him as utterly self-reliant and, like many of his peers, highly disciplined. Through her cloudy, supposedly civilized lens, the boy appeared to be a master of his emotions. She had no behavioral template for what began to unfold before her eyes that day.

Here was a ten-year old boy, clinging to his mother, making a terrific fuss in front of the whole tribe. He had an abscessed tooth but made no heroic effort to remain stoic or conceal his emotional reaction to intense physical pain. Nothing in the boy's past experience suggested he would suffer ridicule if other boys saw him in such a shaky state. Nor would he lose anyone's esteem for "running to mommy" for comfort. Quite the contrary: everyone completely understood. The other boys readily accepted his sudden withdrawal from their fearless ranks.

A cluster of children, many of whom were the boy's playmates, hovered around while Jean extracted the tooth. They gave off none of the subtle signals modern boys would use to mock or shame the lad. His mother remained close, not overly concerned, just quietly available while Jean began the procedure. He blanched at the pain (she had no novocaine) and let out a shrill wail when she finally worked the tooth free. She plugged the bleeding hole with gauze. It was over.

Exhausted, the boy went straight to his hammock, not even turning to look at his mother. He felt no need to assess the reaction of his peers. An hour later, he approached Jean's hut. The color had returned to his cheeks. He said not a word, just played with some rocks nearby as if to let her know he was okay. Then he wandered off to rejoin the other boys.

Likewise, a man of about twenty arrived one morning just before dawn. He was leaning on his wife, who waved at Jean to come out of her hut. Her husband had tears in his eyes. With every small step, he winced in pain. Jean followed the pair toward a fire and examined his foot with a flashlight. He had the beginning of gangrene on his toe. Jean motioned him to sit down on a log. His wife sat down beside him. Jean began to scrape the wound with a hunting knife. He began to weep without restraint, pushing his head into his wife's breasts. Like the boy's mother, the woman remained serene, accessible, not so much detached as centered in herself while staying close by and available to her husband. When the pain became unbearable, he dropped his head into her lap and wept. He had no concern that his loud sobs might disturb the fellow members of his tribe. In short order, half the village arrived on the scene, including Anchu, the tribal chief. Their presence did not require the patient to repress his emotions, nor did he need to dramatize and thus justify them.

Similarly, there is a complete absence of drama when a Yequana woman gives birth. An herb called *merkura* is fermented and made into a cordial to be sipped during labor. With the support of two other women, the pregnant woman gives birth in a squatting position. The umbilical cord is cut with a wooden knife, and the placenta gets wrapped in a big leaf and taken to the top of a tree. Within a few hours, the women are back at their chores, the newborn snug in a sling on its mother's body. Meanwhile, her husband goes through a "sympathetic pregnancy" known as *couvade,* disappearing into the forest where he suffers the pains of delivery and spends the night alone. Away from the village, he asks Wanadi, the son of the sun god, for the child's name.

At the time of these experiences, Jean did not comprehend or even contemplate their significance. Not until after her third expedition and repeated exposure to the indigenous people's norms did the sophistication of their behavior become apparent. The Yequana's lighthearted manner of dealing with challenges made our addiction to struggle seem absurd. She began to question the basic assumptions that those of her "tribe" accepted as sacrosanct, just "how things are."

On her way home from the expedition, Jean had a powerful realization that blew apart a key assumption held by civilized people as an absolute: that mankind must have laws to live by lest anarchy break out. The cornerstone of the Yequana way of life was the polar opposite, based on the unarticulated recognition that people who know who they are don't need laws.

But Jean had not yet formed a general theory in her mind. She had not yet acquired sufficient objectivity to recognize the many erroneous assumptions that we, in the civilized world, have made about human nature. What she had acquired was a profound hunger for more understanding.

PART TWO

14.

The Yequana Way

In January 1962, Jean put the word out: she'd be leading another expedition, her fourth, into the jungle. She set the departure date for the first of March and got busy assembling a three-man crew. Daredevil entrepreneurs and adventurous swashbucklers, both experienced and inexperienced, jockeyed for position. She knew some of them, met and interviewed others, and talked at length on the phone with still others. She left New York in mid-March with two experienced Yugoslavs and a cameraman, Ernst Nukanen. When they arrived at the Orinoco River port of Ciudad Bolívar, she ran into her old friend, Andre Ladeuze, a Belgian who'd spent 11 years in Venezuela hunting diamonds. She asked him to join the expedition.

She chartered a twin-engine Beechcraft and crammed it full of provisions: pasta, powdered milk, canned tuna, milk and tea, as well as an array of equipment. They also brought along several tin boxes of medicines Jean had convinced the drug companies to donate.

On her second expedition in 1953, Jean had become "doctor" in the minds of the Yequana. It happened during that second trip when she and the Italians, accompanied by their three guides, were canoeing up a narrow tributary of the Orinoco River one hot afternoon. Through endless turbulence, their winding course looped one way then bent in another with little warning. They had pulled up on the riverbank for a mid-afternoon break. Enrico stepped out of the canoe and, at that very moment, a loud crack split the air. A large piece of tree seemed to fall from the sky. Enrico gasped as the branch missed him by less than a yard. But it hit one of the guides.

Already onshore, the other Italian, Beppi Orlando, turned at the sound and saw the blood. The branch had left a five-inch gash in the side of the guide's head. Jean looked to the two men. Surely they would know what to do. But one was shaking from the shock of his near miss, and the other had withdrawn at the sight of so much blood. It was clear neither of them would be of any help. Without even thinking, Jean overcame her lifelong squeamishness, pulled out her small first aid kit and attended to the man's wound. She used a needle and a strand of dental floss to sew up his scalp, and then she gave him a shot of penicillin.

In the eyes of the Yequana, that incident made Jean a "doctor."

Now, in the spring of 1962, Jean and her four-man crew left Ciudad Airport and headed south, flying over the vast green carpet of Venezuela's pristine rainforest. A unique combination of excitement and fear she'd experienced on each of her three previous expeditions bubbled through her body.

They landed at a small airstrip and spent the night in a ramshackle encampment that consisted of half a dozen dilapidated sheds and an old school bus. The following morning, two men from Anchu's tribe greeted Jean. She hadn't expected the chief to send a welcoming party and wondered how he had divined the time of their arrival. The two small men had just paddled day and night, taking turns sleeping in the back of the canoe, and yet they did not look at all fatigued.

They welcomed Jean with characteristic Yequana enthusiasm and walked her to where they had beached their canoe. It was the small, lightweight type—clearly not sufficient for the journey ahead. It took another day to find and purchase a hollow-log canoe big enough for all their supplies, five foreigners, plus the four indigenous men she'd hired as paddlers. They set out the following morning; the long canoe trailing behind the smaller one, as the Yequana guides paddled upriver.

The last time Jean stayed with the Yequana, she often had leisurely "chats" with Anchu. They'd developed their own private language—a combination of hand signals, gestures, guttural noises, facial expressions, and the occasional charade. Sitting near the river late one afternoon, Anchu launched into a rather animated pantomime. His usual regal bearing shifted markedly when he suddenly stood up, hunched over slightly, gave her the "come with me" signal, and began whispering in his native Cariban tongue. Jean only understood about one fifth of the words, nonetheless, his message was clear: he wanted, needed to share some kind of confidential information, what Jean would later refer to as "jungle intel." She'd kept his secret to herself ever since.

After three days on the river with her crew of daredevil types, having watched Andre finesse many steep challenges, Jean decided to take him into her confidence. That evening, after a delicious dinner of fish stew, she followed him out of camp when he wandered off for his after-dinner smoke. She wasted no time grabbing his attention by asking a pointed question: "Can I entrust the you with a bit of privileged information?"

Andre nodded and took a deep drag on his hand-rolled cigarette.

"Last time I stayed at Anchu's village, he told me he knows of a faraway place where there is an abundance of diamonds," she said. "A distant region in a remote area further west from the vicinity where diamond hunters have been mining for years."

Andre nodded, remaining blank-faced, stoic.

Jean continued, "Deep in the jungle where no white man has ever traveled, he has seen a riverbed blanketed with diamonds. He's kept it hush-hush to protect his territory from an influx of miners. He promised he would take me there if I ever came back to his village."

She felt a tinge of disappointment when the delight she'd hoped to see on Andre's face did not appear, then remembered what she'd learned to be true of explorers. Reflecting on that moment, she explained, "Yes, they needed plenty of daring and courage to embrace life in the jungle. But the ones who truly thrived in the wild had an equal measure of discretion and caution."

Rather than ask Andre what he thought of Anchu's disclosure, she left him to mull over it alone.

Anchu's village was an eight-day journey up the Merevan River. A tributary of the Orinoco, the Merevan was a mere 100 yards across in its widest parts with at least a dozen treacherous rapids. Upon their arrival, Anchu greeted the outsiders with so much warmth, they hardly noticed his scarred face. In the jungle, such disfigurements were not repulsive, they told a story—in Anchu's case, the story of a long and fearless life.

The chief handed Jean a beautiful basket as a welcome gift. Later, at the evening meal, Jean reminded him of his promise to take her to the secret river. Anchu feigned ignorance. Her initial response was one of relief. Her personal reason for making a fourth expedition was not to make an arduous journey into the jungle but to observe the Yequana. But she was always good for her word and would not fail to fulfill her promise to Andre and the others, so she continued to press the issue with Anchu.

A month and a half passed. Jean continued to urge her friends to wait it out. She was certain Anchu was playing a game and would eventually come around. One of the Yugoslavs and Nukanen fell ill. The second Yugoslav, fed up with Anchu's game and hungry for familiar food, jumped at the chance to leave and took them back to Bolivar. After the three men left, Anchu continued his charade. Another month went by. Andre made regular daylong and three-day trips into the bush. He had a small bag of diamonds but not enough to make the journey worth his while. He was happy to stay until Anchu was ready to go.

Another three weeks went by. Jean had given up counting the weeks and settled into village life. She enjoyed weaving baskets with Anchu's wives and the other women of the tribe. She loved to sit and listen to the women talk and laugh while they went about their daily activities.

Initially, on her first trip to the jungle in 1951, the ways of the indigenous people appeared irrational to Jean. She wasn't able to see the simple brilliance in their way of life. She'd been especially mystified by the women. Their habit of fetching water several times a day made no sense whatsoever. She judged it as a colossal waste of time. Until, on her second trip, one of the Yequana women invited her to join them.

A group of five women left their fireside. Each carried two or three small gourds. Some carried their babies along, wrapped snug in their slings. They walked partway down the mountain before arriving at a narrow trail that led to a stream one hundred feet below. Jean was tense with anxiety as she picked her way down the precipitous slope, taking great care with each step not to fall on the slippery rocks.

Once per day, each woman would place her gourds on the riverbank; remove her *cache-sexe* (a small garment to cover the genitals); take off her ankle, knee, wrist, upper arm, neck, and ear beads; and bathe in the river. Of the entire experience, Jean wrote: "...the bath had a Roman quality of luxuriousness. Every move bespoke sensual enjoyment. Infants were lifted out of the sling and bathed like objects so marvelous that their mothers felt compelled to put a mock-modest face on their pleasure and pride. Walking down the mountain was done in the same accustomed-to-the-best, almost smug style. Their last few perilous steps into the stream would have done credit to a Miss World coming forward to claim her crown. This was true of all the Yequana women and girls I saw, though their distinct personalities rendered the manifestations of their coziness quite various." Jean could not think of a better way to use the water-fetching time, at least from the point of view of well being.

Jean reflected on that early experience while she sat weaving baskets with the jovial circle of women. If it weren't for Andre, she would have happily stayed in the village the rest of their stay. But for Andre's sake, she continued to goad Anchu. Finally, one day, the chief told her, "Today we set out."

They headed up a tributary that was little more than a trickle of a creek in parts. All along the way, Anchu peppered the air with jokes. Jean had become accustomed to this joking; in the village it was an ever-present soundtrack. Often, in the middle of the night, a member of the tribe would wake up and tell a joke. All those within earshot would wake wake up, listen, then fall right back to sleep after the wave of laughter died down.

While watching the steady, rhythmic movement of Anchu's paddle going in and out of the water, Jean fell into a hypnagogic state. A deep peace came over her as her eyes brushed over the perfection of the scene: the muscles of the small chief's back, the smooth flat of the paddle, the ripples that formed in the water with each stroke. Again, she felt the power of The Glade. But the moment she returned to ordinary awareness, she reminded herself that the jungle is a dangerous place. She must never forget that.

They were moving through a particularly dense passage where the tributary had narrowed to little more than a stream when a feeling she'd come to know, but never anticipate, rose up in her. This was a sense of absolute, unshakable belonging. Here she was free to be herself. A startling idea passed through her mind: that she ought to consider making the jungle her permanent home. In that very moment, Anchu turned to look at her and smiled such a knowing smile that Jean thought, *He is most certainly telepathic.* But she immediately dismissed it, muttering to herself, "That's just ludicrous."

After three more full days of paddling, they came to a fork in the river. It was nearly sundown and the forest was growing darker by the minute. Anchu used sign language to explain: "This is the Canaku River. We will make camp before night falls. Tomorrow I will show you the place where you will find the diamonds."

Morning came. They left their campsite intact and climbed into the canoe. The Canaku was not a river at all. It was a creek not more than four feet across. The canoe ran aground so often that Jean and Andre walked together in front, wading through the water, pulling the canoe behind them. Anchu sat in the middle of the canoe smiling and laughing at their efforts.

They walked upstream until there was a break in the trees. Rays of sun seemed to flood a small canyon. The walls of the canyon flashed with light. The river bottom glistened. It appeared to be carpeted with diamonds. Andre ran ahead, splashing through the creek. He scooped up two handfuls of the glittering stones and held them up to the light. His face fell as he saw the truth. The creek was carpeted with rock crystals.

Jean turned to look at Anchu. "They are worthless," she said.

For a millisecond, Anchu's face revealed his surprise. Jean caught that tiny slice of a moment before he burst into a fit of laughter. *He didn't know they weren't real,* she thought. In time she would realize he'd laughed to defend himself from reproach.

But Andre did not see that split-second flash of truth on Anchu's face. He assumed the chief was mocking them, had brought them up river to toy with them, to prove how small they were, how little they knew compared to him. He threw the worthless stones back into the creek and said, *"Je zoon van een teef"* ("You son of a bitch"). Jean didn't need to know Flemish to understand that Andre had just cursed at Anchu. Had the chief understood, had he seen the extreme anger hidden beneath the Belgian's stone-cold face, he may well have abandoned Andre. He would not abide being cursed and could easily have left Andre for dead and returned to the village pretending nothing was amiss. Andre's existence would never be mentioned or acknowledged again. No one dared to insult a chief. Anchu's stature, his authority, the all-due-respect of his station—these were givens. Ignorance of this fact was the reason many diamond hunters went into the jungle and never came out. But Andre had spent enough time in the bush to know his place. He knew that no white man could survive in the bush alone. He would not confront Anchu. He would not blame or shame him. He would behave as the guest he was in this remote land.

They headed back to their campsite and arrived just as the sky clouded over and the rains began to fall. Two teenage boys from the village stood waiting for them. After speaking with the pair, Anchu told Jean that he had to return to the village right away. He pointed to the two boys and motioned to Jean. She understood what he meant and turned to Andre, saying, "They will bring us back to the village." With that, Anchu walked into the forest and disappeared from view.

Jean and Andre spent another week looking for diamonds, but their hearts weren't in it. Andre was horribly disappointed and kept going deeper and deeper into his distinctly Belgian funk. Jean was increasingly bothered by a parasite that had infected her foot. There was nothing to do but return to the village. "And then we go home," Jean told Andre. Her romantic feelings about staying in the jungle had been erased by the constant pain in her foot, a stabbing, itching, burning reminder that this was not her natural habitat.

15.

Jungle Captive

When they arrived at the village on the riverbank several days later, all members of the tribe were busily packing up their huts, gathering up tools and kitchen utensils, and packing baskets until they were full. Anchu explained that the rainy season was coming; they needed to move deeper into the forest to protect the village from floods. Jean didn't mention the failed diamond hunt, but made her disappointment known when she said, "We must leave immediately; we're going home."

Anchu ignored her.

Jean had always found it difficult to look directly at Anchu. He'd lost his left eye[20] and the remaining muscles twitched whenever his right eye moved. But Anchu's keen

---

[20] Jean did not know how he'd lost his eye and felt it would be impolite to ask, so she simply conjectured: "some unfortunate accident, perhaps an encounter with a wild beast or wild fire."

intelligence had gained him so much respect among his tribesmen he became their leader. As chief, he proved himself fair and competent, so much so that his people rarely, if ever, questioned his authority. Moving into the bush away from the river might seem a questionable decision, but Anchu's people—one hundred in number—happily followed his directive. It would take a bit more time and effort to make the daily trek for water, but the Yequana had only a vague sense of time and no aversion to effort whatsoever. And so they went about their task, dismantled their thatch-roofed huts and collected the children and elders. The Yequana chief led the entire village into the jungle, a twenty-minute walk from the river his people depended on for water.

Anchu and his tribe lived as they had for centuries in the nearly impenetrable rainforest in the north of Venezuela. Jean met Anchu on her second of five expeditions to the region. Over time, they became friends, conversing as best they could with gestures, her growing Yequana vocabulary, and the few Spanish words he understood. Before she arrived, it was an accepted fact that when a member of the tribe became ill, they would die. Jean's presence had changed that.

She had no formal training in nursing or medicine, but was called on to perform a wide array of interventions from relieving headaches (aspirin seems like a miracle drug to the uninitiated) to pulling abscessed teeth. On a number of occasions, she stitched up wounds, some of them quite severe. The basics she'd brought with her, penicillin and topical antibiotics, made her a savior in the jungle. On each subsequent expedition, she brought as much medicine as she could carry. More often than not, her ministrations were successful. Many a tribe member who would have died without her medical interventions survived. Thus did her value among the Yequana increase a hundredfold. She did not, however, gain the high level stature that would have been conferred had she been a man.

The day after the village moved into the jungle, Jean approached Anchu. He was sitting outside his hut, whittling. She waited for him to acknowledge her. When he waved his small knife at her she said, "It's time for us to go home."

The chief did not look up. "Before you come, Yequana have much sickness, much death," he said, his eyes on his whittling. "While you here, nobody dies."

"No, Anchu, I must go," she replied.

Anchu ignored her protest. She'd suspected he had an ulterior motive for moving the village in the bush, and now it was confirmed: he wanted to make sure a search party would never be able to find them.

Jean pressed on: "I have no more medicines."

Anchu was not fooled. "Much medicine is left. And once it is all gone, you will still stay with us to pull teeth, sew wounds."

Jean understood that, from Anchu's point of view, he was protecting his tribe. He feared that sickness and death would again plague his people if she left. But she feared for her own health. She had grown too thin due to parasites and poor nutrition. Having lost 30 pounds, she had little of her usual strength and endurance, causing her to wonder how she would fare on the return journey should Anchu give them permission to leave.

"My friends will come for us," she told Anchu.

He smiled an almost sinister smile. "They will not find you."

It was one of the rare moments when she questioned herself, thinking: *What in the world am I doing here?*

She went to the far side of the village where Anchu had put up two rudimentary huts for her and Andre. "He's holding us prisoner," she told him. Once she said the words aloud, she began to realize the implications of what was happening. It dawned on her that the chief might have lured her back to the jungle with his promise to show her a riverbed of diamonds. She shouted, "This is ludicrous. Impossible! He cannot do this."

She approached Anchu again the next day. This time she pleaded with him to let her and Andre go home.

No stranger to real feeling, the chief's demeanor softened. "We have to finish my new house first," he said. His would be the largest house in the new village.

"How long will that take?" she asked.

"Five days," he said.

Jean knew the difference between Yequana-time and civilized-time so she wasn't surprised that a week went by before work on the house got underway. Once the work began, Anchu changed his mind several times about the size of the house. The only thing he seemed certain of was that he wanted one large room with no interior walls. The Yequana worked slowly most days and not at all on other days. Some days they went fishing. Some days they went hunting. Some days they sat around and did nothing. Two more weeks passed.

All the while, Jean watched from a distance and waited it out. Meanwhile, Andre grew more and more restless. But Jean knew there was no point in pushing Anchu. He would only get more stubborn if she did.

Jean wasn't uncomfortable in the village. During the day she spent much of her time sitting and watching the children. She wasn't "minding the children"—they didn't need any minding—nor was she observing them and making notes as an anthropologist would. She simply sat and observed in a passive mode. These children stirred something in her, something she could not name and would not name for another decade.

Finally, the house was the size Anchu wanted. The roof was in place. The Yequana were in a celebratory mood. Anchu appeared to be happy with their work. He looked at the men, and said, *"Bo' otik"* ("Thank you") to each man in turn. Then he announced, "Now we need walls."

The Yequana all laughed and nodded as if to say, "But of course!"

Jean knew Andre would be livid; her fear of what he might do emboldened her. She caught Anchu alone later that afternoon and said, "We cannot wait while you build walls."

"We build walls," he said. He turned in her direction, made the hand gesture that means *I have a gift for you,* and said, "And we build you a house, too."

"I don't need a house," she said.

Anchu looked genuinely hurt that she did not appreciate his little surprise.

Jean was about to lose her temper. "We are going out of the jungle. You must take us out now."

Anchu said nothing. The next day the village men started to work on a small hut right next to Anchu's big mud house.

Jean had known for some time that Anchu admired her. Initially, he'd been impressed with the power of her medicines but had little regard for her as a person. On her first stay with the Yequana, she and her Italian companions were housed at the periphery of the village. The second time she visited, they built her a hut closer in with the families. Her hut was still there when she arrived this trip. She'd been there less than a week when Anchu motioned her to sit with him on a rock near the river. He made it clear that he wanted her to live in his house with him. This was his way of proposing marriage.

"No comprendo," she said.

He dropped the idea and never brought it up again. His next best move was to build her a house right next to his. This had supreme significance: he intended to detain her indefinitely.

She could no longer hide this from Andre.

"He has no intention of leading us out of here," she said. "That's why he moved the village away from the river. A rescue party would be unlikely to find us here."

From that point on, Andre talked about nothing but escape. Every morning he made his way to the river, watching and waiting for help. He urged her to slip out of the village with him before dawn. But Jean knew better. They would have to travel down the Savaru, a small winding river, to get back to the airstrip. She had taken that route on her last expedition but could not remember how many days down the river they'd gone, nor was she certain which fork in the river led out of the jungle. Andre had not been in this territory before, so he would not be able to guide them either. Even if he could, the most difficult passage would require that they portage their canoe four miles over land. Two people would surely die trying.

Growing angrier by the day, Andre wanted to turn to violence and use their shotguns to force Anchu's hand.

"But we can't hold up the entire village of 100 people with two shotguns," Jean said.

"We can if we take hostages."

Andre's idea was preposterous. The hostages would have to be young, strong men who could paddle. How could they hold their guns on them for seven to ten days? It was still the rainy season. Not only was his plan ridiculous, it was offensive in the worst way.

"They have never used violence against us. To introduce it would be a huge mistake, " she said. Her tone of voice was stern. "We would be banished and never allowed back into Yequana territory. These are peaceful people. I will not go along with your plan." Her decision was absolute.

Andre's frustration kept eating at him. He insisted Jean refuse to treat the Yequana, and even went so far as to suggest she throw all the remaining medicines in the river. "If you stop being useful, they will get tired of feeding us."

"But how could I refuse a child in pain?" she asked, not really interested in his answer.

He answered anyway, "Just imagine you are where you ought to be—on your way home. These people got along before you came; they'll be fine if you leave. Why worry about a bunch of savages anyway? Especially this ungrateful bunch."

She took umbrage with his use of the word savage, saying, "You think these people are savages? You obviously haven't spent much time on the streets of New York."

Nonetheless, she could see his point and reluctantly agreed.

That day she turned away three Yequana who came for doctoring. A little girl had burned her arm. An old woman had a headache. Anchu's son had a bad scratch on his cheek. Jean refused to treat them all. She looked up and saw Anchu watching from the entrance to his house. His face was hard, expressionless.

The next day no one came for medical attention. This went on for three days until a woman showed up talking fast and gesticulating madly. Jean understood. A crippled woman who'd been carrying a child was in labor. She could not expel the afterbirth and had a fever and chills. Jean rushed to her aid. The woman was pale as ash and losing blood. She could not push out the afterbirth due to her twisted spine. Worse, the umbilicus was infected—the baby's fragile immune system would not be able to handle it. Jean massaged the mother's pelvis and belly, coaxing the afterbirth toward the birth canal while the tribe's midwife worked to get it out. When the woman finally gave birth, the baby was placed in her arms. Jean gave the new mother three injections of penicillin and asked for the baby. She cleaned the infected area around the umbilicus with alcohol and covered it with Terramycin ointment and a bandage. When she looked up, she saw Anchu standing watch just outside the hut. He smiled at her and walked away.

Andre was clearly disappointed, but he understood and did not complain. Two days later, he reminded her of the plan. "Jean, if you keep curing them, they'll never let us go."

Once again, she promised to stop treating their injuries and ministering to their complaints.

A few days later, Anchu came for her—an old man had cut his foot with an ax. Jean refused to help. Anchu stood there staring at her for several long minutes, then pronounced: "You will have no more cassava."

She could no longer contain her anger. "That's unacceptable." No woman had questioned his authority, not since he was a young man. Anchu's face became contorted. Dare he banish her? She stood up and went to the river to talk with Andre.

"Starving to death isn't going to help," she said. Her eyes were glistening with tears. This was getting to be more than she could endure. "I'm going to help the man," she said. Andre was outraged. Jean went back to her hut, put some medicine in her knapsack, and went to the old man. It was not in her nature to refuse a person who needed her help.

Over the coming days and weeks, Jean grew weaker and weaker. By now she had lost 40 pounds and had no appetite for the scraps they were given to eat. She and Andre were being forced to subsist on pineapples that were turning bad and the tops of sugar cane where there is very little sugar. They were allowed as much cassava as they wanted (Jean had begun to feel nauseated at the sight of it). When the villagers came home with meat or fish, they were allotted a small portion. She was constantly surprised by the villager's indifference to their plight. Surely someone would show their gratitude and bring extra food. But their loyalty was with Anchu, which made it all but impossible to do so. Were it not for the two women who had the stealth and courage to steal away with scraps of meat and fish, they surely would have died. "But then again," Jean said, "it's quite possible their stealth was a charade performed at Anchu's behest. It wouldn't surprise me in the least. The Yequana, like the rest of us, do whatever it takes to get what we need to survive."

The logjam started to give way when Jean was put in charge of two very difficult cases. She was treating a boy who had a fever of 104. He had appendicitis. "I can keep him alive for awhile with antibiotics," she told the boy's father. "But if we don't get him to the hospital, your son will die."

At the same time, she was treating a man with an enormous cyst on his back. A shaman had pierced it with a barb from a poisonous fish. It was draining blood and pus. Jean treated him with penicillin, but he did not respond. His wife begged her to make another incision. Jean refused. The wife said she would do it herself, taking the fish barb in her hand. "It's not sterile," Jean said, snapping the sharp object from the woman's hand.

A day and a half later she came upon the woman again. She had a fresh barb in her hand and was trying to get up the courage to pierce the cyst. It was even larger now, covering his entire shoulder blade. He had developed a fever and was clearly in unbearable pain. Her conservative approach had failed. He would die if she didn't do something. She could not allow his wife to do the surgery with a fish barb, so she agreed to do the procedure.

She fetched her knife and sterilized it over the fire. She was worried what she might hit or puncture as she pushed her knife deeper and deeper into the man's shoulder. Sweat poured down her face. It took four hours to drain the cyst and reduce it by half. But the surgery only served to slow down its growth.

Jean went to Anchu along with the woman and the sick boy's father. It was a huge risk to bring them along; their very presence put subtle pressure on Anchu. If he saw this as betrayal, he might banish them all.

"If you do not get these two men to a hospital, they will die," Jean said.

Anchu looked away, clearly uneasy. He had no choice but to let Jean go. "We will have to build new canoes," he said.

"Well, hurry," Jean replied.

That night she heard the sound of rattles and gourds pulsing rhythmically next door. Anchu and the shaman were chanting, singing in rounds. Both of them were painted blue with red stripes; their necks were draped with bright blue beads. Both patients had been moved into Anchu's house and were lying on the floor in the middle of the main room. The chief and the shaman were invoking Wanadi and the animal spirits that watched over the sick men. The chanting went on, day and night, for two days. When either Anchu or the shaman needed to sleep, another tribesman would step in to continue the ritual.

Andre kept pacing back and forth between the village and the river. The canoes were now ready to go. "When will they give up this foolishness?" he asked. "If those two die, we'll lose our reason to be released. I would rather risk death and try to get back on my own than continue living here in captivity."

Jean feared for Andre. Would he actually do it? Go alone into the jungle? She felt responsible for his life. "No!" she said. "I got you into this; I'll get you out."

"Well this is your last chance," he replied. "If we don't leave soon, I will go—with or without you."

By now the man with the cyst was little more than a skeleton. His face was a waxy gray; death was not far away. She begged Anchu to let them leave. Finally, he agreed.

The condition of the man had certainly influenced his decision, but it was a messenger from a nearby tribe who ultimately convinced him. A small plane had been seen circling the region where the messenger's village was located. It would not be long before they reached Anchu's territory. Once the location of his village was discovered, a rescue party would not be far behind. He would lose his doctor and the two sick men. He relented at last.

Jean ran to find Andre. "We're leaving in the morning."

Half the tribe showed up on the riverbank to say goodbye. Jean approached Anchu. He glared at her with his single eye, pointed a shaking finger and spat out the words: "You Shirisana." It was the greatest insult among the Yequana. Compared to themselves—a sophisticated people—the Shirisana were barbarians: a sub-human species that did not have protective animal spirits and had been forsaken by Wanadi for their horrible deeds.

Jean did not answer the chief. She turned and climbed into the canoe with Andre, three paddlers, the two half-dead men and their families. They pushed out into the stream.

On the afternoon of their sixth day on the river, they arrived on the shore of an *Arecuna* village. Also known as the *Pemón,* these Cariban people made their home in the area surrounding the headwaters of the Caroní River. Jean was surprised to see the village inhabitants wearing store-bought clothes. The wife of the chief owned a sewing machine and had altered the clothing to suit the villagers. There were scrambled eggs to be had. And orange juice. Jean and Andre felt like they'd arrived in Paris.

In the evening, she heard an outboard motor pull up on the riverbank and cut its engine. It was Ernest Nukanen, the photographer. At the urging of people in New York, he'd agreed to lead a search party, and Jean's friends funded the five-man crew. They accompanied Jean and her group on the four-day trip to a village that featured roads out of the jungle and the occasional taxi. Jean arranged for her patients to be taken to Ciudad Bolivar where they would have the greatest chance of recovery. Andre and Jean made their way to a small outdoor café. They ate fresh beef, potatoes, and all the tomatoes they could eat.

At the Ciudad Airport, Andre was barely able to look at Jean when it was time to say goodbye. They were both reluctant to part ways. They'd survived captivity together. They both knew that they would never see one another again. He would take time to recuperate and then return to the jungle. This world had become his home. He would not let Anchu take that away from him. A heavy silence hung in the air between them.

Although their friendship had been peppered with arguments, their shared ordeal and shared love for the jungle had forged a bond stronger than any Jean had ever known. After several long moments, Jean stepped forward, kissed Andre on the cheek, and turned to board the plane. She took the first step up the metal stairs. Andre reached and took her hand. His eyes said more than his words could express. *"Vaarwel mijn vriend,"* he said, "Farewell, my friend."

Jean opened her mouth to speak. No words came out. Never in her life had she felt so close to another human being.

16.

The Concrete Jungle

After eight months in the jungle, six of those in captivity, Jean returned to New York too weak for normal activities. She needed medical attention and time to recuperate. A dear friend in New York offered her the guest floor of her Upper East Side home. With plenty of time to do little more than rest, she reflected at length on her recent experiences. She now had a far more detailed understanding of the jungle's essential rightness. She had spent time with the Tauripan, Sanema, and Yequana tribes. She'd met whole clans, visited with families in their huts, traveled with them in small groups, gone hunting and fishing, living the life of her own species in its natural habitat.

She'd seen the indigenous people thriving, joyfully prosperous and reasonably healthy, with no outside support other than a few machetes and steel axes they bought in trade to add to their collection of handmade tools made of stone. In time, and much to her surprise, she managed to see Anchu's efforts to make her part of the tribe in a different light altogether.

Reflecting back with deep understanding that only emerged decades later, she explained: "Fact is, Anchu never actually held us captive. We were not tied down or put in a cage. He simply declined our request to be led out of the jungle by one of his men, a circumstance that would have put his tribe at a disadvantage." And while Jean could see this clearly,[21] the pain she'd endured and the insult she'd felt were never fully resolved. Said simply, she understood but could not forgive. Nor did her understanding do anything to diminish her fear of returning to her beloved jungle where she might cross paths with Anchu once again.

To her credit, Jean did not allow this residual hurt to cloud her thinking. She'd seen an undeniable truth: the Yequana, as a people, were happy, their lives filled with joy. They were free in ways outsiders could not even conceive. She hardly noticed this until, back in New York, she looked around and saw the throngs of malcontents. The difference in terms of general disposition expressed itself quite noticeably in their physiologies. The Yequana were smaller and less muscular, and yet they could carry heavier loads far greater distances than the strongest civilized man. While in the

---

[21] Those of us accustomed to making demands, attempting to bend another to our will, or manipulate so we can have our way, would rarely see the situation for what it was: a conflict of interest. One that does not in any way deprive either party of the power to make a choice. Nor would we see that opting to pass on another person's preferred course is nothing more than choosing to put one's own interests before those of another. Anchu's choice to avail his tribe of her medicine and life-saving know-how was clear and unequivocal in his mind. From a larger perspective, his actions were perfectly honorable.

jungle, Jean did not wonder why that was so. Not until she returned to the States did she notice the contrast between the relaxed physiology of the Yequana and the tense, armored bodies of New Yorkers.

Years later, once she had time to fully understand the implications of what she had seen, she would explain it this way: "That much tension would make anyone weak. The indigenous people I lived with were relaxed and at ease, pretty much all the time. They don't waste their natural energy worrying about what might happen. They don't resist or refuse to accept what is happening in the moment. Rather than waste their natural vitality fighting a fight that can't be won, they have plenty of energy available for strenuous activities."

Upon returning to the US, Jean was astonished to see the fierce looks on the faces of people on the streets of Manhattan. "I came upon a number of scenes on the subway or in Grand Central Station, and almost daily in Times Square, that were more savage than anything I'd seen among the jungle people," she recalled.

Of particular interest was the contrast between the faces of the Yequana and the faces of New Yorkers. The jungle people were transparent; their feelings showed on their faces. They had no reason to conceal, censor, or revise what they were feeling in order to fit in or conform to social norms. They simply felt what they felt. When their faces weren't reflecting some emotion, they were in repose. Jean had never seen a New Yorker's face in repose. The faces of the people she saw all around her were seldom clear. Having lived among the unguarded Yequana for a total of nearly two years, she couldn't help but notice that the faces of New Yorkers reflected an inner battle. A fixed look of anger. A fixed smile broadcasting the fear it was meant to conceal. A stone cold, walled-off look of discontent or disdain. Moreover, people often planted the seeds of distrust when the words that came out of their mouths didn't match their obvious emotional state. People consistently scrambled their communication, creating a toxic environment of wariness and suspicion.

In contrast, a Yequana's face was like the sky—host to various weather patterns, but otherwise clear and sunny. They displayed a total lack of emotional complication, but not because their feelings weren't complex and varied. Their faces revealed an extraordinarily wide range of emotional states. But their baseline was joy. They had no need to pursue happiness because happiness pervaded everything they experienced— even grief, sickness, and death. Among their fellow tribesmen and women, they had no need to hide or alter their feelings. The atmosphere around and between them was one of deep trust and respect.

This stark difference led Jean to draw a new distinction. It seemed to her that real feelings occur in the moment and, when fully felt, are a complete experience with no residual emotion to carry forward and color the future. In contrast, feelings that are not fully felt turn into blocked energy that leave the experience incomplete. Jean had never seen the Yequana complicate their feelings by denying them. Feelings were not repressed or disallowed. The Yequana did not hold onto unresolved feelings, become overly emotional, and then act out in a display of bad behavior—a common occurrence among New Yorkers.

"People call New York a concrete jungle, but they have never been to the jungle," she would reflect. "It may sound a bit cliché, but I actually lived in a real jungle and I can tell you—we're the savages. What is natural to our species is the norm in the jungle. In New York, what is natural is far from the norm. More shocking: what is natural isn't even known."

Jean had traveled to the South American jungle with no theory to prove, only a general curiosity about the indigenous people and a vague sense that she might learn something of significance. And that she did—far more than she ever could have imagined. She'd gotten a truly higher education, one that wasn't restricted by academia. In the jungle, life was so stripped down that she could see what had true value, what was important and what wasn't. She was able to let go of the habit of worrying, of bucking up against everything like a good New Yorker, and she'd developed a surprising ability to accept what she could not change.

In years to come, she would sum up her experience by saying: "Weather patterns will change, flies will buzz around you. What's the point of fussing over the inevitable? The Yequana are a no-muss, no-fuss society. That's the bottom line. That's why Yequana men are physically stronger than much larger men here. The same is true of Yequana women. They have inexhaustible energy and never, ever complain."

Back in New York, Jean had time to reflect on all that she'd observed in the Yequana children. She began to wonder why they almost never cried. Why did they not go through the terrible twos? Where were the toddler tyrants? And what could explain why Yequana children were so uniformly well behaved? Why did they never argue, never get punished, and always obey happily and instantly? Why did the admonishment "boys will be boys" not apply in the village? The relationships between mothers and their babies, between adults and children, and adults and adolescents were always harmonious. She'd seen none of the adversarial parent-versus-child dynamic we accept as normal. She puzzled over these questions and pondered her observations. Eventually, the pieces put themselves together: parents in so-called civilized societies *expected* their offspring to be difficult. They expected parenthood to be taxing. "Rather than trust that human nature is innately good; we assume it is flawed," Jean would later explain. "The Yequana never look at their progeny as anything less than perfect."

There was no doubt in Jean's mind that the jungle was right, that whatever she was looking for could only be found there. But the rainforest ecosystem—plants, animals, people, and all—did not add up to a personal solution. She hadn't found the hoped-for healing that would resolve the deep despair at the core of her being. Jean had this wild passion and almost romantic love for the jungle, but she still had not found any lasting rightness in herself. She'd only witnessed the rightness of the jungle and managed to recognize it.

17.

Go Home and Be Free

For the next few years, Jean ran around with a group of East Coast intellectuals in New York. They were mostly writers she'd met through her friend, George Plimpton, editor of the *Paris Review*. Jean wrote in her journal: "George is a great friend to everybody and, for reasons I do not understand, me."

Plimpton was the best kind of friend a writer could have. He valued good writing and made it his job to take care of writers. Jean was not a writer, but everyone always told her: "Write!"

They wanted to hear all about her expeditions and her experiences with the tribal peoples. Everyone wanted her to write a "blond goes up the Amazon" adventure story. But Jean had no intention of putting her jungle experiences into an absurdly limited frame just to appease their civilized predilections. The story she wanted to tell was of a different order altogether. When she complained of a stubborn case of writer's block, her friends suggested she tell her story to someone who would write the book for her.

"Out of the question," she would say. In private, she told George, "Bit-by-bit, it's hatching."

He was the only one who really understood. Plimpton believed in Jean. He told her to do whatever she needed to do. "Just be sure to trust your own process."

Jean delighted at the new world that opened up as Plimpton introduced her, one-by-one, to his inner circle. She became friends with Allen Ginsberg, Jack Kerouac, and Andy Warhol. George's flat in the Upper East Side was the regular meeting place and jumping-off point for their various adventures around New York. Jean loved Amateur Night at the Apollo in Harlem where they often took visitors from Europe to give them a taste of New York nightlife. They would often finish up the night with Nipsy Russell at The Baby Grand.

One night, Jean attended a party at the home of Norman Mailer; she'd met him two weeks earlier at Plimpton's place. Undeniably dashing, Mailer had quite the reputation—rakish, slightly disreputable, a womanizer who nonetheless commanded considerable respect as a journalist. Known for his counter-culture essays, he was one of the founders of *The Village Voice*. In the winter of 1964, he put weeks into revising *An American Dream,* a serial he'd published in *Esquire* magazine that got picked up by Dial Press. The book was due out in the spring. E.L. Doctorow was Mailer's editor.

There was a lot of gossip in that crowd, and it was no secret that, on several occasions, Jean had been seen with Mailer's

chosen mentor and personal hero, the popular French novelist, Jean Paul Malaquias.[22] Everyone heard (and many people
embellished) the story going around about Jean and Malaquias
after they talked for over an hour at a party hosted by literary
critic Alfred Kazin[23] two weeks earlier. And at Jimmy Baldwin's
recent party, she'd been so deep in conversation with Malaquias
that no one dared interrupt them, not even Jimmy.

Knowing Mailer's type, Jean wouldn't have been the least bit
surprised had someone whispered in her ear: "You know Norman's jealous of all the attention Jean-Paul is giving you, right?"

Of course, she knew. How could she not?

Mailer had decided to enter the race for mayor of New York and
planned to make an informal announcement during the party,
a birthday bash for Bronx-born boxer, Roger Donoghue. When
George Plimpton got wind of Mailer's game plan, he supported
his friend's ambitious move, saying, "Norman will represent the
disenfranchised of the city." Mailer's wife, Adele Morales, was
none too happy about any of it.

Norman and Adele hosted the party at their 94th Street
apartment. A packed affair with over 200 guests, the party
spilled into the hallway outside Mailer's apartment. When
Jean arrived, Mailer walked across the room to greet her and
welcome her to his home. All in good fun, he gave her an

---

[22] Malaquais's debut novel, *Les Javanais,* was so admired by André Gide, winner of the
1947 Nobel Prize in Literature, that Gide made him his private secretary.

[23] Several decades later, Kazin would become the first to receive the Truman Capote
Lifetime Achievement Award in Literary Criticism, which carries a $100K cash re-
ward. As of this writing, the award has only been given to one other writer: Fran-
co-American literary critic, essayist and novelist, George Steiner.

elaborate introduction to the gathered guests, at one point calling her a "louche."

In response to his name-calling, Jean whispered into his ear, "Be careful, Norman. Your jel-louche-y is showing." Then she raised her voice so his guests could hear and said, "Of course, darling, I'm the louchest of louches. What did you expect, corrupted as I am by those jungle savages? I'm a regular *American Nightmare,* a veritable threat to our precious norms, Norm."

In the ten seconds it took to utter those words, Jean won a room full of new friends.

Reflecting on that memorable evening, Jean recalled an argument between Allen Ginsberg and Norman Podhoretz who had just been named Editor-in-Chief of *Commentary* magazine. Both men had already put back a few and the ire between them started crackling when Podhoretz proclaimed that Ginsberg's poems would be inconsequential as long as he was one of "the Beats." Ginsberg started yelling at the influential editor. A drunk Mailer stepped in, waving his arms and shouting, "Boys! Boys!" It took him less than a half a minute to break up the argument. "That's the kind of party it was," Jean said.

Later that evening, Mailer made his announcement. Obviously inebriated, he stood on a table and proclaimed, "I've decided to run for mayor." His appeal for support was so earnest and yet unconvincing that everyone laughed. But he was dead serious.[24]

---

[24] Mailer's drunken announcement presaged an actual run for mayor in 1969, at the suggestion of Gloria Steinem and others. He ran unsuccessfully in the Democratic Party primary for Mayor of New York City, proposing the creation of a 51st state through NYC's secession. Mailer's campaign was called "the most refreshing libertarian political campaign in decades."

The party continued into the early morning hours. Jean was among the last to leave. When she approached Mailer to thank him for the invitation, he punched her in the arm a bit too hard and said, "One of these days, Liedloff, we're going to find out who's more intelligent, you or me."

Jean looked at him squarely and said, "I have one advantage over you there, Norman."

Ever competitive, Mailer stiffened and glared: "What advantage?"

"I don't care," Jean said.

It was an odd sort of bonding, this blend of mutual respect marbled with his competitive nature and her dismissive, above-it-all attitude. A few months later, Norman won her respect when she heard him say, "In light of the Second World War, humanity stares into the abyss of its own nature searching for something with which to define itself." After that, the two of them became friends.

March 7, 1965

It had been two years since Martin Luther King gave his famous "I Have a Dream" speech and six months since he'd won the Nobel Peace Prize. Jean was talking with Norman Mailer on the telephone. Both were watching television footage of Sheriff Jim Clark's posse of local police and state troopers in a face-off with civil rights marchers on the Edmund Pettus Bridge, in Selma, Alabama. The posse, including several officers on horseback, charged into the crowd of Black, nonviolent protesters, beat them with billy clubs, and sprayed them with tear gas. The shocking violence, viewed by millions on prime-time TV, would later become known as Bloody Sunday.

Jean vowed to go down and join the protest.

"Call Paul Krassner at *The Realist,*" Mailer said. "Offer to write him an article in exchange for airfare. You can stay with the Baird family; they're good friends of mine."

"What's the magazine like?" Jean asked.

"Very liberal," Norman replied.

Krassner gave her the assignment and a press pass, which Jean refused to use. Dressed in a navy-blue suit and penny-loafers, Jean flew out of LaGuardia and deplaned at Dannelly Field in Montgomery, Alambama. Her un-Southern attire drew unwanted attention, looks of disdain, and shouts of "nigger lover." On three occasions, she nearly got hit by a car in the white part of town. After the third near miss, she realized that these were not random close calls, but intentional affronts by angry bigots.

On March 9, Jean joined King and some 2,500 marchers in another crossing of the Edmund Pettus Bridge. Again they faced a line of police after the crossing, but this time King averted a violent confrontation by inviting the protesters to kneel and leading them in prayer. Jean had always been an atheist, but that day she prayed with all her heart. Everyone was shocked when the police stepped aside to let the marchers pass, and even more surprised when King nevertheless turned the march around and led the protesters back to Selma. This compromise maneuver, which King had secretly negotiated with a representative of President Johnson, came to be known as "Turnaround Tuesday."

Jean would never forget waking up the next morning to the words, "Last night's cowardly attack..." booming through the radio as Martin Luther King Jr. lamented the brutal beating of white civil rights activist, Reverend James Reeb of Boston. Along with two other ministers who supported African-American rights, Reeb had finished dinner at an integrated restaurant and walked outside when they were descended on by white men with clubs. The white hospital in Selma refused to treat Reeb: he had to be taken to a hospital in Birmingham two hours away. When Jean heard King's words, "We must all pray for his protection," she knew she must stay on in Alabama.

Norman's friends, the Baird family, welcomed her into their home. James Reeb died the following day. That night and every night she stayed with the Bairds, Jean joined a group of people, both black and white, who congregated at the sheriff's barrier each evening, singing: ". . . like a tree that's standing by the water, we shall not be moved" and "before I'll be a slave, I'll be buried in my grave, and go home to my Lord and be free."

Reeb's murder, along with the violence perpetrated against unarmed protestors on Bloody Sunday, raised a national outcry. In the weeks that followed, President Johnson held a joint session of Congress asking for passage of the federal voting rights law that guaranteed African Americans the right to vote without harassment. The president's nationally televised appeal to Congress gave public support a sizable boost.

Organizers scheduled another Freedom March, a 50 mile trek from Selma to Montgomery. This time the protest drew heightened support from across America. When Alabama Governor George Wallace refused to provide protection for the marchers, Johnson stepped in and sent a federal command of 2,000 U.S. army soldiers and 1,900 Alabama National Guardsmen to protect the march.

Jean fell in line with the marchers when they started out on March 21. They traveled down Jefferson Davis Highway, covering about 10 miles a day. All along the route, people joined the march. When they entered Montgomery, they were 25,000 strong—blacks and whites alike—campaigning for voting rights.

They reached the capitol and were standing in the rain singing "We Shall Overcome," when a Black professor from Howard University gave Jean shelter under his umbrella. Later that afternoon, the professor invited her back to his host's house. She clearly needed a place to warm up and dry out.

Jean wrote in her journal: "I found myself in the home of the bell captain of the Jefferson Davis Hotel. His wife Juliet, who is short and hefty, offered skinny me her clothes while mine were drying out. I looked ridiculous, but I felt so warmed by her kindness and genuine hospitality, I didn't mind at all."

That evening, Jean joined her new friends for a party in the neighborhood. She was one of only three white people in the room. The mood was festive, people were talkative, and she was a journalist on assignment—a perfect opportunity to gather material for an article on the ignorance of racist Southerners.

"It didn't take me long to discover that questioning works better than directness," she explained, "especially when trying to convey the realities of Black people's position vis-à-vis their white bosses who have wheedled them shamelessly with endearments and flattery: 'Mammy (or Sammy), you're just like one of the family.'"

Jean became particularly frustrated when she met a man called Papa Beard. Papa had worked at a local drug store where he cleaned floors for thirty years. He sincerely believed the white owner of the store was doing him a special favor by giving him a five percent discount on his diabetes medication. "That medicine had a 300% markup!" Jean exclaimed, her fire still burning 45 years later.

Jean puzzled over the way Big Mama Beard boasted about her husband's white boss, citing his exceptional goodness and generosity. The Beards' subconscious acceptance of the white man's view disturbed Jean. She mulled over what she called "the indoctrination" that instilled in Blacks the belief that they were inferior to white people and should be grateful for the crumbs that fell from the tables of their former owners. This led her to pivot and, rather than write an article about the protests as promised, focus the piece on what sociologists later termed *internalized oppression*.

But the article never made it into the pages of *The Realist*. Upon her return to New York, Jean learned that the magazine, in self-righteous guise, had taken to printing examples of pornography, which it claimed to decry. And while the editorial department feigned ignorance, publishing the images effectively expanded the magazine's readership. More put off by the hypocrisy than the pornography, Jean declined to lend her name to the paper and refused to submit the promised piece. "I simply could not associate myself with *The Realist*," she said. "As a matter of principle."

18.

The Algorithm
of Beauty

O n another journalism assignment, this one from
George Plimpton, Jean travelled to Chadds Ford,
Pennsylvania, to interview the famous artist,
Andrew Wyeth. Plimpton had commissioned Jean to write the
article along with her friend, Barbara Butler, a well-known art
critic. Jean had tremendous respect for Barbara. She arranged
for a friend who owned a car to drive them from the city to
Wyeth's farm. Barbara Butler showed up with a clipboard.

Wyeth lived in a farmhouse surrounded by fields. He'd
turned the windmill next to his home into a beautiful, completely circular art studio with open windows all around.

Still amused years later, Jean said, "And windowsills!
Those windowsills. They were full of things Andrew had

collected. Beautiful-shaped stones with subtle colors and shadings. Bones of various sizes. All sorts of found objects from beads to bullet casings."

In her travels, Jean had picked up similar articles and brought them home. The things she'd collected were very similar to those on Andrew's windowsills. In what she referred to as her "so-called art career," she'd picked chicken bones out of soup and glued them on canvases with other found items to make odd compositions.

She and Andrew wandered off alone, walking around and talking. They were total strangers, and yet Jean had a strong feeling about him; she recognized him as a kindred spirit. Just chatting together for those little moments in time, she could relax and just be herself. She recognized that feeling of kinship as exactly what she always craved, the one thing that could fill the void at the center of her life.

During the course of their circumnavigation of the windmill, she asked him, "What is an artist?"

Wyeth replied: "To answer the question we must first ask: what is art?"

Jean didn't need to contemplate the question and immediately responded, "Beauty itself...which is commonly believed to be created by the artist, but my feeling is that Beauty resides in the original object—could be an apple, a flower, a twig, a tree, or the hand of a child. It could be some juxtaposition of things found in the bottom of a creek. The artist sees the beauty and is thrilled by it. His impulse is to share it with others. Say the beautiful thing is the moon in a dark sky, and you're standing next to me. Maybe you're even a stranger. I, as the artist witnessing this magnificence, can't help but say: 'Isn't that gorgeous?' This is my impulse, to share it with you, having been thrilled by the beauty. And I want to give it with love—'look at that!'"

"Yes," Andrew said. "That's the algorithm of beauty."

Jean felt the sense of kinship well up again, building on itself with each turn, each nuance explored in their conversation. She wondered if he felt it as well. Then his wife, Betsy, came in to claim her other half.

"I wanted to put arsenic in her junket," Jean wrote in her journal. "I wanted him for myself forever after."

The three of them went back to the house where Barbara had been waiting, clipboard in hand. Trying to hide her smoldering impatience, she lasered in on Jean and said, "There you are."

"She seemed on the edge of a nervous breakdown," Jean wrote. "I just wanted her to be happy, so I was very protective of her state of mind. I did not want to compete. I mean, she was the one with the pencil and the clipboard, so I turned Andrew over to her."

As they were walking out the door at the end of their afternoon visit, Barbara said, quite graciously, "Thank you Mr. Wyeth. I think I've got everything I need. If, by chance, there is something else I'd like to ask, may I telephone you?"

Wyeth replied, "If you want to know what Andrew Wyeth thinks, ask Jean Liedloff."

Two months later, Andrew invited Jean to join him at a cocktail party in New York. While there, she met Adam Yarmolinsky, a former member of the Kennedy "brain trust," a dynamic team of advisors who had served the young president before his assassination. During the Johnson administration, Yarmolinsky became deeply involved in the War on Poverty.

Jean and Yarmolinsky hit it off straight away. They met at about six o'clock in the evening and talked through the night. By sun-up Yarmolinsky had mastered all her ideas. He became her greatest advocate.

Soon thereafter, Yarmolinsky called his friend, Margaret Mead. At that time, the famous anthropologist served as chair of the Division of Social Sciences at Fordham University's Lincoln Center Campus.

"You must meet this young woman," Yarmolinsky told Mead.

At another cocktail party that same week, Yarmolinsky introduced Jean to Raymond Rubinow, the administrator of the Kaplan Fund, founded by Jack Kaplan of the Welch's Grape Juice empire. Rubinow also grasped the importance of her ideas within an hour after the two were introduced.

Not so with Margaret Mead. The well-loved anthropology professor with a Ph.D. from Columbia University had an office, in Jean's words, "literally in the belfry." Jean arrived for the appointment and was told she'd have to wait. An hour passed. Jean approached the secretary's desk and asked if it would be much longer. The young woman excused herself and walked down a long narrow hallway. She returned twenty minutes later and summoned Jean to the turret, saying, "Dr. Mead will see you now."

After the usual introductory niceties, Mead began to question Jean about her "field work." Jean explained that she had not gone to the jungle to do research nor work on a thesis paper. The conversation more or less ended there. Jean began to talk about what she would later name the *in-arms phase*, explaining that Yequana babies are always with the mother, kept close to her body after they're born, even throughout the night. Mead interrupted her to say, "Is that all you have to contribute to anthropology? Ben Spock and I call this *rooming in:* having the baby in the same room."

Ordinarily, Jean would have corrected her. It took herculean self-restraint not to say, "Having a baby in the same room with Mum and Dad while they sleep is a far cry from carrying an infant in a sling, snug against mother's body all day long then cozied up in the family bed at night." But Mead's body language and demeanor made clear to Jean she'd be wasting her breath to attempt any further explanation of her observations and ideas.

The rest of the interview didn't go any better. Jean could barely complete a sentence without being interrupted. Finally, after twenty minutes, Mead stood up and said: "My message to you, young lady, is stop going around bothering important people." Later Jean heard that, after the meeting, Mead had said of her, "She's a young, un-credentialed creature who has somehow been granted an audience."

Mead's disparaging remarks ate at Jean. She knew that her ideas would never be taken seriously if she didn't write a book. By then she had started calling her writer's block, "The Beast."

Not long after, Raymond Rubinow introduced Jean to the widely respected British-American anthropologist, Ashley Montagu. A frequent guest on *The Tonight Show,* Montagu had published numerous studies on the significant relationship of mother and infant. Initially, her friendship with Montagu was merely cordial, until one memorable evening when they sat next to one another at a philanthropic event. The two of them had a grand time. At the end of their meal, Montagu said: "I'm going to introduce you to Johnny Carson's producer. What do you say? Would you like to be a guest on *The Tonight Show?*"

More so than his flattering offer, Jean thrilled when she registered Montagu's keen interest in her observations of the indigenous people. He listened to her thinking and considered the implications for humanity, taking her observations to heart. He acknowledged her fresh perspective, calling her an "original thinker." This grew her confidence that her ideas did, indeed, have merit.

When she got a call from Carson's producer a week later, she told him she wasn't ready to go public with her theory. She had yet to get answers to her remaining questions about certain topics. How do the Yequana conduct their business dealings? How do they handle infidelity? Is there anything similar to divorce? Are Yequana children present during the sexual act? These and dozens of other questions ping-ponged in her mind.

One evening, while attending a party on East 63rd Street, a friend from George Plimpton's circle introduced her to Aaron Asher. He was the soon-to-be Vice President of publisher Holt, Rinehart and Winston, and one of New York's most beloved editors. Whilst sipping cocktails on a green terrace overlooking the city, Jean spoke with Asher, sharing what she'd learned about human nature in the jungle. She also spoke of her struggle to write an outline and secure a publisher. Reflecting on that conversation decades later, Jean wrote to Asher in a letter, saying, "You were the saint who did not say 'If you really wanted to, you'd write,' or 'Just put it down any old way and fix it up later,' or 'When you're ready, you'll write,' or some other version of 'Don't be silly, just do it!' You listened to me talk, questioned me carefully, understood the value of the potential book, and bid me try again and, *mirabile dictu,*[25] told me that if I didn't produce a proposal soon you would write one for me! I have never ceased to be warmed and encouraged by that evidence of your faith in me."

But it would take more than Asher's faith in her, more than Montagu's interest in her ideas, more than Yarmolinsky's advocacy and Rubinow's enthusiasm to vanquish The Beast.

Jean could hardly believe that two years had passed since her return from the fourth expedition. Feeling stagnant in Manhattan, she decided to leave her native New York for good. A few days before her departure, she arranged a meeting with George Plimpton to say goodbye. She met him at Stillman's Gym where he often boxed with former world light-heavyweight champion Archie Moore.[26] Jean watched with fascination as Archie coached Plimpton on his style, wincing every time her friend took a punch. After the two men finished their workout, Jean and Plimpton walked up 8th

---

[25] The Latin phrase, translated variously as "wonderful to relate" or "strange to say" is believed to have originated with Virgil's second major work, Georgics.

[26] Archie Moore was the longest reigning world light heavyweight champion of all time (Dec 1952 – May 1962). In 1990, he was entered into the International Boxing Hall of Fame. Moore is the only man to have faced both Rocky Marciano and Muhammad Ali in the ring.

Avenue to Central Park. She told him of her plan to leave New York, avoiding the topic of her writer's block altogether. She finished what she called her "valedictory," successfully fighting back the tears she felt she had no right to have. Plimpton smiled and put his hands on her shoulders, stared into her eyes and said good-bye with a single word: "Write!"

19.

Diamonds Are Not
a Girl's Best Friend

In 1967, Jean left New York and moved to London. She continued to answer a constant stream of requests for interviews and talks. In the years since her maiden speaking engagement back in 1952, she'd become a seasoned public speaker and sought-after lecturer.

That very first public talk was held at the Art Students League where her parents met back in 1924. Robert Hale, the curator of American Art at the Metropolitan Museum, asked the 25-year-old explorer to speak. He and his assistant, the lovely Muriel Oxenberg, offered to coach her in public speaking before the talk. For a week before the lecture, Jean suffered such severe stage fright that she could eat nothing but mashed bananas and an occasional bowl of egg drop soup.

The Art Students League is located on West 57th Street in Manhattan. Since 1875, the League has counted among its members and students many historically renowned artists who have played an important role in a number of developments in the art world.

Reflecting back on that pivotal event, Jean talked about what happened that day: "Stewart Klonis, the director of the League, introduced my talk, saying: 'Jean's parents met here and she is the result.' I'm sure there were some in the audience who assumed I'd been conceived in the building."

She walked on stage with her pet monkey, Frooky, on her shoulder. Sometimes looking this way and that, sometimes clinging close to her neck, Frooky seemed uncharacteristically nervous. "I was wearing a décolleté black dress. It was Bob Hale's idea," she mused, "his vision of the stalwart explorer astonishing the bourgeoisie by looking like an air-headed debutante."

Less than a minute into her talk, the microphone went dead. Jean stepped to the front of the stage, raised her voice and asked whether she could be heard at the back. She momentarily lost her nerve at the thought of Frooky relieving himself on her dress. She handed him to her sister in the front row. All ended well, and she never again felt nervous when asked to do a public talk or interview.

The day after she spoke at the Art Students League, the *New York Times* published an article titled: "Diamonds Not a Girl's Best Friend if Snakes and Alligators Get in the Way." The piece featured a photo of Jean with Frooky and began: "Miss Jean Liedloff, a tall, tanned, green-eyed blonde who spent seven months digging diamonds out of Venezuelan riverbeds, is back in New York with a pet monkey, the skin of a leopard she shot, and an Indian canoe paddle among her souvenirs—but wearing no diamonds. Yesterday, in fact, she wore rhinestone buttons on her dress."

But the reporter got it wrong. She hadn't killed the leopard herself.

It happened near the end of that first expedition. Jean had been kept awake many a night by the hunting cries of leopards and jaguars, cries the tribespeople could hear from a quarter of a mile away, but ignored unless they came within 200 yards. Jean learned that she could scare off an ocelot (a dwarf leopard) by singing loudly. But she had no interest in having a close encounter with a *kaicuse* (the Cariban word for a panther, leopard, jaguar, lion or tiger).

Years later, she granted: "The last thing I expected was to meet a giant pussycat face-to-face. But, as usual, the jungle had a plan of its own."

They had canoed three miles upriver from their base camp: Jean, the Italians, two indigenous men, and their pet dog. Jean felt fatigued and wished she had stayed behind to relax in the shade of the *tarimba,* a rudimentary hut made of broad palm leaves. The men spent two days breaking apart the upper crust of a diamond-bearing formation, while Jean made trial digs in a pool nearby. Suddenly, she noticed a change in the dog's demeanor—his pricked-up ears, nose flicking the air, the flutter of his coat up the center of his back. A whiny-growl seemed to be stuck in his throat.

Jean looked in the direction the dog was facing, but heard nothing. She turned to signal one of the indigenous men, but he was already on point. She watched in amazement as he made a bird-like sound and the dog crept forward and lay down between his legs. He stood completely still for several long moments. In a single flowing motion, he reached for his hunting bow, brought it over his shoulder to the front of his body and strung it with an arrow. Footfalls shook the earth. Then a crashing sound, not 100 feet away. Jean grabbed her rifle. Two tapirs bushwhacked through the undergrowth and bolted toward the river. Ten seconds behind them, a pair of leopards leapt out of the jungle; their long, sleek bodies flew through the air several feet off the ground. The dog charged after the leopards, barking and growling and snarling all at once. Without thinking, Jean darted after the small stampede. About thirty yards upriver she came upon the two big cats. One was on the back of the larger tapir, the other had sunk his fangs into the smaller animal's throat. Blood spurted out of the creature's neck. Jean watched the animal's body go limp. The leopard looked up, his muzzle and teeth covered with blood. He stared, blank-eyed, at Jean. Pure instinct found her raising her rifle; she felt none of the usual dread at the prospect of killing. But the hunter's arrow flew through the air and skewered the leopard's throat, killing him instantly. She looked in the direction of the other cat; it had disappeared into the jungle, leaving the larger tapir wounded, writhing in agony. The hunter walked toward the animal, determined that his injuries were fatal, and slit his throat with a knife.

For Jean, the sight of the three dead animals did not elicit the usual revulsion. Had the echo of beasts attacking one another, the primeval reality of death ceased to horrify? Had she accepted that the beasts of the forest perish at a fearless pace?

They spent the rest of the afternoon butchering the two dead tapir, smoking the savory flesh over a fire and rendering the lard. It was the best meat Jean had ever tasted.

In the evening, the hunter who had killed the leopard lashed the dead animal's front and back feet to a tree limb. He hung the corpse upside-down, suspended between two trees near his hammock. To his people, leopards and panthers were the scourge of the forest, their worst enemy. Killing one was cause for celebration. The following morning, he led the way back to base camp. He and one of his tribesmen carried the dead leopard, laughing and singing with the all jubilance and abandon a great triumph deserves.

The process of skinning and tanning the big cat was by far the most disgusting of all Jean's jungle experiences. But if she wanted to take the leopard skin home—and she did— she had to submit to the gory lesson. She felt horrified at the prospect of skinning the dead animal. She felt both regret and revulsion at the sight of its massive carcass. When the hunters began the process of tanning the hide using the animal's own fetid brains, she vomited. Terribly woozy, she would do her best to stand up, but the smell made her vomit every time. She felt as though the base of her pelvis had fallen out of her body. Her face was so tinged with green that the men excused her long before the job was done. Nonetheless, her brave attempt to stomach the process was rewarded, and they gave her the skin once it had dried.

Jean took the skin with her when she moved to London in 1967. She took a flat at 11 St. George's Terrace near Queen Mary's Rose Gardens and displayed the leopard skin prominently on the wall of her flat. She firmly believed it would prove a magic totem and inspire her to write.

20.

Wild-eyed and Deeply Inspired

Full of anticipation about the book that had been gestating inside her for so long, Jean settled into her London flat ready to give birth. But The Beast continued to hold her captive, disallowing her the joy of writing. Nonetheless, her reputation as an explorer and original thinker grew as word spread of her radical ideas.

Months passed, then a year. Meanwhile, Jean met a Londoner, David, and the two of them became engaged. To hear her tell the story: "He said he was in love with me, moved in, took care of me, and did simple cooking so I could put my attention on writing. There was no sexual attraction, but I enjoyed his company. I viewed marriage proposals as an embarrassment of riches, the decision of whom to marry a tyranny of choice. Had I been less attractive, or attractive to fewer men, I would not have felt the pressure to choose one rather than be left alone. But there was always someone else, someone else, someone else. With David, I accepted. I suppose when he asked, I just decided it wasn't worth holding out anymore. And, I must confess, I did have this wild idea that having him around to watch over me would help me relax and just write. But alas, The Beast continued to hold me captive. And then David died. Brain tumor."

Just as when her grandmother died, Jean did not grieve. She did, however, attend David's funeral but declined when asked to speak.

In 1969, Jean went to Paris to meet with the French anthropologist and ethnologist, Claude Lévi-Strauss[27] at the Ecole Des Hautes Etudes.[28] She'd been commissioned to make a documentary for the BBC about the plight of tribal peoples in South America. She wanted to interview Lévi-Strauss about his views on the "savage" mind, which he argued had the same structures as the "civilized" mind. Between takes, Lévi-Strauss showed her a book written in the first person about a Brazilian peasant girl by the name of Helena Valero who had been captured at age eleven by the *Yanomami* tribe.

---

[27] Claude Lévi-Strauss played a key role in the development of the theory of structuralism and structural anthropology. He received numerous honors from universities and institutions throughout the world and is considered to be the father of modern anthropology.

[28] Ecole Des Hautes Etudes is a highly selective grand établissement in Paris, France. One of the finest research and higher education institutions, its degrees in religious studies and history are among the most prestigious in the world.

Twenty-one years later, the girl—now a woman—escaped and returned to Brazil to tell her story. An Italian anthropologist taped her account. Levi-Strauss recognized the exceptional circumstance: Helena Valero had not only lived with the natives but had a couple of husbands and two children while there. Her insider's knowledge of Stone Age life inspired Levi-Strauss to declare her story the greatest of all contributions to anthropology. He explained this to Jean and she concurred: having the informant speak directly eliminated the prejudices of anthropology, an academic discipline for which she had little regard.

A month or two later, Jean obtained a copy of the book, *Yanoama: The Story of Helena Valero, a Girl Kidnapped by Amazonian Indians.* Upon reading of Valero's life with the Yanoama, Jean realized that the tribe described in the book was the same one who called themselves Sanema in the far reaches of their stomping grounds. It occurred to her that a Sanema friend of hers, Walema, could tell an equally valuable account. As a boy, a Venezuelan captured Walema. He escaped several years later and went back to his people. In time, he became his tribe's shaman. His account of the Stone Age male subculture would be quite different from Helena Valero's description of the female subculture.

Jean mentioned this one evening while dining with a London literary agent. Supremely excited about the idea, the agent persuaded her to write a brief proposal for another expedition to South America so she could interview Walema. She would capture his story on tape then transcribe and edit his autobiographical account into a book. Jean had been feeling the need to go back and clarify the insights that had coalesced in her mind since her last trip. Sensing this could be a real turning point, she became wild-eyed and deeply inspired by the agent's faith in her. This man, a publishing professional, truly believed she had something of value to offer. Well aware that big name editors in New York and London loved to commune with a writer's mind, she believed the agent when he said, "I know an editor who will accept your proposal." She took his advice to heart and immediately went to work.

Jean had no difficulty pulling the proposal together. Within a week, the agent had piqued the interest of several publishers. In short order, he secured two advances, one from Gollancz, Ltd.[29] in London and another from Holt, Rinehart and Winston in New York. Jean immediately began to organize what would be her fifth and final expedition.

A month later, when she was set to leave London in a week's time, she received a letter from her sister. She rarely opened Fran's letters straightaway—they were a font of depressing news and maudlin complaints—but this one had arrived by aero post so she knew it was important.

In the letter, Fran had written: "Mother is being kind to me. We're sharing a studio on 234th street and getting along quite well."

Jean had never stopped craving Helen's attention. She wanted her mother to notice her, to accept her and be proud of her. She thought, *if there's love going on there, I don't want*

---

[29] Victor Gollancz founded Gollancz, Ltd. in 1927, publishing writers such as George Orwell, Daphne du Maurier, and Franz Kafka. Upon his death in 1967, Gollancz, Ltd. was taken over by his daughter, Livia Gollancz who eventually sold it to Houghton Mifflin in 1989.

to miss it. She postponed the expedition in hopes of basking in her mother's love, if only for a minute. But by the time she flew to New York, Helen had stopped being motherly.

So, I missed it, she told herself, trying hard not to care. But the incident poisoned her feelings about herself. And poor Fran was devastated when Helen reverted to her cold, hard self.

A few days before she was to depart for South America, a concern that had been niggling at Jean refused to be ignored any longer. What if she couldn't find Walema? What if his group had gone even deeper into the jungle? What if he was dead? She brought her concern to Tom Wallace, then head of Holt, Rinehart and Winston. Then she phoned Livia Gollancz in London with the same concern, asking: "What if I cannot find Walema or discover he's no longer alive?" She would, after all, spend most of the advance money the two publishers had given her to mount the expedition, charter airplanes, and procure canoes and provisions. Wallace and Gollancz both seemed unconcerned and said she could just give them her "next book." Whereupon Jean replied: "Then I'll give you my real work."

Both of them responded by muttering, "Sure, sure," and made no further inquiry.

21.

The Final Expedition

After four trips to the jungle, having lived with indigenous people of the Amazon for a total of twenty months, the blinders were off. Jean could now see the distorted faces of "her" people. She could sense and feel some of the forces that cause those distortions and give rise to the common neurotic fixations we have come to accept as normal.

She had returned to New York with a head full of jungle memories and a point of view stripped of presumptions. She held her observations like separate pieces of a jigsaw puzzle, resolving to resist the temptation to develop a working theory prematurely. All she knew for certain was that the behavior patterns of the jungle people hinted at a principle of human nature diametrically opposed to the prevailing view among her people.

She wrote in her journal: "After the fourth expedition, I began to reverse the tearing-down process. Bit by bit, I began to perceive the order that underlay not only my South American observations, but also the naked fragments of my experience of civilized life."

It took time for Jean's conditioned views to unravel but, as they did, a startling new perspective began to emerge. She spent considerable time examining an idea that kept circling back to the front of her mind—that innate human expectations and tendencies could be shaped by evolution. It occurred to her that the feeling of perfect rightness she felt while in the jungle was due to factors beyond the jungle itself—something about the people, something they knew that civilized folks had forgotten.

She simply had to go back and live with the tribal people one more time. Determined not to romanticize her observations of the Yequana, she hoped to find an explanation for their high state of wellbeing, their tangible happiness, their stable joy. She wanted to clarify and enhance her new ideas with deliberate study. As much as she despised the idea of academic research, she felt equally passionate about finding any hidden flaws in her own reasoning. To do that, she must do her best to observe the Yequana methodically. She would interview Walema then make her way through the jungle to Yequana territory. But each time she contemplated this course of action, her thoughts became tangled up in the big question: *what about Anchu?*

It had been nearly seven years. She didn't even know if the chief was still alive. But she had to go. There was too much at stake; the implications of her hypothesis were too important. Compared to what she wanted and needed to know, her fear of ever being held captive again was, in her words, *piccole patate* (Italian for "small potatoes").

Or was it?

What if I do not return this time? she thought. *What good is my momentous theory—as yet unwritten and trapped in my head—if I am dead?*

Perhaps she could find another tribe who would welcome her. But such an expedition would take time, for nothing could be learned until she built the necessary trust.

She began to ask around, questioning her explorer friends in New York if they knew of a tribe she might approach. In the course of her inquiries, she heard a story about the death of a well-loved tribal chief in the vicinity where she'd traveled. Jean put on her journalist hat, determined to find out more. No one she spoke with could confirm the chief's identity. In fact, no one could even substantiate the story. But knowing what she knew of the enduring dangers in the jungle, Jean had no difficulty believing it was true.

It was early spring, 1965. The rainy season had come to an end, and the chief wanted to see how the relentless storms had transformed the river. He brought along one of his adult wives and her sister, a 10-year-old girl.[30]

The three of them canoed upriver to an isolated spot away

---

[30] Polygyny was commonplace among the Yequana. Men often had more than one wife, and the wives were often related by blood. It was not unusual for a man to take a new wife and essentially marry her sisters as well. If the sisters were not of marrying age, he would take responsibility for rearing them. Until they became women, the young girls were treated like daughters, not wives.

from the village. Late in the afternoon, they went down to fish for dinner and came upon a new feature of the river: a pool of crystal-clear water. Just past the pool, the chief saw a massive tree that had fallen to form a dam.

His wife came up beside him, her arm shaking with excitement as she pointed at the young alligators cavorting on the far side of the pool. The chief nodded in agreement—they would have young caiman tail for dinner that night. He crawled along the bank of the river, looking for the young alligators' mother. A full-grown alligator could kill a man with one flick of the tail, but the mother was nowhere in sight. She would not be far away, so the chief worked quickly to make a lasso out of a length of liana-rope.

The girl, full of excitement and anticipation, climbed up on the trunk of the fallen tree. She scooched along the tree-trunk, her legs dangling on either side, until she sat above the young alligators frolicking three yards below. She turned and smiled at her sister, who signaled her to come back. The girl smiled again and stood up. With her arms akimbo, she began to prance along the tree trunk. Displeased with the girl, the chief let out a loud whistle. She wiggled her hips and giggled. He turned his attention from her to the task at hand and climbed onto the trunk, gripping his lasso. He walked toward the girl with a stern, chiding look. She dropped her head and plopped down onto the tree trunk. He sat down next to her and waited for one of the baby alligators to separate from the others. The waiting didn't take long. With one swift movement, he dropped his lasso around a young caiman's neck and lunged toward the riverbank. With primal power, the four-foot-long reptile whiplashed along the surface of the water. The chief made his way along the trunk, as careful and confident as a tightrope walker dragging a wild pendulum behind him. Thrilled, the girl skipped back and forth along the fallen tree, while the chief struggled with his thrashing prey.

He reached the riverbank and began to haul the baby alligator out of the water. The mother alligator appeared on the far shore and yowled. He looked up to see the girl standing on the fallen tree a few yards back, frozen in fear. He dropped the rope, brandished his knife, and leapt onto the tree trunk. Aflame with vengeful wrath, the mother alligator blasted across the pool and walloped through the air, snapping her massive jaws. The girl scurried toward the chief who grabbed her outstretched hand and flung her small body to safety. The mother alligator yowled even louder as she made her way onto the tree-trunk and stalked toward the chief. He reached overhead, his arms flailing toward an overhanging branch. The massive reptile flung her tail in his direction, slapping his hips and toppling him into the water. She leapt on top of him and crushed him with her massive jaws.

The thought of this unnamed chief dying the way he did sent a wave of deep sadness through Jean. Only much later in her life, did she recognize the feeling as grief. She had always been unable to grieve, so why now? "Perhaps," she would say, still trying to explain it to herself so many years later, "it was precisely because I *didn't* know him, didn't know if it was Anchu or not. Maybe I could feel sadness over death only if it was from a distance." But in accord with the Yequana way, her sadness did not last. "They do not carry their grief around the way we do," she would reflect. "Their attitude toward death and toward the ever-present dangers of jungle life is one of total acceptance. The demise of that chief would be regarded as an honorable death. Following the initial shock, the people of his village would celebrate his sacrifice and immortalize him by making the story of his heroic end part of their oral history."

Although Jean felt the story quite plausible, she still had no way of knowing if the dead chief was, in fact, Anchu. Never one to let fear stop her from going after something of value, she decided to make the trip and conduct further inquiries once she arrived.

As soon as she landed in Caracas, Jean learned that Walema and his clan had succumbed to smallpox brought in by an invading missionary. Freed from her official assignment, she set out to do what she'd really come to do. She asked around about the Yequana. How many of the tribes had survived? How many Yequana villages had matured[31] and split into two once they had more than 80 inhabitants? Had they, like the Sanema, been ravaged by disease? Were they facing the threat of extinction?

She felt heartened to learn that the Yequana had been spared. The people of the river remained essentially unchanged, other than developing a passion for canned sardines, and the

---

[31] Yequana villages go through three distinct phases in their maturation process. The first is an incipient phase with a single three-generation family of anywhere from ten to twenty-seven people. In the next phase, the family grows to some thirty or forty people, becoming a stable entity that is likely to survive into successive generations. Once stable, in the third phase, maturity, the village may grow to as many as 80 people and even more in territories where there are plenty of resources.

shirts and shorts some of them now wore with great pride. She also got word that Anchu had died.

Jean and her party stayed in Caracas for a week while they purchased needed supplies. They bought sugar, pasta, dried meats and coffee. Jean made sure she had two extra pairs of shoes. It took some doing, but she scoured the nearby shops until she found special gifts and articles to bring the Yequana. At last, she was ready. She stepped back and looked at her baggage. One army duffle bag held all of her personal belongings, including a camera, recording equipment, and a happy supply of sugar and pasta. She had stuffed a second duffle, filling it to the zipper with canned sardines and Levi's 501 blue jeans.

Jean woke up unusually early the next morning filled with a sense of dread. Had she forgotten something? Was there danger ahead? Was this just another folly to feed The Beast? Would she ever be able to sit down and write? Filled with nervous energy, she couldn't bear to stay in bed. It wasn't yet dawn and all of her travel companions were still sound asleep. She spent the next hour unpacking and repacking both duffle bags. When the sun announced its arrival with the glow of first light, she chased away the lion's share of her nervous energy. But she remained hyper-alert all the same. She decided to go out for a walk.

When Jean first arrived in Caracas back in 1951, the city was home to some 700,000 South Americans. By the early 70s, the city housed 1.7 million, with another half a million living around the urban rim.

At that hour of the morning, the streets were still relatively quiet, but she was amused by the proliferation of motorcycles and brightly colored Chevrolets. She walked down Avenida de Sabana Grande and stopped beneath the Savoy Chocolate marquee on the Pigalle Building. She knew a little bit of history about the chocolate company; it had been founded when the Beer brothers of Austria (Rodolfo, Roberto, and Fernando) teamed up with a Venezuelan by the name of John Miller, who invented chocolate-making machinery.[32] But it wasn't the Savoy Chocolate sign that caught her attention that morning. It was a sign hugging the side of the next building on the street. Jean stopped and stared at the sign with its letters, V-O-G-U-E, stacked in a vertical line. She wondered why she hadn't seen the sign before. How many times had she walked down Sabana Grande on previous visits to Caracas? She stared up at the sign, the morning light glaring in her eyes. A bead of perspiration ran down her temple. The temperature was on the rise and she had a long, sweaty day ahead. *They'll all be awake by now,* she thought. Turning back toward her hotel and walking quickly, she mused about how far she'd come since her modeling days at *Vogue Paris*.

Jean had all but forgotten her earlier unease when she took a seat in the hotel restaurant. She ordered a cup of coffee and two eggs. "Sunny side up," she said to the waiter with a bright smile.

---

[32] The company name, Savoy, was Miller's idea. He'd stayed at a hotel by that name in London and, along with a small crown that became part of the company's logo, felt it a symbol of regal excellence and good taste. It was also a word that was easy to pronounce in any language.

Before her coffee arrived, the proprietor approached her table. He said, "*Buenos días señora encantadora,*" ("Good morning, lovely lady") and handed her a telegram.

Jean unfolded the paper. It read: "Your sister has died; she committed suicide."

That's why I woke up feeling such dread, she thought. But she was not one to give any currency to psychic phenomena and, truth be told, she wasn't all that surprised. She had seen the look of complete defeat on her sister's face when they'd said their goodbyes in New York. For Jean, it made perfect sense that Frances had decided to take her own life.

When the waiter brought her breakfast, she thanked him without making eye contact, and sat looking at the overcooked eggs. Rather than send the plate back as she ordinarily would when a restaurant meal wasn't up to snuff, she just sat there staring into space, letting her coffee get cold. After twenty minutes of glazed-eye numbness, she pulled out her journal and wrote:

My sister never recovered from the early horrors with our mother. She never had a moment of confidence, or perhaps she did, some few moments, with her beauty and her talents for sculpture, drawing, and music, or with her daughter, Janet. But I only remember her on the edge of despair, on the brink of disaster, year after year. She was cheated of any reward for her creativity, her designs for clothes and hair and shoes. Her demon kept her failing, losing all men and most friends. She felt undeserving of love because our mother was unable to love us. When we grew up, she was only ever passionately interested in men who had already chosen me.

Poor Fran. She'd been starving for the love she imagined I had gotten from Mommy when, in fact, I was agonizingly neglected as well. What might she have become if she had been loved, cherished, adored, recognized, respected by Mommy?

Jean went on, her handwriting powerful, making deep rivulets in the page:

What a waste! So much energy put into fear, so little into love. And so much need for love, for each blossoming personality to extend itself in loving, in kindness, in creating beauty to bestow upon others. And however the love of each of us might have emerged, been expressed to us and to one another and on, outward to others and back to ourselves, enriching all around, expanding, satisfying, warming, seeking new opportunities always, to give, to receive graciously—to live, smiling, trusting, expecting to love, expecting to be loved. But no. We lived in need, in want, with all our talents and material comforts, and yet starving, each alone, for that sense of rightness, of welcome. Poor lost little Francie, so vulnerable, no mercy, no tenderness for her.

Jean often reflected on what had been a materially rich and yet emotionally impoverished childhood. But her reflections were largely devoid of feeling. Once again, with Fran's death, she found herself touched by sadness, and yet unable to grieve. But she was in Caracas, about to return to her beloved jungle, and wasn't about to concern herself with emotional stagnation.

22.

Questions Asked and Unasked Find Answers

The next morning, Jean and her crew left Caracas in a small, chartered plane and flew over Amazonia. At last, she was back in the rarified atmosphere of the jungle.

The airstrip she helped clear on the second expedition had become the site of a small church and weather station by her third. Both had since been abandoned. The runway appeared to be one large puddle, bordered by overgrown weeds. The pilot, undaunted, said not a word as he circled the muddy airstrip.

Among aviators, the DC-3 Dakota was legendary. Pilots who'd flown the plane would insist that the only replacement for a DC-3 was another DC-3. Fans of the dogged aircraft described it, in all good humor, as "a collection of parts flying in loose formation." The Dakota was well known for its ability to take off and land on grass or dirt, making it especially suited to unpaved runways. But Jean did not know this. Even if she had, that knowledge would not have prevented the panic attack she had to fight off as the pilot made his approach. Only after the Dakota came to a full stop on the soggy runway did she remember how to breathe.

On the second day of the ten-day trip up the Caroní into Yequana territory they broke camp early. Not far upriver, they would have to cross the most treacherous rapids. The guides she'd hired heard the distant roar first, twenty minutes before Jean's ears could detect the sound. When they reached fast running water above the falls, they beached the canoes. Two of the guides hiked along the bank of the river to assess the passage ahead. Enchanted by her beloved jungle, Jean tagged along. They scouted the waterfall from atop a massive boulder that guarded the cataract. Jean scrambled out to the edge with the guides and felt a familiar pull of terror in her groin. She stepped back, bursting with the kind of vigor that arises only when a person is in fear for his or her life. She inched forward again, stayed behind the guides on the boulder, looking down at 60-foot drops and deep rock channels. She remembered her previous passage through this series of rapids. It featured lock-like steps little more than a yard wide that barely accommodated their canoes. At the bottom of the waterfall, she saw the familiar crystal-clear lagoon shrouded in green foam.

The crossing was a two-hour ordeal. As they neared the final set of rapids, the first canoe got caught in a whirlpool and capsized. Jean and her companions were able to retrieve most of the supplies that went overboard; only a hunting knife and their supply of sugar were lost.

By the time they reached the village nine days later, Jean's sweet tooth was aching. Before long, her craving for sugar became an obsession. She would've traded her entire supply of sardines for sugar cane, but then thought better of it.

Only the Yequana women are allowed to cut sugar cane, but they are not permitted to negotiate a trade. Jean approached one of the men and struck a deal: a piece of Venetian glass costume jewelry for a supply of sugar cane. The next day, she left the village early with the man, his wife, and their son. They hiked over two mountains. It was a difficult trek. But the moment she saw the huge sugar cane field drenched gold in the sun, Jean's weariness disappeared.

She sat on a log alongside the two men. The woman walked into the field. She came back a few minutes later carrying two large stalks that were eight feet long and two inches in diameter. The man looked at Jean, cocked his head and nodded.

Jean shook her head and said, "More!"

He waved his wife back into the field with a quick flip of his hand.

She brought out two more stalks and lay them down with the others. Her husband opened his hand, palm up, and nodded at his offering.

Again, Jean said, "More!"

The man nodded in agreement.

Jean was surprised by the equanimity on his face. Then it suddenly dawned on her: she was being greedy! She shouted after the woman, "*Toini*!" ("Only one!")

Now she understood how the Yequana conducted business. Bargains were made on the basis of trust. She could have exacted a price of 15 stalks for the trinket and the man would not have objected. Per Yequana custom, trading goods involved no competition, no pitting oneself against another.

They had no motive to "pull one off" on someone, only to keep the faith and maintain good relations. Fairness, balance, harmony, justice—that was the Yequana Way.

Her lessons of the day were not yet complete, however. It was time to head back to the village. The man gave his wife a wave and told her to go on ahead. She left all seven stalks on the ground. The man and his son picked up three stalks each and balanced them on their shoulders. Jean stood looking at the last stalk on the ground. Did they intend for her to carry the cumbersome thing? How would she manage its weight over two mountains? The two men were already fifteen yards down the narrow path when the elder one turned around. He pointed at the sugar cane, shouted, *"Aamadeh!"* ("You!"), commanding Jean to shoulder the heavy stalk. She was incensed that two strong men would make her carry her share of the load. The pleasure she'd enjoyed while sucking on sweet juice at the sugar cane field turned into indignation. She sulked as she caught up with them. The two stocky men did not appear the least bit burdened; their faces, as usual, were in repose. Half an hour passed. Jean was sweating and cursing under her breath when the older of the two men stepped aside and gestured that she should lead the way. She continued to sulk as they made their way up the mountain. Her grumbling resentment multiplied every time she stumbled and had to struggle to get her balance—a challenge that was difficult enough when her hands were free.

Back on the trail after a break for lunch, she once again took the lead. Anxious the men might grow impatient over her slow pace, she waved them to go ahead. They both shook their heads and motioned her to continue in the lead. They showed no sign of impatience for her slower pace, no judgment of her lumbering and bumbling, and no disdain for her lack of strength. She was thunderstruck. Not only did the Yequana have no concept or apprehension of work, they had never once demonstrated a self-righteous attitude over perceived delays. Unlike the white man, they had no words for "Hurry up." Jean realized that her feelings of shame over her clumsiness, her fear of being judged and thus losing her hard-won cachet created tremendous tension in her body. She saw the folly of adding the weight of defending her honor to that of the sugarcane. The need to muster up enough determination to prove herself and belie the notion of "the weaker sex" evaporated into the humid jungle air.

She later wrote of the incident: "Gone was any sense of competition. The physical strain turned from an imposition upon my body to a satisfying demonstration of its strength. It surprised me to feel a burst of physical energy as I let these engrained misconceptions go. My teeth-gritting will power in the face of martyrdom no longer applied. All of these habitual ways of being did nothing but drain my mental power and undercut my physical vigor. In the wake of this startling realization, a new pleasure arose adding itself to my freedom: I was aware of carrying not just a stick of cane, but part of a load shared by my companions."

It was in this same manner, through random experience, that many of Jean's questions, asked and unasked, were answered.

By this time, she'd grown accustomed to naked children, bare-breasted women, and the Yequana's habit of roasting iguanas alive. Their routine snacks had ceased to bring on disgust, but she still refused to eat fat, juicy grubs the size of a man's finger.

"Even when rapaciously hungry," she would say, scrunching up her face, "I simply could not stomach picking up a dung beetle and snacking on its legs as if they were corn chips."

But her curiosity about their spousal and sexual relationships was not yet satisfied. Some of it made sense, other aspects continued to baffle her. Moreover, she had witnessed what, in her estimation, was the most bizarre marriage rite known to man.

Before the wedding, a groom's family would make a basket large enough for the couple to stand in upright. When the time came, the man and his bride climbed into the basket. The woman's family would then approach the large basket with a small basket full of rolled up leaves. Each of the leaves held a dozen or more red ants. All the men of the village circled around the couple, playing drums and rattles. The women emptied the leaves into the basket and began a ritual dance. The newlyweds were expected to suffer this torment in silence. A rite of passage that symbolized life's adversities, it impressed upon their minds and bodies the value of facing adversity together.

On earlier trips, Jean had found the sexual customs among the Yequana quite strange, at times offensive. But on this trip, she no longer felt shocked when a hunter would come home and grab his wife. "Yes! By the hair!" she would joke, mocking the stereotype.[33] The hunter would then lead his wife away

---

[33] The cartoon version of a "caveman" grabbing a woman by the hair dragging her along on the ground behind him is just that, a cartoon. Not to be confused with the highly erotic, primal experience of having a strong set of fingers go up the back of one's neck, spread out and gently massage one's head before those fingers slowly tighten into a half-fist, then firmly pull one's hair and take subtle, consensual control in the manner of the greatest lovers of all time.

from the village center to copulate behind a tree without so much as a coy smile to disguise his intent.

She marveled at the equanimity of women who were one of a man's four wives; she never detected resentment between them. There were no jealous tantrums and none of the back-biting that was so common among civilized women when competing for a man's attention.

She thought highly of their attitude toward unmarried girls: a man wouldn't dare touch a virgin who was eligible for a husband. But she couldn't help but question their rigid attitudes toward adultery.

One afternoon, she spoke directly to the third wife of one of the well-respected hunters. She wanted to understand their odd mindset toward adultery. By now, she had acquired a rudimentary Yequana vocabulary. In conjunction with a whole lot of hand gestures and pantomime, she could engage in lively conversations. The woman explained the fierce taboo against adultery: an unfaithful wife could be burned alive and have her ashes scattered in the river rather than have them buried as was customary. But if her husband had approved the liaison, or if he forgave her transgression, she went unpunished. If her husband sent her to "entertain" a distinguished guest, it was looked upon as a great honor. This highlighted the one aspect of Yequana life that continued to offend Jean's modern sensibilities: a woman belonged to her husband—she was his property.

The Yequana attitude toward sex, while equally divergent from that of her culture, more intrigued than troubled Jean. Men and women felt no shame about sex; the urge to copulate was not a private matter. Although she had noticed this on earlier expeditions, her conditioned embarrassment always compelled her to look away. Now she would deliberately observe their behavior as well as the reactions of the tribe, in particular the children. To her surprise, both adults and children displayed no reaction at all. They neither watched nor felt the need to look away.

Further observation[34] revealed that certain couples enjoyed a richer sex life within the confines of the hut. Sex outside the hut was a perfunctory matter, devoid of passion. A woman was perfectly happy to relieve her husband when his need arose. This was evermore true when he returned from a successful hunt with his testosterone levels sky high. Women knew instinctively what a man needed and gave it to him. After the release, he would take a refreshing nap and wake up ready to do the hard work of slaughtering his kill. To Jean, this seemed a clever deal.

Sex inside the hut was a different matter altogether. It had a playful quality to it and could continue for hours. Children were not made to sleep in separate quarters nor chased out of the hut during these erotic escapades.

Once home from what turned out to be her last expedition, Jean continued to contemplate this aspect of Yequana life for many years. Their sexual behaviors would seem outrageous

---

[34] Jean's observations were entirely casual and non-intrusive, what one would notice in passing while going about whatever there was to attend to during the day or when moving about the village at night. There was nothing clinical (not even "in-milieu") about her approach, she was simply in a quiet, discreet inquiry.

to Westerners. Her puzzlement was not focused on why they behaved the way they did, that she understood: it was in keeping with all of their un-self-conscious ways. The Yequana trusted and, in fact, had never denied or strayed from the natural rhythm of life, which included sexual activity. But a larger mystery with far-reaching implications continued to trouble Jean. What did the stark contrast between their attitude toward sexual expression and our experience of human sexuality reveal about her people?

It was her association with Arthur Janov some years later that expanded her thinking on this question. Upon her return to London in the early 1970s, Jean worked and trained with the author of *The Primal Scream,* hoping his method might have a palliative effect on the wounds of less-than-ideal treatment in infancy and childhood. This promise did not deliver. However, the work afforded her a roundhouse-view of what Freudians labelled the Oedipal or Electra complex.

Jean was, by this time, whole-heartedly convinced that our common neuroses develop as compensatory mechanisms when we are deprived of the essential experiences that evolution programmed us to expect. She reasoned that our Paleolithic ancestors would not have cordoned themselves off from their infants and children during the sex act. To do so would put the little ones at risk. She'd observed the Yequana's laissez-faire attitude toward nature taking its course between a man and a woman. Parents and children shared the same bed. Even in such close proximity, children rarely woke up during their parent's nighttime romps. If their parents were particularly rambunctious and a child did wake up, they typically fell right back to sleep.[35] All in all, couples never showed shame or concern about their sexual behavior. To the Yequana, sex was as natural and everyday as eating.

The net effect on the children was a passive education about the nature of sex relations; children acquired a subconscious understanding of adult sexuality, resulting in the knowledge that "This is what mommies and daddies do, and therefore, what I will do with my mate one day." Children would simply know that father and mother were sexual partners at an intrinsic level; it needed no explanation, required no attention at all. Likewise, sex education. As was the case with every other adult activity, the young learned through passive exposure. They were gently marinated in tribal ways, which included man-woman dynamics. This was in keeping with the experience of their evolving antecedents, the successful *Homo sapiens* who had come before. Jean reasoned that,

---

[35] A client spoke with me one day about a dilemma he'd been struggling with for many years. He and his wife had read *The Continuum Concept* and were co-sleeping with their eight-month-old daughter in the family bed. One night, their daughter woke up while they were making love; he was worried that she'd been traumatized. He didn't say it out loud, but I could tell from his facial expression he was carrying deep shame about the incident. I asked him what happened when his daughter woke up and he said, "She looked at us and went right back to sleep," to which I replied: "That doesn't sound like a traumatized child to me." His face relaxed as he *saw what he'd been unable to see*: the benign nature of what had occurred. He was prevented from seeing the event as benign by a *blinding cultural taboo*. Once I named it as such and explained, "It was a perfectly innocent, even natural event that fit her innate expectations," his shame evaporated.

The point of this story is that cultural taboos have no bearing on the true authority of the continuum. That doesn't mean a cultural taboo can't play havoc in someone's psyche—as this story shows, it can. The biggest hurdle in applying continuum principles is our own conditioning, especially when continuum parenting practices go against the grain of our upbringing.

in the absence of this essential experience, a boy child might easily project his sexual feelings onto his mother and develop what Freud called an *Oedipal complex.* Likewise, a girl child might project her sexual feelings onto her father and develop an *Electra complex,* the term used by Carl Jung, a one-time student of Freud.

Although intrigued by this emerging insight, Jean was not yet convinced of its veracity, so she kept it to herself. She wondered why she had no noticeable signs of an Oedipal complex and wrote in her journal: "I never slept anywhere near my parents. And even if I had, I doubt they made love after I was born. "

Jean had heard that it was possible to access the unconscious by taking LSD and became determined to experiment with the drug. She wrote about that experience in her journal:

> I wanted to try it out, but even at that age I was a cautious, prissy girl, so I got David, a famous neurologist[36] to sit by my bedside and administer the LSD. I was lying down; he was sitting next to me. I had already explained to him that I wasn't dropping acid just for the trip, not even to "open the doors of perception" as Huxley admonished an entire generation. My motive for going on an acid trip was quite specific. I wanted to understand Freud's Oedipal complex in the larger context of what I had started thinking of as the continuum.

---

[36] The famous neurologist was the Swiss-born Dr. David Gurevitch who received his medical education in his native Switzerland. He trained as a neurologist in Berlin and London then practiced medicine in Palestine before immigrating to the United States in the mid-1930s. He worked and taught at Columbia-Presbyterian Medical Center, held the position of medical director to the United Nations and, following FDR's death, became Eleanor Roosevelt's private physician and trusted friend.

I could not comprehend why Freud's—well, doctrine is really the only way to describe it—was held as universally true by every psychoanalyst in New York and London.

I told David it was impossible for me to imagine being attracted to my father. I shared what the big man, Pop, said to me when I was six, while helping me put on a sweater, "You have a very beautiful neck."

I felt repulsed. I still feel a physical revulsion just thinking about it. Fortunately for me, David was a neurologist, not a shrink and he had no opinion on the matter. I made a bad pun, and said, "Who's a-Freud of the big bad wolf?" and asked him to administer the drug. When it took effect, I spent a little time getting familiar with the territory of my unconscious, then traveled, quite intentionally, back to my earliest memory of my father.

We were walking in Central Park and came upon one of those stands where they sell souvenirs. I saw a little sailor doll. His suit was made of blue velveteen and he had a sailor's hat on his head. My father bought me the doll along with a box of Cracker Jacks. There I was, lying on a day bed in a London flat, and I could taste the candy in my mouth and feel the excitement of finding the prize inside the box as if it was actually happening. I hugged my little sailor doll close to my chest and looked at my father. I was utterly startled as I recognized— actually, sensed is a better way to put it because I did not have any words for it at the time—that my body had a stronger response to the sailor doll than it had ever had to the presence of my father. I truly loved that doll. The contrast between the joyful feeling I felt in my body for that doll and the absolute void of feeling I felt for my father, it was alarming to me even at that young age.

Then my memory jumped to the last time I saw my father. I was probably twelve. Pop was a religious fanatic. I, on the other hand, was an atheist. When I told him I was an atheist, he said, "It doesn't matter, you're a good girl, God will take care of you." He had no regard for what I thought, just floated over what I believed. I had a mind of my own even then—especially then. Imagine. Twelve-year-old me, being dismissed that way by this oaf. I found it really insulting.

After her LSD experiment, Jean continued to ask deep questions about Freud's Oedipal theory. She knew him to be a controversial figure in the field of psychology and soon found out that his theory of the Oedipus complex was one of his most contested ideas.

She completely agreed with Freud on some of his points but insisted that he was blinded by the limitations of his experience. After all, he had never seen humans whose experience during infancy and childhood afforded them a subliminal understanding of sexuality like she had witnessed among the Yequana people. There simply was no fertile ground in which that type of neurosis could grow.[37] Yequana children would be

---

[37] This was the crux of Jean's argument with many of the "experts" and a point she struggled to make throughout her career as a thought leader in the area of human development: if we've never seen what optimal development looks like, we're hamstrung when we make assumptions about human nature.

far more likely to develop an Icarus complex and fly toward the sun on wings made of wax than develop an Oedipal complex and feel jealous of their same-sex parent. Jean whole-heartedly agreed with Freud's point that humans are sexual beings from birth and that pleasurable sensual experiences, caressing, cuddling, kissing are not only completely normal, they are essential for our development. But she called into questioned his assertion that a child's natural curiosity about sexuality leads to the development of sexual fantasies about the opposite-sex parent. Such fantasies, in Jean's view, arose as a result of not having received information at the right time and in the right way—in a preverbal state in a passive manner as was natural and normal among our evolving antecedents. This deprivation, as Jean called it, is why children develop the Oedipus or Electra complex.[38]

The more she questioned and opposed Freud, the more Jean clarified her own theory. "Who's A-Freud of the Big Bad Wolf" became a sort of mantra for her. Freud's theory was the stone on which she sharpened the blade of her own ideas. The more clarity she gained, the more convinced she became of the value of what she had to say. When, at last, she shared her ideas with Arthur Janov, he said, "That's the best explanation for the Oedipal/Electra complex I have ever heard."[39]

She gained further recognition for her original thinking from the Marshall Field Foundation of New York when she

---

[38] The risk for those with this type of complex is the potential to be traumatized if they see their parents in the act, what Freud termed the "primal scene." In the absence of the complex and with continuum-correct experience, there is no trauma.

[39] As of this writing, I've had no response from Janov or his people to confirm or disconfirm this quote.

looked to them for backing on a research project to make the point. One of the foundation's board members, the famous Harvard professor Dr. Robert Coles, was called in as an expert in the field. "After I explained to him my theory," Jean reported, "He told me there is nobody that's an expert in the field because the field doesn't exist. You are the only authority."

23.

Commissioned by
the Cosmos

Jean returned to England with a giant anteater cub she'd
adopted and, at last, began to write. In years to come,
she would explain it this way: "I was liberated by two
block-busting requisites: an advance and a deadline. It did not
seem to bother my temperamental muse that the advances
were not for the book I was writing. No one knew what my
book was going to be about. Maybe I felt I had been commissioned by the cosmos. Or perhaps the publishers' commitment made me feel welcome in the world of grown-ups, and
thus, able to offer what I had of value, demonstrate my worth."

It took her just shy of eighteen months to write *The
Continuum Concept*. Both Tom Wallace and Livia Gollancz
were alarmed by the manuscript and asked if she could make
it more autobiographical. They also wanted her to include
photographs. Jean declined; she felt what she had written

was too important to dilute. Wallace was generous and said that, despite the fact that he felt the book was not "salable," he would take it to his editors at Holt without revealing his opinion. If they accepted it, he would, too. But his editorial team shared his view. Livia Gollancz asked for a bibliography and was outraged when Jean told her that her observations and conclusions were formed without reference to those of anyone else. In the end, both publishers rejected the book.

Oddly enough, Jean was not discouraged. She felt certain of the truth and value of what she had written. She thought it only needed the blue pencil of some fresh-eyed editor to, as she put it: "dis-convolute [*sic*] some of my less felicitous paragraphs." She eventually did that job herself.

The turning point came when Jean discussed her book with Sir Jonathan Miller. Both a medical doctor and theater director, Miller was quite famous at the time for his role in the satirical comedy revue, *Beyond the Fringe,*[40] with Peter Cook, Dudley Moore, and Alan Bennett. Jean had met Miller in New York through Bob Silver, editor of the *New York Review of Books,* who ran around with Plimpton's crowd. Miller insisted on seeing her manuscript and bravely read it through in a single afternoon. He proclaimed it a very important work and said it would sell a million copies. He asked Jean if he could propose it to his neighbor, Colin Haycraft, who just so happened to be the head of Duckworth of London.

Founded in 1898, Duckworth had been an important publisher of English literature. In the first half of the twentieth

---

[40] First performed at the Edinburgh Festival, *Beyond the Fringe* continued in London and New York. In 1963, Miller, Moore, Cook, and Bennett were recognized with a shared Tony Award as well as a New York Drama Critics' Circle Award.

century, the firm published writers such as Virginia Woolf and D.H. Lawrence. Jean sensed right away that this was the break she needed. The contract was signed within a month. Six months later, in the spring of 1975, Duckworth published the first edition of *The Continuum Concept*.

About this time, Jean came across a book by Ashley Montagu that had been published in 1971, some years after their conversation in New York. The book was titled, *Touching*. Although she barely gave the book a cursory read, Jean concluded that he had stolen her ideas. In her mind, Montagu, not believing she would overcome her writer's block, took her insights and presented them as his own. It was a preposterous assumption on Jean's part, but no amount of reason could get through her stonewall of scorn.

Montagu's *Touching: The Significance of the Human Skin* was a scholarly book that drew on the author's lifetime of study; this was not the first time the prolific author had written about these matters. But Jean wasn't having it. She insisted this was a blatant case of plagiarism. She became morally outraged. The wound inflicted at Oakwood Boarding School decades earlier was torn open. All the wrath and indignation she'd repressed when the headmaster wrongly accused her of plagiarism rose to the surface. Her friendship with Montagu soured. But she vowed she would not let that deter her from contacting Johnny Carson's producer when the time was right.

The Continuum Concept drew excellent reviews. The iconic George Leonard, founder of Esalen, wrote: "Here, at last, a book that can shake some sense into our heads about child-rearing. Jean Liedloff's case is clearly, passionately and tenderly argued. Rather than indicting, she presents alternatives toward which we as individuals, as well as society, can move. If I had to choose one book to give to parents-to-be, here it is."

The review in *The Sunday Telegraph* (London) was likewise full of praise: "An urgent, gracefully written plea to Western parents to rear their young in the natural, good-humored and unfussy way that the Yequana rear theirs. Reduced to its most fundamental terms, it is really a thesis about achieving fulfillment . . . it is time we reappraised ourselves and discovered what sort of animal we are. We have a standard of living, while the Yequana have a quality of life."

Jean was especially tickled when she received this endorsement from Shurin, the leading exponent of Zen in Great Britain: "I am so excited and so delighted; I never thought a Westerner could see with those eyes. My Western students are always asking me for books to explain Zen. When I tell them we don't use books, they always look a little disappointed. Now at last I can tell them there is a textbook on Zen, even though that's not what *The Continuum Concept* is supposed to be about. Jean Liedloff is a great philosopher."

Perhaps most pleasing of all was the lengthy piece published in the *New York Times* on October 16, 1977, in which book reviewer Alix Nelson wrote:

> . . . Liedloff's thesis, which stems from her observations of the Yequana Indians—a Stone Age tribe she lived among in the jungle of Venezuela—is that our modern childrearing methods deprive children of the crucial "in-arms" phase of infancy (i.e., being carried around

casually but constantly by one person or another), which forms the foundation of the "secure" personality during the first five or six months of life. Our ancestors, for millions of years, adapted to a "continuous chain of experiences," the expectation of which became part of our evolutionary design. If there is a gap in the necessary sequence of early experiences, the emerging self remains unfulfilled—impaired for life by feelings of longing and unease, as well as by deficiencies similar to the reduced verbal ability now known to result in children who have missed out on the "crawling and creeping" phase of motor coordination.

[The book moves] with a swift grace and persuasive eloquence when she describes the differences between the way a Yequana baby is raised and the way we raise our own. The contrast is indeed astonishing—as is the outcome of these disparate modes. We produce children, and adults, who are shy, combative, anxious, dependent, unruly, accident-prone, temperamental, delinquent, unmotivated. The Yequana, who continuously carry their newborn "in arms" while attending to the rhythmic routines of daily life (until the increasingly agile infants move off to explore wider horizons of their own free will), produce children, and adults who are cooperative, confident and relaxed.

Yequana children grow up in an atmosphere where "innate sociability" is the expected norm—they are not coerced or "socialized" into appropriate behavior. Yequana parents also assume that self-preservation is instinctive—no one hovers about with overprotective, self-fulfilling prophecies of the "Don't do that, you'll fall" variety, nor do they tell their offspring when to sleep or how much to eat. Motivation comes from the child, and every experience strengthens the child's ability to cope with successively more complex situations in a smooth, self-propelled continuum from infancy to maturity...

Nelson's recognition and support for Jean's ideas resulted in a curious invitation: Hans von Meiss-Teuffen wanted to expand her experience as an explorer with a trip to the Hunza Valley, the original Shangri-La. Son of a Swiss baron, von Meiss-Teuffen was well-known for his book: *Wanderlust: One-Man Swiss Navy*.

"He was the Richard Branson of his day," Jean would say. "He once sailed alone in a 30-foot sloop across the Atlantic in fifty-eight days." But it was his reputation as a double agent during World War II that put Jean off. "As intriguing as it sounds, I simply cannot abide the idea of traveling with a sea-going spy."

Support for the book continued to grow, as did the number of requests Jean received for radio interviews, public talks, and television appearances. She didn't have to wonder if the time was right to contact Johnny Carson's producer: he called her.

"Johnny wants you to come on the show. He's not taking no for an answer."

"Well, alright then," she said, containing her glee. "But he can't have me without Clovis."

"Clovis?" the producer asked.

"Yes," she said. "He's my pet anteater."

It would be the first time Johnny Carson hosted a guest with an anteater, and—much to her disappointment—the last time he hosted her on his show. Her banishment from *The Tonight Show* was not due to any misbehavior on Clovis' part; in fact, Clovis behaved like a model *Vermilingua*. No, it was Jean's misbehavior that got her nixed from Carson's Rolodex. She simply could not resist toying with the Latin meaning of *Vermilingua* (literally "worm tongue") when Johnny asked, "Is 'anteater' what zoologists call them?"

Ever the master of sophisticated wordplay, her comeback must've been a bit obscure, or perhaps obscene.[41] Either way, Johnny apparently did not take well to her humor because Jean and Clovis were never invited back.

---

[41] Per Wikipedia, the show aired on February 8, 1963. When I contacted Carson Entertainment Group hoping to view the episode, they responded to my email saying: "Unfortunately, the archives are not complete, many shows from 1962 until May of 1972 do not exist." To my logical mind, "many do not exist" and "that show does not exist" are not at all the same, so I persisted and finally reached someone who agreed to check the data base. He explained that, during the digitizing process, nearly a decade worth of shows suffered water damage and that, indeed, that episode of The Tonight Show no longer exists.

24.

Allowing Human Nature to Work Successfully

J ean's book struck a deep chord in readers. It wasn't long before *The Continuum Concept* was picked up by Penguin, then Arkana, then Addison-Wesley. Every time the book went into another printing (seventeen by 1990), Jean giggled with pride. When the second edition came out, she became visibly radiant, like a mother holding her precious newborn in her arms. Over the years, the book was translated into more than twenty languages—French, Italian, Japanese, and Hebrew, to name just a few. The German translation sold more than half a million copies. Her baby was all grown up and traveling the globe.

John Holt, a pioneer of the homeschooling movement who coined the word "unschooling," recommended *The Continuum Concept* to Merloyd Lawrence, a publisher at Addison-Wesley. Lawrence enjoyed the book and added it to her list of Classics in Child Development. This placed Jean among a number of esteemed authors, including Donald Winnicott. An English psychoanalyst and pediatrician, Winnicott was a leading scholar in the emerging field of Object Relations Theory. She was delighted at this development. Her intent to present the concept to the world was coming to fruition. Uniquely positioned to offer a new view of our species' promise and potential, Jean provided both an explanation of, and remedy for, the rampant neurosis humanity suffers. Year after year, her following grew.

When her publisher decided to do a second edition, they asked Jean if she'd like to add any updates or comments on new developments. "But of course!" she replied. The second edition included a new introduction that gave a picture of the impact the book was having on parents. In this new addition to the book, Jean took great care to console those who feared they had harmed their child with their lack of understanding of the continuum. Thrilled at the prospect of the new edition, she became vocally annoyed when the publisher refused to give her creative control over the cover art. This sticking point continued to vex her on various translations, printings, and editions.

Jean was particularly unhappy when Addison-Wesley gave the book a new subtitle: *In Search of Happiness Lost.* She felt it trite and, worse still, misleading. The phrase "Happiness Lost" echoed the title of *Paradise Lost,* John Milton's epic poem in blank verse, and that irked her. She had a sensitive spot—better yet, a feverish spot—when it came to anything that smacked even vaguely of plagiarism. She was incensed that the publisher insisted on the subtitle. She preferred the more accurate, albeit less romantic subtitle on the 1986 edition from Addison-Wesley: *"Allowing Human Nature to Work Successfully."* But the publisher refused to change it back.

Jean took issue with Merloyd Lawrence when she sold the mass-market paperback rights to Dell Publishing, which presented her work as a baby book. Jean felt this positioning diminished both its importance and reach. In her mind, placing *The Continuum Concept* on the shelves among childrearing books or texts on child development meant others who would benefit from her ideas would not see it. Furthermore, she insisted, if the book did fall into the hands of readers who weren't parents, they would be embarrassed to be seen carrying a book with a "Gerber baby" on the cover. Over the years, she persisted in her complaints to Lawrence. During one passionate tirade, she even questioned the wisdom of putting her book on a list of child development classics, insisting it was actually a book about *human development*. Jean would never forgive Lawrence for these "offenses," and harped on her publisher for not promoting the book in the manner she felt it deserved. Jean held the grudge despite all attempts by her inner circle to smooth her ruffled feathers. Her behavior toward Lawrence and her other publishers, many of whom were ardent fans of her work, was consistent with her tendency to push people away—to reject, find fault, be dismissive and, in the process, re-enact family of origin dramas.

Disappointment in her various publishers notwithstanding, Jean delighted in the enthusiastic reception of the book, and the many accolades for her writing. She collected them all, printed a little booklet titled *Reviews & Comments, The*

Continuum Concept and carried several copies in her purse everywhere she went. It was her way of spreading the word without being too ostentatious. Rather than talk about the book, she let the words of other people promote her work. The most treasured among the many compliments came from John Lennon who called her ideas "deeply comforting home truths."

Still and yet, Jean felt deeply frustrated, and often disparaged herself for failing to write a follow-up book. When she moved back to the US and settled in northern California, her writer's block tagged along behind her. In her words: "I am still under the spell of my ancient and dishonorable writer's block, until (or unless) my muse is released by the kiss of commitment in the form of an advance and a deadline from some frog of a publisher."

She worried that her mission would not be complete if she didn't summarize the fundamentals of continuum-correct childrearing in book form. She would bemoan her block and explain her dilemma to anyone and everyone who would listen: "I need a book contract. That's the only way I was able to write *The Continuum Concept.* As soon as I put my signature on the line, my writer's block no longer stops me. The Beast immediately disappears into its cave because I simply have to be good for my word."

As the influence of Jean's ideas grew, so did her reputation as an expert in childhood development and optimal childrearing practices. She wrote a number of articles for *Mothering Magazine,* including "Who's in Control?" and "The Importance of the In-Arms Phase," a term she'd coined. So beloved by the magazine's readers, *Mothering* named Jean "A Living

Treasure" in 1996. The accolade pleased her, not for the sake of personal recognition, but for the fact that it celebrated her ideas. *The Continuum Concept* had gained acceptance; it was the greatest triumph of her life.

But Jean remained blocked, unable to write her next book, provisionally titled: *Non-Adversarial Childrearing.*[42] She enlisted any number of willing volunteers to "aid and abet" the project. She promised to give Edward Mills—a man who had applied continuum principles with his children—co-author credit if he helped her finish the book. She promised a woman who loved *The Continuum Concept* a percentage of the royalties on the new book if she would just help her write it. But despite her considerable means, Jean refused to consider paying an editor or ghostwriter to help her complete the book. Regardless of the details of the bargain each person struck with Jean, and despite the enthusiasm they brought to the project, one by one, these volunteers gave up.

I was one such volunteer. Again and again, we would meet at the Depot Café and catch up on new developments in our lives. Again and again, she asked me to find her an agent who specialized in foreign rights to track down all those unpaid royalties. "Only my German publisher ever sends a check," she would say from her high horse of moral indignation. No matter my many attempts to bring her back to the matter at hand and get the job done, we could not get past the Introduction. This was due in part to Jean being distractible in the

---

[42] Jean did write and leave behind an outline and detailed overview for that book.

extreme. We'd be sitting at the Depot, ready to get started, and she would start to chat it up with someone at the next table. Any man of any age was an invitation to flirt. Even people who did not grasp her puns were worthy distractions. If she saw someone she knew, she would turn away from me and talk with them at length. And Jean knew a lot of Mill Valley locals, "Millbillies" as she liked to call them. Whenever she heard some passerby speaking Spanish, Italian, or French, she would start a lively conversation in their language. On the days when she felt particularly upbeat, she would sit at her table on the café patio, put on her bashful act, reveal the fact that she was a minor celebrity, and proceed to hold court. I always thought she would have made a great actress.

And so the afternoon would slip away. I'd walk her to her car and listen while she berated herself yet again: "It's my writer's block. I am the worst procrastinator ever."

This impasse tortured her; at times, she wondered about her sanity, and that of those around her. In one of her journals, she wrote:

> What is going on? I fear I am going mad or losing my mind—physically—my memory, my "normal" sense of the present. Such a delicate thing, this normal consciousness. Here at the Mill Valley Book Depot, there are a number of "looneys." I often see people who are detached from the usual, or normal, sense of reality. I feel I might be joining them. I am known here, served lunch at the counter several times a week. There are "regulars" here who greet me and sometimes talk, but mostly I am reading or writing at my table. My book

is constantly selling well inside, in the bookstore. I was asked to do one of their author's evenings here, soon after I made myself known to the owner, Mary Turnbull. I feel welcome here and sometimes chat with people at nearby tables. It's easy, pleasant. There are numerous dogs and birds on the terrace. There's always an assortment of children and youths practicing street skills, playing netball, and skateboarding in the plaza. Last year there were unicycles—gone now. Adults play chess or backgammon, surrounded by redwood trees. Parking spaces with meters—two hours for forty cents. Many languages are heard on the terrace. Some bring laptop computers and write. There are house newspapers and piles of free papers inside. On weekends, there are sometimes wine tasting festivals, or bands playing, or guitarists seated on the stone planters playing and singing. Children smoking—rebelling. Cyclists in spandex and helmets abound—sub-species in non-human sunglasses. Clattery shoes, a separate way of walking (strutting). Endless variations on shirts, trousers, dresses, shorts, hats. People chewing with their mouths open. Smokers unheeding of the destiny of their smoke. But many exchange smiles, without sequel—first friendliness. Quite a lot of hugs among friends. More chaos and color, more variety in behavior, socio-economics and dress than a café terrace in France or Italy where custom is deeply embedded in café culture. It's nearly 5:30. There is a sudden extra chill in the breeze from the Pacific Ocean to the west. I have a client telephoning me from Chicago at six. I'm away.

25.

Strong and Agile or Fearful and Fragile?

In her consulting role, Jean would listen carefully to the challenges and difficulties parents were facing, take their stories to heart, and mull them over in the light of what she'd learned from the Yequana. Then she would offer pointed suggestions. Usually, her suggestions worked. When they didn't, Jean's instincts, which had been roused and refined by her years living with indigenous people, could identify what went wrong. The impasse was usually due to some subtle, unconscious habit, generally left over from the parents' own upbringing. Jean could readily recognize when these conditioned responses disturbed the peace and thwarted the parent's intentions. She would educate and advise, offering parents specific ways to overcome their conditioning so they could remain true to continuum principles. The parents would then give her feedback, helping her further refine her thoughts on practical solutions common to the challenges of modern parenting.

In her words: "Readers of *The Continuum Concept* often write to me saying how upset they were when they realized what they had been doing to their children. They want me to tell them, specifically, how to make the transition to behavior that respects our real nature. When I wrote the book, I did not anticipate that I would become thought of as a childrearing expert. Nonetheless, when asked, I always try to help. Often, for questions from my readers, I can offer no precise example from the Yequana. So, I do my best to extrapolate principles of human nature from my observations of life in a tribal village. I then make educated guesses about what is likely to work. In my private practice, I ask parents to try a certain approach and report back to me with the results. When it works, I can then offer the method to other parents with similar concerns."

Jean shared these educated guesses with parents at weekend workshops in the U.S. and Europe hosted by fans of *The Continuum Concept*. She travelled to Germany, England, Italy, and France at the invitation of parents who wanted to mine her understanding of what fans of her book began to call the *Yequana Way*.

On one occasion, Jean gave a powerful ad-hoc demonstration of the contrast between conventional mothering (that sometimes crossed the line into smothering) and the Yequana's "continuum-correct"[43] approach.

---

[43] In alignment with our inbuilt expectations as prescribed by the continuum of our species' experience over the long, formative years of evolution.

It happened at a seminar at the Sheraton Hotel in Los Ange-
les. During a long lunch break, Jean joined several of the mothers
at the hotel swimming pool. Four of the moms had brought small
children along; they were clustered on the steps in the kiddie pool.
Meanwhile, in the adjacent big pool, a group of older children
were playing pool tag in the shallow end, which was sectioned-off
from the deep end by a colorful safety rope.

One 14-month-old boy walked back and forth on the first
step of the kiddie pool. He took a few steps, stooped down,
splashed the water with his chubby little hands, and looked
to his mother for reassurance and approval. Obviously concerned, she smiled nervously, reached for his hand and moved
closer to him, at which point he became helpless and threw his
arms around her neck. This sequence repeated every time he
moved more than a couple of feet away from his mom, who
watched his every move.

This went on for at least ten minutes. The women were
discussing the challenges of changing the game with their kids
and establishing a non-adversarial parent-child relationship.
At a break in the conversation, Jean addressed the watchful
mother, asking, "Denise, would you be willing to do a little
experiment?"

Denise hesitated for a moment then said, "Sure." The
other moms were clearly interested in seeing what came next.

"Remember our discussion about the child's natural tendency to meet his mother's expectations?" Jean asked.

"Yes," Denise said. The other mothers nodded in agreement.

"I want you to move away from your son and turn your
back on him," Jean signaled the mothers to follow along as she

walked backward into the middle of the kiddie pool, putting some distance between mother and son. "This is just an experiment, remember. I will keep an eye on him to make sure he doesn't drown."

"But Timmy's only been in a pool once before," Denise said. "He doesn't know how to swim."

"I understand," Jean replied. "I will make sure Timmy is safe. Let's just see what happens."

Denise glanced at the other mothers. They gave her reassuring looks. One said, "We're right here. We won't let anything happen."

The women moved with Jean as she stepped away from Timmy a foot at a time. She stopped when they were about three yards away.

"Just make like he's going to be totally okay, Denise. Fake it if necessary."

Denise did her best to follow Jean's instruction, resisting the impulse to turn around and walk back to her son.

Jean encouraged the other mothers to avoid hawk-eyeing Timmy, rather to glance at him with certainty in their eyes. "The point," she said, "is to affirm his ability to take care of himself. He'll send out a clear signal if he gets in trouble."

They all agreed, and the women began to chat about their own habitual hyper-vigilance.

Meanwhile, Timmy continued to walk back and forth on the top step. He leaned forward and splashed the water with his hands. He wasn't even aware his mom had moved away from him and, in fact, paid no attention to her at all. He was just having fun getting to know the water. Nothing about his demeanor suggested fear or anything less than complete competence.

Between the kiddie pool and the larger pool was a foot-wide divider about three inches above the surface of the water. Its bright blue tiles shimmered in the sunlight. Timmy was attracted to the color and clearly curious to learn what it was. He moved toward the divider unafraid. When he got there, he plopped himself down, his little round belly resting on the divider. He reached his arms into the big pool and continued his splashing. He hollered at the kids playing tag, but they did not respond. He started slapping the water to get their attention, splashing himself in the face and laughing. This went on for a couple of minutes. The little guy was having a blast. Denise was so agitated that she had to hold Jean's hand to keep her cool. The other moms kept reassuring her, "It would be hard for me, too. But he's just fine."

Then Timmy scooched up on the divider and swung his legs, one at a time, into the larger pool. He stood on the top step, dancing in place and clapping his hands as if to applaud the bigger kids, then sat down on the top step and continued his splashing. He made no move to venture further into the pool and was perfectly happy to sit on the step and participate from afar. Denise couldn't take it anymore. She broke away from the group and dove across the divide between her and her son. The moment she entered Timmy's field of vision he once again became helpless, reached toward her as if in distress, and threw his arms around her neck. Her son responded to her distress, to her expectation that he needed her to keep him safe. It did not matter that he'd been competent and confident until her look told him otherwise. The moment he registered her expectation, he stopped trusting his ability to take care of himself.

Jean's explanation of what had just occurred made perfect sense. "Nature abhors duplication," she said to the women still circled around her. "If it's being done for us, we stop doing it for ourselves."

Another spontaneous demonstration occurred when Jean was speaking at the La Leche League International Conference in Cork, Ireland. She began her talk, "The Importance of the In-Arms phase," with a slide show presenting photographs of both Yequana moms and modern moms breastfeeding a child or carrying them around in a sling. The final slide showed a mother turning and walking away from her distraught baby who was red-faced and crying, reaching toward her from his crib.

"This is what she's been told to do by so-called experts: Leave him alone, show him who's boss or he'll turn into a demanding little brat," she said to the room full of women. "In other words: ignore your instinct to hold him close to your body where he belongs, where he feels safe and secure, where he learns the world is a loving place that supplies what he needs."

She went on to explain that Yequana babies were never "put down" for a nap. They did not need peace and quiet, nor to be sequestered away from others to go to sleep. Quite the contrary, when they got tired, they snoozed blissfully in a sling tied to their mother's body while she carried on with her normal activities. The need for scheduled naptime was non-existent, as was the struggle to get the baby to go to sleep so mommy could finally get a break. "Yequana mothers don't need a break for one simple reason: there is no stress involved in caring for a child," Jean explained. "If, for some reason, she needed to hand the infant off for a bit, another adult or older child was always available.[44] I often saw older children carrying little ones in a sling or simply on a hip while they danced, ran, walked, shouted, or paddled canoes.

She continued, "Babes in arms almost never cried and, amazingly, did not wave their arms, kick, or arch their backs. They sat quietly in their slings or slept on someone's hip. Their bodies were soft and relaxed. They did not throw up when fed, nor require pats on the back in order to be 'burped.' They did not suffer from colic. Never once did I see an adult bouncing a baby in hopes of calming him down the way we do."

Jean never saw Yequana adults keeping a close eye on children when they began creeping and crawling. Nor did they hold toddlers' hands high above their heads and waddle along behind them in an attempt to ensure they did not fall down as they learned to walk. This practice, so common among modern parents, interferes with the natural learning curve from crawling on all fours to walking. Well-meaning

---

[44] It's important to emphasize (more than Jean did) that the abundance of alloparenting support is partly why Yequana moms didn't "need" a break. *Alloparenting* is defined as care provided by individuals other than the biological parents. It is a universal behavior among humans that has shaped our evolutionary history and remains important in contemporary society. Among the Yequana, moms were *given* breaks as a matter of course; they never needed to ask. In our culture, with stay-at-home moms (or dads) often being the *only* caregiver, on-duty 24/7 while handling the unavoidable stresses of modern life, they really do need a break. Not a break from babycare, but a break from the inhumane conditions under which they are required to provide care.

parents essentially scramble the information children would otherwise acquire through trial and error to fully develop *kinesthesia,* our awareness of the position and movement of our own body.[45]

Likewise, as Yequana children begin to venture away from their mother, to explore their independence after having their very real dependency needs met, they possess the precise instinct and self-sense to do just that. Of their own accord, children move away from mother, then turn back to her for the measure of reassurance they need. Once the need for reassurance is satisfied—sometimes by a look, or by being picked up and held for a bit—they resume their explorations. Without supervision, even the smallest tots rarely get hurt.

"Are our children more clumsy or inept when they start walking?" Jean asked. "Is our human nature different from that of the Yequana?"

Most of the women shook their heads; a woman in the back of the room shouted, "Of course not!"

Jean continued: "Some people actually imagine it is, despite the fact that we are the same species."

What can we learn from the Yequana? We can do our best to fully grasp the formative power of the in-arms phase, which begins at birth and ends when the infant can depart and return to the caretaker's knee at will. Quite simply, human infants ought to have 24-hour contact with an adult or older child until their behavior signals they no longer need it.

Over the course of five expeditions, Jean had lived among

---

[45] Also referred to as proprioception, this physical self-sense of location and movement by sensory organs (proprioceptors) is often referred to as our "sixth sense."

the indigenous people of the Amazon for a total of nearly three years, with time in between each expedition for reflection. She slowly, incrementally, grasped that our human nature is not what we have come to believe. If our essential nature was so untamed, even naughty, that children need to be "broken" of their wildness lest they become hoodlums, how could the behavior of Yequana children be explained? Toddlers played together without fighting. Among older children, there were no bullies. All children obeyed their elders and did so instantly and happily. The notion of punishing a child did not occur to these people, nor did the adults demonstrate permissiveness. No child would have dreamt of interrupting, nor expect to be waited on, by an adult. Children were not regarded as an inconvenience, quite the opposite: by the age of four, they joined the family work force and completed various tasks with little instruction. They had learned what was expected by passively observing the activities of their family members.

On early expeditions, Jean merely observed the in-arms experience and noted its obvious benefit for both babies and adults. Babies were relaxed rather than tense and squirmy. They were no trouble to manage and did not place a burden on their parents. Their small, soft bodies conformed to any position convenient to their bearers who, at times, even dangled their babies down their backs while holding them by an ankle or wrist. The Yequana treat babies as precious, not fragile. Adults instinctively trust what she termed a child's "roughness cues," i.e., how much roughhousing they want.

"He'll let you know how much is enough," she would explain, "or let you know when he wants to be treated more roughly, thrown higher in the air. Your manner of handling baby signals either 'you are strong and agile,' or 'you are fearful and fragile.' The Yequana pick their babies up by a hand or foot; their limbs do not come out of the socket. Adults will dance while holding a baby whose head is bouncing up and down, but he doesn't even wake up, nor does his head fall off."[46]

As if on cue, a stray baby crawled down the aisle toward Jean. She smiled down at the tot and said, "Well, hello." Then she gracefully picked him up by one arm, held him up and asked, "Does this belong to anyone?"

The baby was perfectly happy. The audience was shocked, but enlightened.

Jean explained that she was not advocating for this position, simply demonstrating the fact that being handled thus is within the scope of what constitutes comfort for a baby. In contrast to this is the desperate *discomfort* of infants laid down oh-so-carefully in a crib or carriage, tenderly tucked in, and left to go rigid with the desire to be in contact with a living body that is, by nature, their expectation and rightful place. They expect to be welcome in arms that belong to someone who trusts their cues and unquestioningly fulfills their need to be close to a warm body.

Why the ignorance in our society? From childhood on, we are conditioned to ignore or distrust our instinctive knowledge,

---

[46] This is not to say that a baby can't be injured by excessive shaking, only that injury doesn't happen when a Yequana mother dances with her sleeping baby in arms because they have both developed a high degree of kinesthetic intelligence through their natural way of life, which includes a fully integrated awareness of each other's bodily states in relation to their own. To the degree that modern modern parents have been deprived of this development, they need to be mindful while their latent continuum sensibilities are coming alive.

perfect as it is, having allowed our species to survive for millions of years. We are taught that parents and teachers know best. We feel too hot in a jacket and report this to a parent, only to be told that we must keep it on because it's cold out. Often parents insist with intense emotion, essentially telling us our experience is dead wrong. In this manner, parents instill in children a foundational distrust in their inbuilt ability to regulate their own temperature. The more such mistaken parental admonitions are foisted on a child, the more troublesome basic discernments about what is "good for me" or "bad for me" become. In time they may find it difficult to trust the signals from their own body. This can include everyday signals such as "I've had enough" before their stomach is over full.

Conditioned to disbelieve our feelings and ignore our instincts, we grow into adult parents who do not believe that a baby's cry says: "Hold me! I need to be next to your body!" or, "Don't leave me alone!" Instead of trusting these signals, adults overrule their natural response and follow the going trend as dictated by so-called "experts." This loss of faith in our innate baby-care expertise leaves parents turning from one book to another as each successive fad fails.

In talks, interviews, articles, and private sessions, Jean often emphasized that parents must recognize that they themselves, and their children, are the real experts. "The second greatest baby-care expert is your instinct, your native intelligence," she would say. "The greatest expert of all is your baby, programmed as he is by millions of years of evolution to signal by sound and action when his care is incorrect. Every surviving species, by definition, and evidenced by the fact that it has survived, must know how to care for its young. Evolution is a refining process that has honed our innate behavior with magnificent precision. The signal from the baby, the understanding of the signal by his people, the impulse to obey it—all are part of our species' inbuilt character."

PART THREE

26.

Where's Gloria?

Since the start of our friendship, I'd been aware of the landmine in Jean's psychology. Intent and direct at our first sit-down, she delivered the warning: "There is something I do to push people away, but I don't know what it is. I so wish someone could just tell me when I do whatever it is I do."

Just as she'd done with many new friends before me, she told me her version of the story of her friendship with Gloria Steinem, which had ended abruptly two decades earlier. The inner corners of her eyebrows raised as she spoke. "She just stopped returning my calls. When she came to San Francisco, her publicist told me she had no spare time in her schedule." Jean blamed herself for the cessation of their connection and puzzled over it throughout her life. "I may have offended her with a remark about the man she'd been dating," she said, trying to figure out how she'd alienated one of the few women of her generation she viewed as her intellectual equal. Obviously distressed, she hoped that, in me, she had finally found a friend who would stay the course and help her gain insight into this mysterious, self-defeating behavior.

"Pussycat," she had pleaded, "promise me you won't go away."

I promised. And I kept that promise for twelve years.

Sure, we had the occasional falling-out, but we always managed to slog our way through rough terrain. Per her request, I attempted to point out her off-putting behavior several times. One such attempt occurred while we ate lunch on the outdoor patio at the Depot Café.

As was our habit, we sat at the edge of the fenced-in patio, right near the square. I loved to watch the comings and goings of all the lovely people, especially a group that often gathered to practice *Capoeira*—a Brazilian martial art/dance form. Meanwhile, Jean loved watching the children. Whenever she saw a mom making a fruitless attempt to get her child to obey, Jean would walk up to her, apologize for the intrusion, pull out one of the *Reviews & Comments* booklets, and say, "You might find this of interest." Then she would offer a knowing smile and walk away.

Jean didn't need to look at the menu; she always ordered a turkey sandwich. I, on the other hand, liked variety. I took a few moments to consider my options and decided on a taco salad. She waved to the waiter, a Latino man she knew by name, and ordered our lunch in perfect Spanish. Then she launched into a not-atypical critique of my appearance: "Darling, you really shouldn't go out of the house without mascara," she said. "And your upper lip is so thin, you really must use a liner before you put on lipstick."

I didn't bother to argue. ("But I like going au naturel.") I just shook it off with a little humor: "What? You don't like the lipless-wonder look?"

Over the years, Jean had taken it upon herself to critique me on everything from my style of dress to my choice in men. I always did my best to be gracious. I even managed to brush it off the day she clipped me at the knees after my first book signing and public talk in San Francisco. That morning, I decided to wear an outfit that was less Marin-casual and more city-chic. Deciding to go all black, I put on a short skirt and black turtleneck with fetching boots and fishnet stockings. Jean had invited me to stop by her houseboat on my way back home to San Rafael. I pulled into the parking lot at Issaquah Dock feeling quite pleased. The book signing had gone smoothly. My nervousness had vanished as soon as I'd stepped up to the microphone. Eager to share this with Jean, I rapped her brass knocker. She opened the door, looked me up and down and said: "You look like a tart." And here I was so proud of myself for wearing a sweater that didn't show my cleavage.

Before bringing our meal, the waiter dropped off the standard basket of chips and salsa that comes with a taco salad. I was unusually hungry and dove in straightaway. I hadn't munched down two of the salty chips when Jean swiped at me like a cornered alley cat. "Stop crunching!" Her words were sharp and definitive; they stung as if she had indeed reached across the table and scratched me, breaking the skin and leaving tiny drops of blood.

"Jean, they're tortilla chips," I said, bewildered.

She gave me a look of scorn, and shook her head almost imperceptibly saying, "Naughty girl" with her eyes. My appetite ran out into the square and hid behind a redwood tree. I sat in my chair, eyes cast down, vaguely aware that it had happened again. I excused myself to go to the bathroom to lick my wounds. I looked at myself in the mirror, my face host to the twisted look of a little girl who'd been chastised without cause. I vowed to say something, to let her in on the effect her caustic statement had on me, the fact that it had killed a perfectly pleasant mood. I knew better than to do so while actually showing my hurt, a demonstration she despised. I stiffened my nearly non-existent upper lip, walked back to the table and sat down.

"Jean, I would appreciate it if you would refrain from criticizing me so much. First, it's my makeup, then the way I chew my food. Tortilla chips are crunchy, for the love of God! It's not like I was chewing with my mouth open. It doesn't feel good to be scolded like that." I took a deep breath and said, "That's the type of treatment that makes me want to go away."

"You're being too sensitive," she said.

There it was again: dismissal of any feedback. A short puff of breath—almost a snort—came from the back of my throat. Fortunately, she was looking at her plate and did not see me shake my head from side to side.

We ate our meal, Jean joking while I sat nibbling my taco salad in silence. She was truly unaware that anything had happened.

A few days later, I headed over to *White Elephant*, her houseboat in Sausalito. We were relaxing in the Adirondack chairs on the upper deck, enjoying the view of San Francisco, Tiburon, Alcatraz, and Angel Island. There was no fog swirling over the Marin Headlands, nor chilly wind blowing in off the bay. The typical microclimate of Sausalito had succumbed to the bright, early summer sun. The temperature was perfect.

We were discussing the details of setting up a non-profit organization to support her work and spread the word about *The Continuum Concept*. The conversation turned toward our ongoing discussion of an appropriate name for the non-profit. We toyed with any number of names, most of which Jean had already rejected: Liedlovian Childrearing ("I don't like Liedlovian"), The Continuum Association ("too ordinary"), The Continuum Parents Alliance ("sounds like we're going to war"). Her favorite was *Che Continua,* which I rejected on the grounds that its meaning made sense to her but would mean nothing to potential members.

We were in a particularly jolly mood that day. Jean's eyes were all a-giggle; she was in her "you are so welcome, so worthy" good-mother mode. This made me more articulate in her presence, although I still couldn't begin to match her way with a pun. She always referred to punning as "the lowest form of humor," but I would disagree saying, "Uh-uh. No way. Sarcasm is the lowest form of humor." This seemed obvious to me. Punning required a quick mind and mastery of language, whereas sarcasm required only a hypercritical eye and snarky tone of voice.

An idea struck. I didn't realize it at the time, but now it is clear that in the presence of her high regard, I became inspired. My mind was free of the fear of her criticism.

"How about The Liedloff Society for the Continuum Concept?" I asked.

"Darling, that's it! You're a genius!" It was a word she generally reserved for herself and a few special friends: Jonas Salk, Adam Yarmolinsky, Andrew Wyeth.

At last, the naming conversation could be put to rest.

She smiled a satisfied smile, stood up, and winced at the stabbing pain in her knee. She sighed. In a millisecond her face had turned from satisfied to exasperated. But this time she did not complain.

She sat back down in her chair. Another wince. "It's a little early yet for tea."

She looked at me again; it was clear she was pleased. Her eyes overflowed with affection. I raised my hand in a high-five gesture and, as we had countless times before, said in unison, "Damn we're good!"

I was feeling so close to her, so simpatico, that I decided to bring up a tender topic. I tiptoed toward it, and asked her permission as if I were a lady's maid: "I've been thinking about something that I'd like to run by you. Might now be a good time?"

"Yeaaah . . ." she said, dragging out the vowel and giving it a musical lift as she always did when she was in a mischievous mood. It was a signature Jean-response with a subtext that said, Bring it on!

"What is it?" she asked, leaning forward with concern when she sensed my hesitation.

I took a deep breath. "Remember early on in our friendship when you asked me to promise I would never leave you?

That you always do something to push people away, but don't know what it is?"

She tilted her head toward her right shoulder, scrunching her eyebrows together. There was a long moment before she spoke. "What are you saying?" she said, clearly annoyed. "Am I not a good friend?"

"That's not what I meant."

"What did you mean then?" she asked, jutting her chin toward me half an inch. Her statement was more of a criticism than a question. Notably, she had not begun her sentence with the usual affectionate "Darling . . ."

I felt an urge to bolt, silenced by her scorn, unspoken, and yet clearly communicated. Her facial expression and tone of voice said everything. She would pounce if I said or did anything to offend her or question her authority.

Resisting a strong urge to excuse myself and go get us afternoon tea and biscuits (in this case, ginger cookies), I managed to stay present. But I had to tread lightly.

"Just hear me out, okay? I want to help you, not hurt you."

"What makes you think I need your help?" She sat upright, placing herself above me and looked at me as though I were a commoner asking for an audience with an aristocrat.

"Never mind. Let's just drop it," I said, too low for her to hear.

"Speak up, darling. Don't swallow your words."

I repeated, "Let's drop it."

She softened a bit and adjusted herself in the chair as if I'd just pulled the catnip away. Now she wanted it. "Go ahead, pussycat."

Another deep breath. "Do you remember the first time we met at the Depot for lunch? It was the week after I met you at the talk you gave at that mansion in Pacific Heights."

"Sure," she said. Her welcoming facet was back.

"You talked about Gloria Steinem. You told me the two of you struck up a friendship right around the time her article on female genital mutilation came out in *Ms. Magazine*."

"I don't remember the conversation but go on."

"You told me that you had somehow pushed her away, that your friendship ended, but you didn't know what you had done."

She reflected a moment, then said, "Yes. I still don't know what happened. We met for dinner in San Francisco. After that she never returned my calls."

"Yeah. That's what you told me. The very first day we met."

She shrugged. "Did I?"

"Yes," I watched, bracing for the pushback. "You told me this has happened with other people, too. Many times. I think your words were, 'I always do something to push people away.' You specifically asked me to promise I wouldn't go away. To tell you what it is you do so you can finally see it and stop making people leave."

"Oh," she said. "Well, okay."

I lied: "I've seen it a couple times, but never had the courage to say anything." I had, in fact, attempted to point it out many times only to be dismissed with more of the same. She would quash me with, "Don't be silly," or, "Darling you really must grow a thicker skin" or, most stinging of all: "You're an idiot."

But this time I was strategic in my approach. Speaking directly to the offense when it occurred always proved futile.

Maybe if I addressed it when we were filled with the joys of friendship, she'd be able to hear me.

She softened. "Really? Darling, you must tell me what it is. I have helped so many people. But nobody has ever been able to help me see the pattern."

I ventured a little further into tender territory. "Well, I was thinking it might be easier for both of us if we agreed on a code-word. That way I can point it out in a way that won't offend you."

She thought about this. "What might the code-word be?"

"I don't know," I said, which was true. I'd already given this some serious thought. I wanted to come up with a code word that brought Gloria Steinem to mind rather than make it personal to me. Her friendship with Gloria had been a real loss to her, more so perhaps than any other.

Time and again, she would wonder aloud, "Maybe something I said about the man she was dating . . . perhaps I was too harsh about what happened when she allowed mothers to bring their infants to work at the magazine . . . the mothers should've been given slings to carry the baby . . . but they put them in a bassinet and perched them on their desks or on the floor near their chair. How ridiculous!"

But with all her recursive thinking, she could never put her finger on it, and the mystery still pained her decades later.

Suddenly, I was struck with an idea: "What if I just say: 'Where's Gloria?'"

Her eyebrows lifted up; a satisfied smile jumped onto her face. Without hesitation, she said: "Okay!"

27.

The Push-away

In the twelve years we'd been friends, Jean and I had never gone out to dinner together, so I offered to treat her for her 80th birthday. On November 26, 2006, I picked her up at Issaquah Dock and we drove to her favorite Chinese restaurant at the end of Tiburon Boulevard where the main road meets the San Francisco Bay.

We ordered hot and sour soup and pot stickers; then we haggled over which entrees we would share for our meal. When the waiter returned with our soup, I placed the rest of our order: sizzling Szechuan lamb and asparagus beef with black bean sauce, plus an order of moo shu pork just for fun.

She objected, "Darling, it's too much."

I insisted, "Leftover Chinese is always good. Take it home, you'll have it for lunch tomorrow."

I handed the menu to the waiter and said, "Please dovetail our entrees rather than bringing them all at once."

Apparently, he did not understand the meaning of the word "dovetail" and only heard, "Bring them all at once." Ten minutes later, he arrived at our table with plates stacked up his left arm in a tier. A second waiter stood behind him with a sizzling platter of lamb on a tray. A familiar scowl took over Jean's face, announcing to anyone within eyeshot that she was none too pleased.

Our table was still cluttered with soup bowls and half-eaten pot stickers. A busboy appeared, reached under the waiter's arms to clear the table, and make space for our meal.

"I'm not finished!" Jean snapped.

The waiter shot the busboy a look, nodding toward a table nearby. The busboy quickly moved the additional table next to ours. Naming each dish as he set it down, the waiter presented our meal, then bowed and backed away.

Jean and I looked at the steaming food: two big plates piled high with colorful shiny vegetables, a sizzling iron platter of steaming lamb sitting on a carved-out wooden board, a large bowl of white rice, a small bowl of plum sauce, and a basket of pancakes for the moo shu pork.

"What a feast!" I said. I reached for her plate and asked, "Do you want rice?" She nodded yes.

"And some of this beef?"

"Yeah!" she said, adding a lilt to the word as if to give it wings.

"Moo Shu Pork?"

"Later. Not just yet."

"Lamb?"

"Yes please."

Jean loved lamb, but rarely ate it, so I spooned some onto her plate, then some more. She received the plate with delight in her eyes.

Keenly aware that our appetizer course had pushed me out-of-bounds on my latest weight loss attempt, I served myself a small portion of beef and an even smaller portion of lamb.

Jean furrowed her brow, tilted her head slightly to the right.

"I'm watching my weight," I explained.

"Don't be silly, darling. You look just fine."

I shrugged and let it rest. There was no point whatsoever in trying to explain. Jean had been tall and thin throughout her life. I was both height- and weight-challenged and had battled an extra ten to twenty pounds since age sixteen.

After we'd finished our meal and shared a small bowl of green tea ice cream, the waiter dropped off our check along with two fortune cookies. I reached into my bag for my wallet, but Jean already had the check in her hand. She said, "You know, you could have just asked me to pay for our meal."

"That's ridiculous. I'm paying. It's your birthday."

"Nonsense," she said. "You hardly ate anything."

"Jean, give me that. I invited you, and I am buying your birthday dinner."

"But you didn't eat much and I'm taking most of it home." Her eyes chastised me.

"That's crazy. Hand me that check. Dinner is on me," I said in disbelief.

She ignored my protest.

I thought: *She actually believes I planned it this way so she would pick up the check?*

I explained why I'd eaten so little: "Jean, I'm on Weight Watchers. The appetizer course alone was over my daily points!"

But she continued to push back and assert her interpretation of what just occurred. "You knew I wouldn't let you pay if I ate more than you and took the leftovers home."

"Jean, that's not true," I said.

"It is true," she said. Her back was arched: "I don't like it when people try to pull one over on me."

I was so stunned, so completely flummoxed by her version of reality that I forgot who I was talking to for one deadly moment and said: "Why, that's just crazy."

No longer a pussycat arching her back and swiping me with a claw, Jean morphed into a she-lion crouched for a lethal pounce.

"Now you're implying I'm delusional."

I said, "That's not what I said. I'm just trying to explain."

She said, "Don't make excuses for yourself. It's not attractive."

I thought about using our code and asking, "Where's Gloria?" but I knew better. There was no opening whatsoever. Her mind was made up. I was the bad guy; she'd been insulted. I knew that any further discussion would only escalate the situation. The only way to calm her down was to let her be right, so I shrugged and gave up the fight. She noticed the change in my demeanor. Hers changed slightly, too, and she went from angry to indignant.

"It's my birthday and I did not come here to be insulted."

I would have lobbed a sarcastic rejoinder: "Oh. Where do you usually go?" But I knew better than to risk my throat. Instead, I rolled over and curled up into a ball. I was numb. My breath became little more than a sip here, a sip there; it was as if all the oxygen had been sucked out of the air.

Six months passed. Not once did I feel inclined to call Jean or drop by The Depot. One day, while running an errand in downtown Mill Valley, it hit me: Jean had finally succeeded—she'd pushed me away.

28.

Here We Go Again

The better part of a year passed before I ventured into Jean's sphere again. I'd pulled up stakes in Marin and moved to the mountains above Malibu to work on a book with a ghostwriting client. In September that year, I planned a weeklong trip to my beloved Bay Area and decided it was time I reached out to Jean. She insisted I stay in her guest room; it was as if nothing had happened between us.

Our visit started to veer off track straightaway. Upon my arrival in Marin, I was to meet her for lunch, presumably at our usual table at the Depot Café. She had suggested this plan a few days earlier in a phone conversation. Actually, she hadn't so much suggested, as asserted, that we rendezvous in a public place before heading to the houseboat. I found myself wondering if she thought it necessary to suss me out before welcoming me into her home again. What she neglected to tell me was that she no longer spent her afternoons at the Depot, and would meet me at her new favorite spot right down the street from the houseboat marina on Bridgeway, Sausalito's main thoroughfare.

I arrived at the Depot unawares and waited half an hour. Jean did not have a mobile phone, so I called her at home. When the answering machine picked up, I said, "Hi Jean. I'm here at the Depot. Hope I didn't mix up the time. I'll wait for you to arrive before I order." I waited another forty-five minutes before calling a second time. Again, I got her answering machine. *It's totally unlike her to no-show,* I thought. Concerned, I drove over to Issaquah Dock.

Her gold Mercedes was in the parking lot. A sense of foreboding rose up from the center of my chest. A couple of years earlier, when my grandmother was Jean's age, she'd fallen and broken her hip. That injury led to her slow decline. I prayed that had not happened to Jean as I walked down the dock toward *White Elephant.* She opened the door and looked at me, her eyes aflame with a mixture of disappointment, anger, and blame. Flummoxed, every muscle in my body gripped my bones as I braced myself for what might come next.

"You stood me up," she said. Her statement was brusque, emotionless.

"I . . . I . . . waited for you," I stammered. "I was sitting at our usual table on the patio for an hour and a half."

"What patio?" she said, her voice graveled with disdain.

I shrugged, my face screwing up in confusion. "On the plaza . . . ?" I said, half reporting, half questioning.

"I told you," she said, enunciating each word, "I don't go to the Depot anymore. You were supposed to meet me down the street at Taste of Rome."

She turned away from the open door, walked into her living room, and sat down.

I stood in the doorway, blinking, unable to feel a thing. I opened my mouth to speak; my tongue was paralyzed. Then a clear, unambiguous thought lit up the marquee in my mind: *Here we go again.*

I wrestled with the urge to turn away from the door and walk out of her life for good. Why stay when still, after all these years, she insisted on mean-girling me every time I saw her?

Somehow, my tongue got the message it was okay to speak and I muttered, "Wha . . . what?"

"Oh, don't play dumb," she said. "You stood me up."

"Jean," I said. I crossed the threshold and slipped off my shoes. "You didn't say anything about meeting in Sausalito, and I didn't think to ask. I assumed we'd meet at our usual place."

"Don't give me a flimsy excuse, of course I told you."

"You didn't," I said, careful to state the facts without becoming defensive or implying she was mistaken. *Tell me this isn't happening*, I thought, taking three steps into the living room. Not feeling particularly welcome in her home, I did not sit down.

"Now you're telling me my memory is wrong," she said.

I took a deep breath, half-coughing to hide my exasperation. By this time in our twelve-year friendship, I'd developed a keen awareness of the slip-ups that could spark Jean's scorn. Her number one trigger was being opposed. She saw herself as the ultimate authority—on everything. On a number of occasions, I'd seen her hold to a strong opinion on some obscure topic she hadn't explored in detail or thought about carefully. I'd seen her slam the door shut on any give-and-take in conversations countless times. It didn't matter if she was talking to a university professor, another author, or someone who was an expert in the field under discussion—she was the one who knew the score. Period. She was the genius. To question or challenge her was to cross an invisible boundary, violate an unspoken code, and be dismissed out of hand. The form of the dismissal was perplexing at times, funny or playful at others, but often outright rude.

Jean was a master at *paronomasia*: the rhetorician's ability to use a word in a different sense or use words similar in sound to achieve a specific effect, typically humor or dual meaning. Punning was, for her, a self-protection strategy. But with me, her dismissal typically took the form of a put-down, a snub, or a comment that elicited shame. In the aftermath of these interactions, I would puzzle for days: *Why do I keep putting myself in her line of fire?*

Reflexively, I withdrew into a protected place inside myself, turned so she could not see my face, and rolled my eyes. The only way out of this pickle was to apologize and admit to a wrong I did not commit.

"Perhaps you said it and I misheard you, Jean. I'm sorry. I did not intend to offend."

"I don't like it when people waste my time," she said.

Waste your time? I thought. Inside my own mind, I could let my snarky side off-leash. *Since when do you do anything other than piss away your time? You would've gone to a café, any café, regardless, just like you do every single day!*

"I'm sorry, Jean," I said. "Really."

She looked at me with eyes that were starting to soften. But she was not yet fully appeased. I didn't see the next dig coming.

"You still haven't grown into a reliable adult, have you?" she said, turning away.

I choked back my anger and, with all the equanimity I could bring to bear, said: "I can see that I've upset you. I'll just go check into a motel."

"Don't be so dramatic," she said. "Sit down. I'll make us some tea. Did you have lunch? Can I get you something to eat?"

"I ate," I lied. "But thanks for asking."

Jean went to the kitchen, filling the air with conversation as if what had just happened was as natural and routine as boiling water for tea.

We spent the next several hours catching up on this and that. She told me about a recent love affair that had ended abruptly.

"I found him hiding in the *Pacific Sun* personals," she said. "He was quite good-looking, a wonderful lover, but . . ."

She didn't have to complete her sentence. I'd heard the story before, about any number of other good-looking men and wonderful lovers who were far from her intellectual equal. Jean found anyone who had difficulty keeping up with her quick mind and quirky sense of humor "rather tedious." It was clear from the look on her face this recent lover was of that ilk. Still and yet, she enjoyed sex—very much. Her solution to this unfortunate impasse struck me as bizarre.

If a potential beau was "easy on the eyes" and followed up after the first date (which few of them did—Jean's subtle disapproval generally pushed them away), she would suggest a visit on her houseboat. Upon arrival, she would invite him in for a sit-down, serve tea, and ask if he'd like to "have a shag." It was one of the many bits of British slang she'd picked up during her years in London. It pleased her no end to watch how a man responded to her brazen proposition and unusual lexicon. Rarely did she get a "No thank you," despite what was often a considerable age difference.

Once the door to having a romp had swung open, she would immediately tell the unsuspecting gent how she expected him to behave. "Wonderful," she would say, "I have only one rule: no talking."

Not a single man chose to opt out of her game—at least not immediately. Once the deal was struck, if he dared to query her as to why, she would gently put her finger on his mouth to shush him before directing the hapless guy to her bed. Most returned for a second go at it, only to discover that Jean's one rule went into effect the moment he crossed her threshold. Thus, did she ensure that no lover would become attached; these "bibelot love affairs" as she called them rarely lasted longer than a few weeks.

"But there's another man whose ad caught my eye the other day," she said. She reached for the small red address book on the table next to her couch and pulled out a 1 x 2-inch piece of newsprint. The look on her face was one of complete delight. I knew that expression—she'd always been a devoted mis-chief-maker in matters of love—but something was different that day. I detected a slight scent of desperation mingled in with her seemingly ageless pheromones. "This one," she said, "is at the top of my list of 'Men I Must Meet.'" She patted the couch beside her, indicating she wanted me closer so I could read the ad with her. Then, with delicate precision, she read the words aloud:

AWARD WINNING WRITER SEEKS LEADING LADY
Young 60s SWM writer with A+ brains,
good looks, and a wonderful personality seeks
slender, tall, elegant A+ counterpart
with the kind of brains, looks and
personality that will send me screaming
your name from the top of Mt. Tam!

But alas, her repeated calls to the anonymous writer's voice-mail at the *Pacific Sun* never led to a date with Mr. A+.

The next few days flew by without event—or so I thought. The evening before I was due to leave, I phoned Jean from Whole Foods Market. "Thought I'd pick up some dinner. Does roast chicken and a nice big salad sound good?"

I expected to hear her say "Yeah!" Instead, she responded with a tepid, "Fine."

Her response was so curt I physically pulled away from the phone. *What now?* I thought. Weighed down with dread, I walked over to the salad bar, built a colorful salad, then picked up a Mary's chicken fresh off the rotisserie.

When I walked into the houseboat ten minutes later, Jean was sitting on her couch with Tulip-the-Abyssinian on her lap. She looked up at me, expressionless. The temperature in the room seemed to drop fifteen degrees.

I ignored the hissing sound in my head and asked, "Is everything okay, Jean?"

I couldn't tell if the zigzag of her head was a yes or a no, but obeyed when she said, "Fix me a plate before the chicken gets cold."

While I divvied up the salad, I gave myself a good talking to, "Geralyn, you will summon your strength and you will listen. She's getting old . . . won't be around much longer . . . give her the benefit of the doubt . . . you can handle this . . ." Meanwhile, another voice in my head said, "I can see this is going someplace absurd. Maybe I should leave tonight rather than wait 'til morning."

We ate in silence. I cleared the plates and did the dishes. Still no conversation. I thought: *If only I had a little bud of that Purple Haze; that would loosen her up.*

Jean turned on the TV as if I wasn't there. I sat on the chair beside the couch. The armrests had grown dingy over the years.

Two-thirds of the way into an episode of *West Wing,* after 40 minutes of working every relaxation technique I knew, I yawned and said, "I'm exhausted, Jean. Think I'll go to bed early. I have a long drive tomorrow."

"So, you're leaving in the morning?" she asked, expressionless.

"Yes."

"Alright, then."

My guard dropped to its knees and the words tumbled out of my mouth before I could think. "Jean, did I do something wrong?"

She looked at me square on: "Why do you keep moving Ganesh?"

"Moving Ganesh?" I asked.

"That's what I said."

"Forgive me, I'm not sure what you're talking about. You mean the deity?"

"Yes. Ganesh. You know. The statue in the guest room?"

"Statue in the guest room?" I said, wondering, *when did you become interested in the Hindu pantheon?*

"You keep moving it. Why?"

Again, that hiss in my head. Again, with the discombobulated thinking I only ever experienced with Jean. I stood there, semi-frozen. Tried not to let my heart turn to ice. Tried to come up with some explanation. No words came.

"Three mornings in a row, I found the statue on the table near the window," she said. "Why did you move it and not put it back where it belongs?"

"You mean the doorstop?" I said, remembering now.

"YES, the doorstop! Did it ever occur to you I put it there for a reason?"

I felt utterly addle-brained, but managed to respond, "Um. I moved it out of the way so I could close the door when I went to bed." I felt it best to omit the fact that she snored so loudly I'd found it difficult to sleep. "I guess I forgot to put it back when I went out."

Jean came back with a barrage of assumptions that were so off-base as to be ridiculous. I was impolite. Ungrateful. Didn't respect her. Self-absorbed. Ignorant. Un-cultured. Selfish. A louche.

I attempted to share my experience, to explain that I had no idea it was that important to her where the statue was, that I hadn't meant to offend.

She accused me of mocking her.

I said, "Not at all, Jean." I coached myself: *Let it go. Breathe, dammit. Breathe.*

But there was really nothing to do other than stand there and endure while my soft parts ran for cover.

29.

Continuum Lessons

I never intended to stay away for two years. Throughout that time, from 2006 to 2008, Jean was never far from my thoughts. I'd see a mother scold her two-year old, saying: "Don't point!" while waiting in the checkout line at the drugstore, and think of Jean. I'd see a mom on the sidewalk suddenly rush to grab her child's hand when he walked a few steps away from her and think of Jean. I'd see a hapless father try to wrestle his six-months old baby boy into a stroller so he'd stop screaming bloody hell in the produce section, and think of Jean. I'd hear a parent talk baby-talk to a toddler, asking: "What do you want, Peanut?" When the child turned away and started to fuss, I'd think of Jean. On many occasions, I not only thought of her, I started a dialog with her in my mind.

In the jungle, Jean had witnessed an instinctive, natural way of rearing children without all the fuss and frustration we assume is just part of being a parent. She did her best to highlight continuum principles and offer a different take on common conflicts between parent and child. She'd explain that the Yequana, too, had a code of conduct, but they never scolded children for breaking the code. They did not view the "misbehavior" as offensive, nor was the child seen as "bad." Instead of a reprimand, they would simply give the child information: the specific information he needed to get along among his people. No scolding. No disappointed glares or even a sugary-sweet, "Honey, we don't ..." Just delivering the information with the assumption that he wants to know what is expected of him and will cooperate—simply because it's in his nature to do so.

Our estrangement did not in any way diminish my respect for Jean, nor lessen my dedication to her work. In fact, I would often tell stories about what I came to call the "Continuum Lessons." For example, one day while Jean and I sat at the Depot, she nodded toward a mom who was scurrying around the square trying to catch up with her toddler. "Luther, go pick up your dump truck. Time to go home and see daddy." The boy ignored her. Again, she said, "Luther, honey. We're leaving now." Thirty seconds passed. The exasperation on his mother's face left no room for doubt: her patience was spent. In fact, she appeared to be running on a negative balance. "Luther. I said, Pick. Up. Your. Toy! Mommy is ready to go." She walked over to the boy, took him firmly by the hand, and all but dragged him over to the dump truck.

Jean whispered to me, "The tone of her voice communicates her expectation that he will disobey."

I said, "She's training her son to ignore her?"

"That's right," she said. "My advice to parents is: never say anything twice. Say it once with complete confidence that the child will obey, then go about your business."

"What if he doesn't do what she tells him to do?"

"Just ignore him. Children hate to be left out of the action."

"So, she should get in her car and drive away?"

"Of course not," she said, "If he doesn't act on her request within a minute, maybe two, she simply walks over to him, takes him by the hand, and gently shows him what she wants him to do. No anger. No scolding. No cajoling or bribing or threatening. Simple confidence and direction that gives him the information, that says: this is how we do it in our tribe."

She must have explained this to me half a dozen times, but I was aware of the immense challenge for parents. It was difficult for even the most devoted mother or father to overcome their exasperation and see the situation through what they typically see as a radical new perspective at first. Many found it nearly impossible to trust their child and break the habit of issuing commands. From what I'd seen, it was almost too much to ask.

"It isn't," Jean would say. "Not if you factor in the long-term benefits." She was always trying to educate me, to impress upon me what she called the *requirements of the Continuum*.

"Think of it this way, darling. How often have you heard parents tell their child: 'You be good.' Mom and Dad are taking Johnny over to grandma's house. Mom says: 'Now Johnny, you be good for your grandmother.' What her tone of voice says is: 'Pretend to be good, because we know you are bad.'

She has just reinforced his growing sense that he is not trust-worthy, which is a tragic mistake for all concerned."

On another occasion, I saw a young mom trying to rein in her three-year-old when it was time to go home. This mom took a different tack, one Jean referred to as *child-centered,* a term she had appropriated to describe a major pitfall of "progressive" parenting.[47]

"Sweetheart, are you ready to go home?" Her voice had that all too familiar sing-song, beseeching tone that broad-casts uncertainty.

"No," the little girl said, turning away from her mom.

"Come on honey, don't you want to go home and have a snack?"

"I'm not hungry."

"Well, Mommy needs to go home and start fixing dinner. What would you like for dinner? Macaroni and cheese? I also have your favorite fish sticks in the freezer."

Once again, I thought of Jean. I heard her voice in my head: "She's giving her child the authority, which makes the little girl feel unsafe. A child that age needs to know the parent is in charge. When she gives her daughter the power, it confuses the girl, so she makes a fuss and defies her. She's

---

[47] Jean's use of "child-centered" had a negative connotation, describing parents who give their children too much control, usually due to the parents' insecurity, fear of being too controlling, or belief that children always prefer to be in control. As a re-sult, child-centered parents frequently fail to provide the calm, confident leadership children innately expect of them. The term also has a well-known positive meaning in progressive education circles, where a "child-centered" school is one that prioritiz-es the individual needs of each child, supporting their unique developmental paths. Such schools may or may not be child-centered in the Liedloffian sense.

pushing the boundary to find the line where mom will take charge so she can feel safe. She actually needs her mom to be the one who knows what's what. Her place, as a three-year-old, is not to be in charge of when they leave, or what's on the dinner menu. That is a mother's job. This kind of role-reversal sets up a pattern guaranteed to cause all sorts of havoc when the little girl gets older. What's more, Mom gets confirmation for her belief that toddlers are tyrants."

The young mother's patience now exhausted, she said, "Honey, Mommy is tired," hoping sympathy would convince the girl to go along with her agenda. "It's time to go home. Mommy really needs you to get in the car." I could see she was doing her best to disguise her frustration, to be the good mom she wanted to be. Finally, she could take no more. Her tone went from sweet to harsh "We're leaving," she ordered. "Now!" Her voice was loud enough to turn the heads of those close by.

Her daughter continued to ignore her.

"Lizabeth. Get. In. The car!" Now on the verge of losing her temper, she stomped toward little Lizzy, hands on hips, and said, "I'm counting to three and if you're not in the car. One. Two . . ."

The child looked defiantly and her Mom, waited until she said "Three" and ran away, singing, "You can't get me! You can't get me!"

Her next tactic was to make her daughter choose between doing as she was told and being given "a consequence." She'd clearly bought into the notion that the way to get her daughter to obey was to give her "options," but the child could *feel* that this false choice between obedience and a veiled punishment was actually a *threat*.

I cannot count the number of times I witnessed these common power struggles between parents and children. I missed Jean terribly at those moments, reflected on the countless times she and I had been sitting together while similar situations played out before our eyes. She would turn her head my way and give me a look that said: "What is wrong with this picture?" She wasn't testing me so much as turning the situation into a teaching moment. She'd explain how the mother's words and actions reinforced the very behavior that results in a mommy-migraine before the day's end. Or how a father's tone of voice told his son that he expected him to be a "bad boy."

Jean frequently emphasized this point with parents she counseled: *children fulfill the expectations of their parents, even when these expectations are only implied.* In fact, they are typically unspoken, even unconscious. Dad believes his son will be difficult to manage. The culture he lives in supports this belief. He doesn't even realize that his attitude, his demeanor, and the distrust in his voice, communicate to the son that Dad expects him to be a problem. In fact, Dad has resigned himself to the fact that parenting is difficult, a constant test of his wherewithal and patience. The boy's innately social and cooperative nature, which has been shaped by millions of years of evolution and etched into his genes, looks to the big people in his world for cues as to how he is to behave. The boy, then, becomes obstinate *precisely because his father expects him to, not because it is his nature to behave badly.* The child's innate sociality has backfired on him and he's at risk of becoming a hellion.

Trying to wrap my mind around this, I would ask: "So parents set their kids up for a power struggle?"

"Yes," Jean would reply. "His expectation—what he's designed to do—is watch, listen, and learn. A Yequana child passively absorbs the ways of his people. He doesn't need to be disciplined, to be broken of his naughty nature. His nature is innately social. He wants to be shown what to do. His brain is built to mimic other's behavior. How else can he survive among his kind? His instinct, passed down to him by his evolving antecedents, is to comply with the ways of his people, to be one of them, and to trust his mother and father. But if they don't trust him, he gets the message that he is not to be trusted, that he is untrustworthy."

She would then continue, "You see, Darling, a child can't figure out his place among his people on his own. He needs to look to the authorities in his world for information about how to act. If his mother's look says, 'You're naughty,' he takes the cue. After all, she's the one who knows. So, he assumes *children of my tribe are naughty* and goes along with the program."

The implications were staggering.

Her insights always seemed undeniably true. Jean did her best to maintain a compassionate attitude toward parents who simply didn't know any better. She referred to their misguided treatment of their offspring as "shenanigans" to lessen the implication of parental wrongdoing. I often heard her sigh: "That's how she was treated as a child," or, "She's taken her cues from other moms who are child-centered."

During the years we were out of touch, I met many women who had read *The Continuum Concept* and swore by it. "Once I read Jean's book, I threw all the other parenting books away," they would say.

More and more, I noticed women carrying their infants in a Snugli[48] or a sling. Many hadn't even heard of *The Continuum Concept.* Nonetheless, their mother-instinct had been given permission to do the right thing, to take the baby out of the stroller and put him on her body where he belongs. But I knew there was much, much more that Jean had to offer parents, any number of principles that could eliminate power struggles, mommy-dependence, bedwetting, nightmares, the terrible twos, sibling rivalries, and adolescent rebellion.

Jean firmly believed that a widespread understanding of the continuum concept was the key to a sane society, one where addiction, crime, the agony of low self-esteem and anxiety, even sociopathic and sadistic behavior are all but unknown.

---

[48] One of the early baby carriers, the Snugli was created by a Peace Corp volunteer who observed mothers in West Africa maintaining physical contact with their infants throughout their daily activities.

30.

Our Secret

In the spring of 2009, I put my hurt aside once again and emailed Jean. It had been three years since we last saw one another. I asked if she'd like to have a visit. She replied right away, "Yes!"

Jean had made a point, any number of times, of telling me she never got depressed. And though she never admitted it, she was clearly lonely. The clearest indication of this was her repeated suggestion that I write a book titled, simply, *Loneliness*. It was if she felt I could find the answer and relieve her of the pain she must have lived with every day.

When she opened her door that chilly, overcast day in May, I was startled. The silent terror of being alone showed in her facial expression when she opened the door, full of anticipation to receive me as her friend. But that fearful look disappeared in a millisecond as her happy-lines winged out from the corner of her eyes, leading her mouth into a sweet, loving smile. I handed her a bottle of Cabernet.

We took up exactly where we'd left off, before the final upset over the doorstop. It was as if nothing had happened between us. Midway through our visit, she shared her latest distraction: Craigslist. She'd discovered what she called the "e-personals." From the look on her face, I knew she'd found a guilty pleasure.

"I posted an ad last week," she said. "So far I've received twenty-three responses." She giggled, put her finger to her mouth, and said, "You mustn't tell. It's our secret."

She started to explain—or perhaps, excuse—her preoccupation: "I'm only looking for someone interesting to talk to. God knows . . . "

I joined in the fun and shared my secret: "I just posted a profile on one of the online dating sites. It can be tedious, but I met one guy who's become a good friend." I suggested she go on Match.com or eHarmony. "You won't have to sift through all those exhibitionists on Craigslist whose idea of seduction is sending you a snapshot of their stiffy."

She made a face I couldn't quite decipher, then said, "I could use a stiff one right now . . . make it a double."

"You're too funny," I said, reaching for my phone. "Here, let me show you." I went to eHarmony, pulled up my account and showed her the screen.

"Nice picture of you," she said.

I read her my profile. In the back of my mind, I imagined that I was showing her how it's done. But she outdid me.

"I'll read you mine," she said.

She reached under the side-table next to the sunk-in spot where she always sat on her fading couch.

"Move, Pussy," she said, chasing Tulip onto the floor. She pulled out an overstuffed expanding file, started going through it and grumbled, "I wish someone would help me get organized." Then, "Ah! Here it is." She pulled out a typewritten page. I glanced at it and realized she'd typed it out on her old Underwood machine.

She held up the paper, put on a pair of tiger-striped reading glasses and sat up in a mock-important way. She cleared her throat and started to read:

Women seeking men. I would love to meet a man who is deeply decent, possesses a deliciously high IQ and concomitant sense of humor, and who is too sophisticated to be pretentious. Naturally creative in the realms of love, he is healthy and cuddly with endearing ways. He smiles readily at my puns and knows how to laugh at my human foibles rather than make an issue of them. A truly rare bird, he skirts psychobabble and shrink-rap in favor of keen insight. He laughs at the human condition when not weeping for it.

Are you a man I can obey without question? Ah, what a luxury! Will you see my vulnerability and count on my strength? Have good taste in ethics as well as aesthetics, tread lightly and adapt with grace? I long for a friend with an agile mind who supports my life's work and has a project or two that I can abet. A man who is Zen enough to work in the kitchen or yard, and has what it takes to recognize and vanquish that sneaky demon: Panic-At-The-Threat-Of-Unaccustomed-Happiness.

She finished reading, looked up at me, smiled and said: "Twenty-three responses!"

I smiled back and asked her to read the last paragraph again; my mind was stuck on three little words that struck me as antithetical Jean: *obey without question*.

A week or two later, I arranged to pay her a visit with my new sweetheart so the two of them could meet. Bob and I had only been seeing each other for three months, but we were very close and had started talking about living together. For some inexplicable reason, I felt it important that he meet Jean. In the back of my mind, I suppose I wanted her approval, even though I resented her for giving a thumbs-down on my past two boyfriends.

Bob and Jean got along like a house on fire. It was the first time I saw her smoke a spliff. She loved it as much for the high as for the pain-relief.

Not long after that visit, I swerved into my busy life with Bob and drifted away from Jean once again. I hadn't intended to pull away. In fact, I had vowed to stay in touch. But time did its usual furious charge ahead, and a year whizzed by. Whenever Bob and I would drive down the Waldo Grade from the Golden Gate Bridge into Sausalito, he would ask, "Have you talked to the houseboat lady lately?"

"No," I'd say. Then, as we drove past the Bridgeway exit at the bottom of the grade, I would say, "I really should call her." But I didn't make the call. I loved Jean, admired her work, her intelligence, her way with a pun. But I was reluctant to put myself within range of her hurtful behavior.

Time and again, I would see yet another parent struggling to get a little one to listen or stop screaming and urge myself to call her. I'd watch a mother ignore her child, thinking this would prevent him from becoming a spoiled brat, and I'd swear to call Jean the next day. But other priorities always got in the way.

The fact that Jean's work had not fully come to fruition troubled and saddened me. I felt that I'd failed my assignment. The reason she had let me into her life in the first place was to help her write that follow-up book. She'd hoped I would bring with me the magic key to lift the writer's block that had stymied her for so many years. She knew she had a second book in her, a very important book. But she just couldn't sit down to write it. No matter what I did to encourage her, she undermined my every attempt to help.

We would schedule an afternoon to get together and work on the manuscript. Jean would answer the door, invite me in, direct me to the kitchen table where her word processor sat collecting dust. She'd complain about how difficult it was to "get the machine to obey" and immediately start to fuss with the stacks of paper on her kitchen table. Inevitably, she'd come upon an unpaid bill she'd been searching for, or an unanswered letter, and start to groan over how little time she had to manage it all. She would insist on making tea and catching up before we dove into working. I'd fill her in on my latest adventures. She'd tell me about an invitation to speak in Europe or a call she'd received from a distressed parent. Then she'd complain about her publisher at Penguin. Or she'd ask me once again, as she had half a dozen times before, to find her a foreign rights agent who could track down her unpaid royalties. I didn't dare speak my thoughts aloud: "What agent would work for so little a payout?" It was an example of a common foible: Jean was oblivious to the needs of others.

On good days, I could coax her to actually open the document that contained a rough outline of the childrearing book, but that was as far as she would go. If I came up with so much as an introductory sentence, she would pick it apart, get lost in thought, trail-off into stream-of-consciousness mutterings, distract some more, then brilliantly revise my sentence. Dragging a single sentence out of her this way could take half an hour. I calculated our progress and estimated it would take eight and a half years at this rate—if we worked every day.

It was early spring in 2010 when I circled around to her again. I'd run into a mutual friend who told me Jean wasn't doing well. "She lives on microwaved food from Trader Joe's," she said. "A dill pickle with lunch is her idea of getting her vegetables."

I dropped by the houseboat marina a couple of days later. Her gold Mercedes was in the parking lot. The poorly maintained lot was in terrible condition as was her car. I walked up the ramp and across the rickety bridge that led to Issaquah Dock, then down fifty yards to *White Elephant*. I crossed over the narrow paint-chipped ramp to her door and popped the brass knocker three times. No answer. I rang the bell. It was still broken, just as it had been ever since my first visit sixteen years earlier. I knocked again then walked over to the kitchen window and peered in. Her counters were exactly as they'd always been, cluttered with boxes of tea and vitamin bottles from Trader Joe's. No sign of Jean. I walked to the end of the ramp where she would leave a hide-a-key when she was going out of town and needed me to feed Tulip. No key.

I went back to the door and called out: "Jean, are you home?" A few moments later she opened the door. A wide smile spread across her face. "Sweetheart! How lovely to see you. Watch your step. Don't step on the white carpet." I dared not tell her the carpet was no longer white, but a dank shade of grayish beige. "Take off your shoes. Come, sit on the couch. You haven't been hiking in the hills, have you? The deer ticks are bad this year, and I don't want them to get on Pussy."

We sat down. "Darling, you look wonderful, but you really shouldn't show so much cleavage."

I looked down. The sports top I was wearing was actually quite modest. I'd been in the house less than two minutes and had already fielded four of her off-the-cuff commands and one criticism, but I didn't mind. It was so very good to see her. But Jean had aged, and not well. She was thin, frail, and very pale. When I asked her how she was doing, she said, "Oh fine!" She told me about her doctor friend, Inga, a lovely woman I'd met a number of years earlier. They, too, had fallen out. Her explanation of why made no sense whatsoever. I knew better than to question her further. She talked about an aborted trip to Germany where she'd been asked to speak. "I couldn't travel because of my knees."

Jean had complained about her knees for years, but no matter what the doctors tried, the pain kept getting worse.

Her mobility had started to suffer. She had a hard time getting out of bed, and an even harder time climbing the stairs. She wasn't getting the right help at Kaiser. I suggested she see a well-known knee specialist, an out-of-Kaiser doc, for a second opinion. She wouldn't even consider the added expense. "I pay Kaiser $600 a month for health insurance; they should take care of it." She continued to complain, going from frustrated to angry to indignant to furious with her doctors. The more she complained the less they listened. She was viewed as a malingerer, a hypochondriac in common parlance.

I suggested we go together to her primary physician so I could advocate for her. She looked at me, hard. I knew that look. If she'd been a cat she would have been up in an arch. She said, "What makes you think I can't advocate for myself?"

Here we go again, I thought.

Fortunately, I'd grown a thicker skin over the years.

31.

Triple Jeopardy

Fall 2010, right after Thanksgiving. Jean and I sat on her washed-out couch, drinking Chardonnay. We were laughing about God-knows-what when she looked at me intently and said, "I've got to get rid of Matt. Will you please help me?"

Matt had been living on the houseboat for six years. In exchange for free rent, he took care of Jean's car, ran errands, and managed her checkbook. What Jean really wanted was a live-in assistant who would also be good company. Matt was only a warm body—and an unpleasant one at that. He was abrupt and reclusive. He had an avoidant personality.

"He respects my work," she would say. "But he is rude and mean-spirited. He barely speaks to me and when he does, he's full of disdain."

She wanted a housemate who could be a friend and companion. "I'm not looking for a boyfriend, just someone who makes soothing noises."

She did not want another woman living in her home, she wanted a man, and he had to be easy on the eyes. A younger man would be best. An artist. Not a musician: "too unreliable." A handyman type: "I love a man with a tool belt." This person should not have a full-time job: "I need help getting up in the morning." And God-forbid he should have a social life: "I want him to be home in the evening."

"Sounds like you want someone to be at your beck and call," I said.

She frowned.

"Jean, you need to be realistic," I went on. "That room would rent for $850, $900 at the most. Divide that by $20 per hour and you're looking at something like ten hours a week. That's about an hour and a half a day . . ."

"Please, Darling. Just post the ad on Craigslist. If you would be so kind as to screen people over the phone and send along the good ones."

I posted the ad. Matt moved out of the boat a few days before Christmas. I was concerned about Jean being alone, so I dropped by *White Elephant* every other day. On New Year's Eve, I got a call from a man named Steve who'd seen the Craigslist ad. He was a sculptor who had worked in construction; he had a tool belt. He was "in transition" and relocating to the Bay Area. He had a car, but no job. He was driving north on 101 right now and had just passed San Luis Obispo. He'd be in the Bay Area in about four hours. Could he meet Jean this afternoon?

I met Steve in the Issaquah Dock parking lot. He was definitely easy on the eyes. I trusted him immediately. So did Jean.

I gave him the lay of the land. "She can be a bit demanding. You'll make her tea every morning. Make sure she gets out of bed. Don't leave the boat until she's upstairs. She'll let you know if there are errands to run. Keep your cell phone on in case she needs anything during the day, otherwise your time is your own until ten pm. No overnight guests."

The arrangement fell apart in a matter of weeks. "This isn't what I signed up for," Steve said. "She's just rude."

Matt, for all his flaws, had possessed the one quality Jean most needed in a companion: he was impervious to scorn. He didn't care if she was rude. He was immune to her disdain. He was resolute and single-minded. No matter how much she protested, no matter how caustic her complaint, he was stalwart. She would have to get herself upstairs if she wanted her morning tea. In that sense, he was a godsend.

Lacking this hell-bent attitude and foursquare resolve, Steve had been steamrolled by Jean. She insisted on having her morning tea in bed and berated him until he complied. And now he'd had enough.

I posted the Craigslist ad a second time and received a flood of emails. Two weeks passed. I'd interviewed a dozen or more people without success. Jean had all but stopped getting out of bed. Now, in addition to complaining about her knees, she began to lament her dependence on a bedpan to "tap a kidney," or "squeeze the lemon." Who was I to argue?

"God forbid I should have a meeting with the governor when nobody's around to get me to the bathroom." I'd never heard that one before, but I immediately understood that "meeting with the governor" meant making a poo.

Another week went by, and Jean had lost her mobility entirely. I should have known better than to ask Matt to leave. Change can cause even the most resilient among us to wobble. Young or old, we like stability; we actually need equilibrium. It's called homeostasis—an inbuilt tendency to avoid making changes that might flip the apple cart. But I didn't see it coming. The wobble. The loss of equilibrium. Yes, I had acted at her behest, but I hadn't considered the consequences of getting rid of Matt.

Then, late one morning, I got the call. It was a Monday.

"Hi Geralyn. It's Inga."

Jean had told me that she and Inga had managed to rekindle their friendship. Inga was in the U.S. with her husband, but she was due to fly home to Germany at the end of the week. Jean's housekeeper had called Inga when she found Jean asleep on the couch, an empty bottle of Vicodin on the coffee table.

"She's at Kaiser Terra Linda, Room 245," Inga said.

"I'll be there in half an hour," I replied.

Jean was awake when I arrived. Inga looked at me with knowing eyes. I knew immediately that Jean had spoken the same words to her that she'd said to me the previous week: "Life isn't worth living bedpan to bedpan."

She had asked me to get her a "lethal dose." I didn't take her request seriously. I could not, would not, believe she would attempt to end her life. I didn't conduct a formal suicide assessment because I didn't believe she had the means or the ability to obtain the means. Surely, she knew that a bottle of Vicodin would only trash her liver, not kill her. Then again, how would she know? Was her attempt a cry for help? Or did she take the pills with a clear intent to die?

Inga and I talked it over. Every time Jean spoke with one of the nurses, she reiterated her wish to die. The hospital staff began making arrangements to transfer her to Unit A, the psychiatric wing at Marin General.

This will not stand, I thought, and went to her with a plan.

"Jean, if you keep telling them you're going to kill yourself, they will send you to the psych ward."

She frowned and let out a groan that sounded almost like a growl.

I told her exactly what would happen if she continued threatening to commit suicide. I suggested she start talking about going home to write her memoir. I promised to help her write the book. I promised to help her regain her strength so she could walk again. I promised to feed her a nutrient-dense diet. I even promised that if she got strong enough to walk and still wanted to end her life, I'd go with her to Switzerland where the laws are more lenient.

"I'll make you superfood shakes and green juice every day," I said, strengthening my promise. "We'll get a physical therapist to come to the boat, and I'll come over every afternoon and make sure you do your exercises. I'll cancel my trip to Maui."

She wasn't so keen on the idea of superfood shakes and green juice, but she took the point about the psych ward. She stopped talking about ending her life. When she told her doctor that she planned to go home and work on her memoir, I vowed to make sure she did. The doctor was satisfied that she'd found a reason to live, gave her a referral for a physical therapist, and wrote up the discharge papers.

Once home, she hired her housekeepers to be her care-givers. When the physical therapist came, she sent him away.

"You can't cancel your vacation on my account," she insisted. "I won't have it. The memoir can wait until you get back."

I knew better than to argue. Bob and I left for Maui the next morning.

We'd spent the morning at Ho'okipa Beach where both surfers and kiteboarders convened every morning beginning at dawn. I uttered one "Wow!" "Whoa!" "Look at him!" or "Oooh . . . wipe out!" after another, thrilling to their chutzpah and skill. Bob, a lifelong surfer, had yet to try kiteboarding and was determined to take a lesson before we flew home. I felt wary, wanted to say, "Don't you think that might be above your play grade?" But I hadn't been asked to grant or withhold permission, so I let it be.

Back at our island getaway, I finished a long outdoor shower, grabbed a towel, and took two steps onto the warm, lush grass. Bob shouted from the lanai, "Phone for you." Then, "You'd better take this call. It's a friend of Jean's calling from Kaiser."

"Not again," I sighed.

I walked across the grass and through the French doors of our cottage, thinking, *I'd better call Hawaiian Air and change my flight.* I flew back to the Bay Area the next day.

After this second attempt, Jean's medical team at Kaiser 5150'd her and immediately transferred her to the psych ward at Marin General Hospital.[49] The staff would do an assessment and, in all likelihood, transfer her to a Kaiser psychiatric hospital on the peninsula.

The nurse buzzed me in through the locked doors of Unit A. I found Jean asleep in a wheelchair near a window. There was no sun. She looked up at me and said, "Oh, Darling. I'm so glad to see you. Come here." She reached toward me, pleading, "Get me a lethal dose. Please. Nembutal. I'm sure you can find it."

I told her I didn't know where to get it and wouldn't get it for her even if I did. "Jean, you are only 84; you still have plenty of life in you. Your time isn't up yet."

She gave me her hardest, *don't you dare cross me* look, then softened. "Well then, take me to Oregon."

That evening, I looked into the Death with Dignity laws in Oregon. She could certainly afford to move up there; in six months' time she'd be able to fulfill the residency requirement. But it was highly unlikely she would be able to find two doctors to confirm her right to die because she hadn't been diagnosed with a terminal illness.

When I told her what I'd learned about the Oregon option, she told me she'd figured as much and had come upon another plan. "As a last resort, I'll just stop eating."

She continued to put a little bird in my ear and say, "Please get me a lethal dose," when I visited each afternoon. Her tone of voice was so intimate, so sincere. "A true friend would do

---

[49] Under California Welfare and Institutions Code 5150, individuals deemed to be a danger to themselves can be placed (involuntarily) in a locked psychiatric facility, for an evaluation for up to 72 hours.

this." Maybe she was right; a true friend would not sit by and watch her starve to death.

I was her true friend, perhaps her only true friend. Who else had stayed close that many years, always circling back despite repeated incidents that would push most people away? Who else was ready and able to stay by her side until the very end? I considered the path ahead. Maybe she would change her mind. Maybe I could still talk her out of her plan. Maybe, maybe, maybe. But part of me knew Jean all too well. She could procrastinate until the wild boars came home, but once she made up her mind, she had an iron will. "Life isn't worth living bedpan to bedpan" had become her mantra.

I googled Nembutal. I couldn't believe I was doing so, but what she'd said kept pinging around in my head: "A true friend would do this." Her words kept me awake that night. Part of me knew those words were true.

I went back to see her in the early afternoon the next day. A male nurse buzzed me in through the thick metal door and waved me toward the nursing station. "We're making arrangements to send her home," he said.

I must've looked startled.

"She proved she isn't depressed," he said. "She's rational. She has a court order stating that she can go home."

That morning, Jean had insisted on speaking to the "head pussycat." The staff sent a senior psychiatrist instead. He conducted a second assessment and determined she was not depressed. She was, in his estimation, quite rational. "But hospital rules are hospital rules," he said. "We won't release you to go home and commit suicide. You'd have to . . ." he swallowed these last three words.

"Have to what?" she asked.

He hesitated.

She demanded, "Have to talk to the chief administrator? What's his name?" Jean didn't need assertiveness training. She had a way of turning people into a spoon she could easily bend to her will.

The doctor didn't have a chance. "You'd have to speak with a magistrate of Marin. Get a court order."

She called the office of the Marin County Court and eventually reached someone in a position to hear her request. She had the relevant medical records faxed over. The psychiatrist had determined that she was not depressed. Her thinking was not disorganized, she was not emotionally labile, and showed none of the signs typical of someone having a psychiatric emergency. Two hours later, she had her court order. The hospital staff had no choice; they could not keep her on involuntary hold, even though she'd started refusing food. The chief administrator gave his staff instructions to send her home with hospice care.

I followed the ambulance back to *White Elephant*, helped her get settled, and made her tea.

"Won't you stay for awhile, pussycat?" she asked. "Bring down a chair from the kitchen table. And hand me that remote. Jeopardy's coming on soon."

"But of course," I said, and went upstairs.

Despite the emptiness she felt inside, Jean had no addictions—except Jeopardy. She faithfully watched it every afternoon. A whiz at the quiz competition, she typically answered the Jeopardy challenge before any of the contestants. But because it was all-too easy for her to win, she only gave herself points if she responded correctly when none of the contestants knew the answer. In Jeopardy-speak, this is known as a "Triple Stumper."

Contestant: "Literary Drop Letter for $200."

Alex Trebek, the game show's host, said: "We're going to drop one letter from the title of a well-known book or novel, and it'll give you something completely different. Drop a letter from a George Eliot novel, and the Tulliver siblings are unwell on a certain river."

The contestants stared at the board. No-one hit their buzzer.

"What is The Ill on the Floss," Jean said, picking up her score-pad. "Two hundred for me."

I was gobsmacked. How did she know to drop the first letter of *Mill on the Floss?* And how in the name of all that is holy did she know that three Holy Roman emperors from the 10th century sported this palindromic name. ("Who is Otto?") Or that Post-Civil War Republicans opposed to civil service reform were called these. ("What are Stalwarts?") Maybe she'd seen the Tony Award-winning Broadway Musical that was based on a collection of stories that won the Pulitzer in 1948. (What is *South Pacific?")*

Or maybe she was some kind of trivia savant.

When the show was over, I excused myself, saying, "I'll be back tomorrow. Can I bring you anything?"

Jean had now stopped eating. That was her plan, her third and final attempt to leave this world in her time and on her terms. She would simply refuse all food. It was the only means available to her. She would take in fluids, nothing else. She was determined to carry out her plan.

"Bring me a box of those little envelopes of chicken broth, the instant kind," she said. "And a case of diet root beer."

32.

The Blind Spot

Refusing to believe Jean would actually starve herself to death, I insisted we start working on her memoir. I spent several hours at the boat every day, waiting for the flurry of activity to subside so we could have some time alone. Then I'd pull out my iPhone, open the voice memo app, and start asking questions.

Every afternoon, the hospice worker, Chip, stopped by for a visit. It was his job to keep her as comfortable as possible. Bedsores can become a real problem for people who are bedridden, so he ordered a hospital bed and gave instructions to change her position every six hours. Jean developed bedsores anyway. He ordered a special mattress and brought in a gurney so we could move her off her bed while we switched mattresses. Jean complained that she couldn't sleep on the new mattress, so we repeated the procedure two days later. This time Chip brought her a special pad. Her bedsores continued to worsen.

Jean's housekeepers-turned-caregivers rotated shifts to ensure she had 24-hour coverage, often sending one of their teenage children to stay overnight. At one point, Jean discovered that someone was making unauthorized withdrawals on her bank account. She called the Marin County Sheriff. The housekeepers were questioned. Debit cards were replaced, and ruffled feathers smoothed.

There was a whirlwind of activity involving the trustee of her estate, who lived on Issaquah Dock with his lawyer wife. Several people got involved in an ongoing kerfuffle over last minute changes to her will. There was the conversation about her paintings, which were not mentioned in the will. Perhaps they should go to Scott Noelle, a loyal friend who had created and maintained continuum-concept.org for over a decade. Anna Ariel, one of Jean's student-trainees who visited her a few weeks before she died, expressed keen interest in a painting of a family that Penguin used as cover art on the 1986 UK paperback edition of *The Continuum Concept*. And what about her cousin Whitney? Should he have one of the paintings?

One afternoon, Jean told me to take whatever I wanted from her file cabinet and her office upstairs. "You might find my journals somewhere," she said.

Other than two leather bound diaries that were falling apart, her "journals" weren't actually journals; they were file folders full of tissue thin typing paper on which she'd poured out her heart banging away on her old Underwood manual typewriter. I also found old appointment calendars, address books, and a photo album. There was one file labeled "Kind Words" that contained dozens of letters she'd received from fans of her work. Then I came across a rough draft of a letter she'd written to Gloria Steinem, but had never mailed. I also found carbon copies of several letters she had mailed to high-profile individuals. She wrote to Steven Spielberg shortly after the success of *Schindler's List* suggesting he consider turning her story into a feature film. She also reached out to Barbra Streisand, having heard she was a fan of *The Continuum Concept.* And she wrote to First Lady Hillary Clinton about the concept and offered a gentle critique of some of the ideas in her book, *It Takes a Village.* I boxed up all of these treasures and took them with me. I thought about taking the paintings but decided to wait for her explicit okay. The following day, her trustee insisted I bring everything back. To this day, I wonder why I complied.

All the while, I continued to make the case for the life she had yet to live and insisted that she eat. She flatly refused, saying: "I've lived a full life. How many people get to make a contribution like I have? No one will be heartbroken."

"I'll be heartbroken," I said.

She cocked her head and said, "You won't be—not really."

I asked Chip for a sit-down, and we agreed to meet at ten o'clock the next morning. He arrived half an hour late, accompanied by a social worker from the county.

The three of us sat at Jean's kitchen table. "She's approaching the stage we call *wasting away,*" the social worker explained. "If she begins to eat in the next two to three days, she can still rebuild her strength. Another week with no calories and we're looking at *cachexia*. That's the point of no return. Extreme weight loss, muscle wasting, loss of body fat that can't be reversed. No amount of nutrition will repair the damage."

"So, she has a few days to change her mind?" I asked.

"Yes," the social worker said.

Chip nodded.

But the pressed lip half-smile on his face broadcast what he knew: once a person as determined as Jean had set her course it was a done deal. To his way of thinking, the point of no return had long since passed. A deathly cold passed through the room. My conviction that I could convince her to live caved in on me. To prop myself up with even a smidgen of hope would be to squander what little time I had left with Jean. She had made her choice.[50]

"How long will it take?" I asked.

"We can't say exactly. People have been known to last as long as 60 days."

Two full months? Surely, giving her a lethal dose was more humane. But I'd looked at that question from every possible angle. There really was no decision to be made. It wasn't a moral or ethical issue; it was a legal one. I could not and would not risk my freedom so she could have hers.

---

[50] Jean's decision to hasten her own death shocked many who knew her. Likewise, many who did not know her personally but had been deeply moved by her work, were shocked to learn of her decision to stop eating. It is tempting to label her choice a suicide, to characterize her decision to die consciously as irrational or cowardly. It is tempting to say she took "the easy way out," but we must not take the easy way out when it comes to our sovereign right to meet death on our own terms.

That day, when Jean and I finally had some time to ourselves, I perched myself at her bedside with my laptop. I looked at my list of questions and set the computer aside. It was time to ask her if she wanted to be buried or cremated.

"Just throw me into the dumpster," she said.

I ignored this comment and asked how the Yequana dealt with death and dying.

"The shaman, *curandero,* sits beside the dying person with a rattle," she said. "He chants and rattles to keep the moon from grabbing your soul when you go by."

I offered to bring in a shaman, "I know a man who is the real deal."

She rolled her eyes and said, "You've been living in Marin too long." She shook her head and smiled that smile that said, *silly girl.*

I was grateful she didn't say the words aloud.

"Just because the Yequana believe we have a soul doesn't mean we do," she said. Jean had always been an atheist; she was not about to change her beliefs now.

Our conversation turned to Gloria Steinem. I could tell by the way she spoke that she desperately wanted closure. She still couldn't forgive herself for whatever it was she had done to push her friend away.

"If only I knew what it is I do," she said. "I don't want to take the mystery to my grave."

It was a matter of personal integrity for Jean. She wanted to know. She needed to know. And it was a matter of personal integrity for me to do whatever I could to help her gain that understanding. My attempts to tell her what she does that pushes people away had failed up until that point, but I had developed a working theory about the phenomenon in general that I felt sure she would accept. If only she would listen with an open mind. This was the opening I'd been hoping for.

"I admire your tenacity, not to mention your vulnerability when you talk about Gloria," I said. "And I want you to know that you're not the only one. It seems to me most people do it to some degree or another."

"What makes you say that?"

I knew, without thinking about it, that citing her contribution to my theory would affirm her authority and help her keep an open mind.

"The first day we met, you told me that you do something you can't see," I said. "Ever since, I've been aware of this in myself, as well as in other people. Basically, you alerted me to an issue that is very common. Not long ago, I started to refer to it as the *blind spot.*"

I explained that her confession had made me aware of my own vexing, repetitive pattern. Over time, I'd become aware that most people have a blind spot of one form or another. I told Jean that my curiosity about this had led me to start a women's group.

"I felt certain that a group could help me see what I couldn't see on my own," I said. "I explained my thinking to my women friends, and told them I *know* there is something I'm doing to shoot myself in the foot, something I can't see. And I'm pretty sure *you can see it* because I can see what each of you do, again and again, that actually hurts you, and prevents you from getting the thing you most want."

"Oh . . . kay," Jean said, a tinge of challenge in her voice that warned: *This better get relevant to me real quick because you're losing me.*

I proceeded: "I had to get to the bottom of that same question I've heard you ask over a dozen times: What is it that I do? It was beginning to eat at me. I had to know. So, I started a women's group with eight of my friends. We did a process I called, the *hot seat*."

I explained the hot seat process in detail. "One at a time, we'd sit before the group and talk about our frustrations, what wasn't working in our lives. The hope was that honest reflection and feedback from people you trust would make it possible to see the behavior that holds you back. Unfortunately, it didn't work. The women would empathize and comfort each other. They'd say, 'Oh, Goddess, but you are so beautiful.' It wasn't at all what I had in mind. But I didn't know how to get around the . . . well, collusion is too strong a word . . . more like *agreement* to let each other slide in those places we fool ourselves."

I paused, waiting to see her response. I feared she'd dismiss me as she had so many times before.

"Go on," she said, waving her hand.

Aware that I was baiting her, I said, "Well, recently, I found a way to revise that agreement."

She looked me in the eye and said nothing. But the message in her silence was clear.

I continued, "A year ago I met an extraordinary woman who practices shamanic healing arts."

Jean rolled her eyes and said, "Don't tell me. She's a medicine woman, right?"

Fully aware of Jean's prejudice against all things New Age, I said, "I know you're skeptical, but this woman is a true seer. She comes from an ancient lineage of healers; she apprenticed with the elders from the time she was 12 years old. Only after training under a master healer for 20 years did she start working with people directly." I did not mention that she also spent a decade getting her PhD in psychology. Jean had an equally strong prejudice against higher education.

Again, that wave of her hand. This time it seemed to carry a hint of impatience mixed with conviction. Despite her reservations, she urged me to go on.

"She led me through the most potent, liberating process imaginable," I said. "But I want to back up a bit and give you some context."

Her impatience flared. "Meaning?"

"Please. Can you just indulge me for a moment? The detour will make the destination clear. Promise."

Her head made a figure eight as she considered my request, then began to nod ever so slightly.

I thanked her.

"You're welcome," she said with a smile, as though she wasn't yet giving up the game.

I looked her in the eye, shook my head from side-to-side and chuckled. Obviously, she was more interested than she was willing to let on.

"So," I said with fabricated authority. "You remember EST[51], right?"

"Yes. I took the training in 1978," she said. "I found it interesting."

---

[51] Founded by author and lecturer Werner Erhard, a self-improvement guru, Erhard Seminars Training (EST), was an awareness course/human potential seminar, conducted in large groups from 1971-1984. In January 1985, the training morphed into The Forum. Erhard sold his intellectual property to a group of his former employees in 1991; they re-branded the seminar, and formed Landmark Education.

"Right," I said. "I did, too. Did it in 1984. I actually did the very last EST training, delivered by Werner himself. A month later, I was in the seminar he called, The Symposium, that eventually became the Landmark Forum."

Jean interrupted. "Didn't you tell me you were on staff at EST at one point?"

I nodded. "I'm surprised you remembered."

"My memory isn't totally shot," she said with a wink.

I winked back. "So, you remember the whole bit in the training about *your racket,* right?"

One of the features of the EST training involved a discussion of the way most people fall back on an all-too familiar way of doing things that doesn't really work. The "racket" as it was called, is a strategy, a defense mechanism that occurs reflexively without our being aware of it. It shapes our in-the-moment experience, so our experience lines up with what we've come to expect our life to look like. We experience the world and our relationships with others in accord with the architecture that lives deep in the unconscious.

Jean looked at me and said, "Yes. I remember the teaching about your racket. That was a difficult pill to swallow. But definitely enlightening."

I smiled and continued, "Got it."

She chuckled in that "I'm dying so everything's funny" way that had emerged in the previous day or two.

I took her amusement as a signal to go on. "Remember how skillfully the trainers would point out a person's racket?"

"Yes." Jean said. "And people with similar patterns could see themselves in someone else's racket."

"Right. But that's part of the problem with the training. Well, not 'problem' really, more like limitation."

"What do you mean?"

"Well, let's think about it. You said 'so many of us had similar rackets.' But what about the way a person's racket is unique? Not at all similar? With three hundred people in the room, EST trainers couldn't provide that kind of specificity. They could only go so far. At most, they would work with half a dozen people and help them get a glimpse of their racket. But it was only a glimpse. Sure, a few people had a profound insight, but for the most part, it faded fairly quickly because the subconscious pattern is so entrenched. As for the other 300-plus people in the room, they were left with a generic sense of what it meant to have a racket, and a vague feel for the various rackets people run. The specifics of each individual's racket and how it functions in real-time remained a mystery. That's part of why I left the EST organization. I was hell bent on solving that mystery."

Jean was still tracking me, so I continued. Cautiously.

"That brings me back to the medicine woman," I said, smiling. "Her name is Tullah. The process of transformation she took me through was not at all generic."

"What do you mean?"

"Her approach is very individual. People go into an inquiry, an expedition into the subconscious terrain of the psyche. The process can take four hours, often more. That's why she works with small groups, just six people at a time. The insight I gained is both profound and totally specific to me and my unique racket."

"Makes sense," Jean said.

"Totally," I said. "One by one, people sit and do their work. It's a marathon hot seat. The beauty of it is, instead of someone telling you what's in your blind spot, she sets up context so you can show yourself."

"Oh." Jean said. Her immediate comprehension of the import of this was evident in her tone of voice.

"Right. *Oh.*" I said.

"So, what did you see?" she asked. "When you got on this hot seat?"

"Uhhh . . ." I hesitated. It didn't feel right to talk about myself just yet. "Let me tell you someone else's story first. It'll give you a sense of what happens. I'll share what happened for me another time."

"As you wish," she said.

"So, there's this man, Steve, in the hot seat," I began. "Only it's more like the sweat lodge with Tullah in the mix."

Jean laughed. It wasn't often she laughed at my humor.

"Steve's second wife is threatening to leave him," I said. "He doesn't want another divorce; he came to the weekend because he wants to save his marriage."

Jean nodded. She closed her eyes and listened.

"Tullah starts by asking a number of questions: What repetitive behavior patterns keep you stuck? Is there a complaint you've heard over and over from key people in your life? That kind of thing. This part takes an hour or so and lays a lot of information out on the table. Steve starts to clarify his core issue and get a feel for what it costs him in his life. He's a self-aware guy, and he has no problem talking about his various issues. After revealing his hidden self to the group, he tells us that all the women in his life, his lovers especially, have said the same thing to him in difficult times."

"What's that?" Jean asked.

"They all have said to him, at one time or another, 'Do I mean anything to you?' And they almost always say it with tears in their eyes, tears he cannot even feel because, to use his words, he feels 'behind a wall'."

"That's his racket. Hiding behind the wall," Jean said.

"Yes," I said. "But wait. Here's where the specifics become so key."

Jean nodded, giving me her full attention.

It felt almost uncomfortably strange to have her full attention, but I continued. "Steve doesn't know why he does whatever it is he does, or how he gets behind the wall. All he knows is he always ends up behind that wall, numb. Barely able to speak."

Jean took a deep breath. I could tell she was tracking every word.

"For Steve, one of the stand-outs from this discovery process is his sensitivity to criticism. And he absolutely hates it when women don't listen to him. He especially hates it when he is falsely accused of something. This turned out to be an important clue. Bottom line: when criticized, not listened to, and especially when falsely accused, Steve completely shuts down. His first wife had a hard time with this pattern. She wanted to feel close to him, but she felt like she couldn't get to her husband—sometimes for days—because he was behind a wall. Steve reported to the group that she would often say, 'I feel like I don't mean anything to you at all!' And now he and his second wife were stuck in the same painful pattern."

"Sounds typical," Jean said. "People tend to recreate the same dynamic in one relationship after another."

I nodded. "Right. So common."

"So, what happened with the guy?"

"Steve," I said. "Well, by this time, he was quite unsettled. The hot seat was getting hotter. He kept saying: 'I don't want another divorce! But I have no idea what I'm doing that drives women away. I really need help here.'" I paused.

Jean's eyes met mine. She blinked, signaling me to go on.

"Tullah speaks to the group at that point. She says to us: 'See how his body language just changed? That's key for this type of transformation. Then she looks at Steve and says: 'You need to give up figuring it out and truly feel that desperation. You must sincerely ask for and genuinely want help. You can't do this alone, Steve.' He nodded in agreement at which point Tullah said, 'I think you're ready to see what you do to push the women you love away.'"

I paused. Once again, Jean nodded her head and said, "Go on."

"Okay. So, I need to give you a little of the backstory on Steve."

"More context," she said, deadpan.

"Yes. More context," I said, matching her deadpan with mine, and delving right into the story. "Steve grew up in San Francisco, in the Richmond District. He has a very clear memory of the day his mother sent him down to the corner grocery for the first time. His mom had never sent him to the store alone before, but she had a newborn, so she gave Steve some coins and told him to bring back a loaf of bread."

I didn't need to explain to Jean that this type of early life event stands out in memory precisely because they are first-time experiences, markedly different from what came before. I used one of her favorite metaphors, saying: "It was one of those fish-out-of-water moments." It was my way of acknowledging that she already knew everything I was saying. I was also, once again, letting her know that she had deeply influenced my thinking on these matters.

Time and again, I'd heard Jean talk about these watermark experiences and was warmed when she described them now: "Right," she said. "It's as though we're fish who've only ever known water. Then someone throws us up in the air just long enough for us to gasp, look around, and realize there's more than water in the universe before we splash back down. That breaks the familiar trance and tags the experience for long-term memory."

I smiled. It had been weeks since I'd heard her speak so articulately, much less string three sentences together.

Between Jean and me, it went without saying that being sent to the corner grocery for a loaf of bread, while a totally new experience for Steve, was not traumatic. It also went without saying that, for many people, their earliest memories track back to a traumatic event so frightening and beyond the familiar they became totally overwhelmed.

Jean and I had talked many times about how early life experiences lead to neurotic behavior in adulthood. She was fully aware that the mystery of her push-away behavior was rooted in childhood. But she'd never been able to see what the specific behavior was or how she could change it.

At this point in the conversation, I wanted to share some of Tullah's writing on the topic. It was a bit of a risk; I knew there was a good chance Jean would dismiss her authority, insist she had nothing new to say, or criticize her writing. Nonetheless, it felt key to the matter at hand, so I ventured to ask, "Can I read you an article Tullah wrote?"

"Is it long?" she asked.

"I'll just read the most relevant part," I said. "It's only a couple of paragraphs."

"Okay," she said.

I opened my MacBook Pro and pulled up a doc containing a blog Tullah had asked me to edit for her a few days earlier. "Here it is," I said. "This is the part I want to read to you."

I reached for a glass of water, took a drink and cleared my throat. I began to read the passage very deliberately and loud enough for her to hear without strain:

> Our identity, our sense of self-in-the-world and in relationship with others, is still forming at age three or four. If intense emotions arise that we are too young and inexperienced to know we will survive, we become overwhelmed. In our child's mind, we don't know the difference between a psychological threat and a physical threat. The feelings are so intense, we don't just fear we are going to die, we think we are actually dying. To protect ourselves, we react in some way and ward off the perceived threat. If we survive (and we usually do since psychological threats are

rarely deadly) the psyche—at a deep, unconscious level—registers, "Hey! That worked!" Next time we feel similarly threatened or overwhelmed, we use the same strategy. And, once again, it works. Now we have the beginnings of a defense mechanism, an unconscious reaction the ego uses to protect itself from anxiety when there is some kind of threat or conflict. That mechanism becomes the cornerstone of an entire defensive structure. We build on the foundation of our successful strategy, incident by incident, brick-by-brick, each and every time we feel threatened. We don't even realize we're building on that initial reaction; it's just the way we cope, the way we navigate challenges—for better or worse. Like a reflex, the defense mechanism kicks in lightning fast, simply because it lives so far below conscious awareness we are oblivious to the influence it has on our behavior, on how we perceive and move about our world.

I stopped and put my Mac aside.

"Sounds like she knows what she's talking about," Jean said.

"She nailed it, don't you think? She doesn't call it the blind spot but it's obviously the same dynamic. The defensive structure is invisible; it exists in a blind spot we cannot see. But others see it, and they feel the effect of it."

I almost said, "And that effect is what makes people go away," but thought better of it. Best not to make it too personal and push the agenda at this point. Jean had a keen mind; she would no doubt make the connection herself. I looped back to the story about Steve.

"So Tullah asked Steve about his other early memories. He talked about his dad, about his first day at school, nothing really dramatic, then his face flushed as a particular memory popped into his mind."

Jean's eyes opened. She was listening with more than just her ears. I had the distinct feeling we were approaching a wholly different point of no return. Again, she waved her hand for me to continue. I told her Steve's story, rather, the story of Steve's marathon hot seat, doing my best to describe the way Tullah worked to position him in just the right way so he could "see" what was previously in his blind spot.

"So, Steve was about five years old. He often played in the vacant lot next to his house with a group of his friends. But on this particular day, he was out there alone, tossing a ball up in the air then catching it. He walked closer to the house and began throwing the ball against the wall. He got bored. He started scuffing his feet around in the dirt and wondering why his friends hadn't come out to play. His foot hit something buried in the ground. He got down on his knees and started sweeping dirt away from the object. It's a hex nut! He'd never seen one quite that big.

"He dug the piece of metal out of the ground. He dusted it off, flipped it around in his hands. He liked the weight of it, liked the way the metal felt in his hand. He tossed it in the air and caught it several times. It was quite a bit heavier than a ball. Next, he tossed it against the wall. It chipped the paint. Whoops! He walked away from the house toward the fence, tossed the hex nut in the air and let it fall to the ground. He liked the thump it made when it hit the dirt. He tossed it even higher. Thud! He tossed it higher still. He watched it go up and . . . uh-oh . . . it came down on the other side of the fence.

"He had no way of knowing the little girl who lived across the street was on the other side of that fence. When the hex nut came down and hit her on the head, she started wailing in pain. Steve raced to the corner of the lot, jumped the fence and ran in her direction. He could see that she was bleeding, but she got up and ran toward home as soon as she saw him.

"Steve's memory of what happened next was in shards. Bit by bit, with Tullah leading and the other participants reflecting what they saw, he was able to piece it together."

Jean sighed and said, "That's not easy to do."

"No kidding," I said.

"So, what happened?" she asked.

"Tullah kept prompting Steve to tell more of his story. He shared that he'd never been in serious trouble before that day; he was always considered a good boy. Now he was dragged upstairs and pinned in the corner of his mother's kitchen with several adults shouting at him—yelling, questioning, and pointing at him as if he'd hurt the girl on purpose. He tried to speak, to explain that he didn't even know she was there. It was an accident! He didn't mean to hurt her. But he couldn't speak. Each time he started to open his mouth to explain, a finger flew toward him and repeatedly poked at the air a few inches from his face. Loud, angry voices kept telling him he was bad, bad, bad.

"The hot seat was getting seriously hot. Steve was clearly reliving the experience fully. One moment, he was talking and describing the scene, and the next he was stiff as a board, as if he was no longer there.

"At that point Tullah spoke to the group, explaining that memories like this don't tell the whole story; we must find a way to open the memory to see what secrets it holds."

Jean reached out and touched my hand. "That makes total sense. I've always hoped someone could help me do that."

"I know. It's no small task."

"A bit like coming back from the dead," she said.

It took some doing to bring the conversation around, but after Jean said her piece, I circled back and continued from where I left off.

"Steve was in the hot seat with Tullah directing him. All of us were very attentive while he attempted to make sense of his memory. He had one foot in the present and one foot in the past. He had no defense against adults; he couldn't deflect the anger flying into his face. Especially upsetting to him was the fact that his mother did not defend him. She knew he wouldn't hurt anyone. Why was she just sitting there? He could no longer think. His body was frozen. That's when Tullah asked: And what did you say to yourself in that moment?

"Steve stretched his arm out straight, his palm facing out as if to say, 'Stop!' When he opened his mouth to speak, it was the voice of an angry five-year old. He said: 'You mean nothing to me!'"

Back in the room with Jean, there was a long moment of silence. Then she said, "That would certainly push people away."

I explained what happened next or, more accurately, shared my interpretation of what happened next. Jean sat riveted, listening intently.

"When Steve spoke the words, something in him shifted," I said. "It was as if the memory dissolved and he re-experienced what had happened that day as a complete gestalt, an organized whole that he could grasp as more than the sum of its parts. It was amazing to watch as he recovered something he'd lost. I think that's what they mean by soul retrieval. His innocence, his purity, and his humanity came back. I got the sense that he was actually letting us in, letting the members of the group mean something to him in a way he hadn't been able to for all those years."

I went on to explain how Tullah had led Steve through a series of inquiries so he could integrate his experience and come back to the present with the insight intact. "Steve looked totally different. Calm. And very dear. For the rest of the weekend, he was completely available to the other people in the group. His sensitivity and vulnerability were beautiful. His face was in repose. The heavily guarded, hidden man was nowhere to be seen."

Jean held my gaze for several long moments. She was clearly moved.

"I hate to sound trite," I said to Jean, "but he was reborn."

A heartbeat later, Jean asked: "Do you think you could do that with me?"

33.

"You be my Boswell"

I sat at her bedside, plinking away on my laptop while Jean told me more of her life story. I was fascinated, fully engaged as she told me about that day long ago when an anteater scared the bejesus out of her by crawling up in her lap. And the way the Yequana children giggled when she displayed such fright. And how the whole village celebrated when she adopted the little creature and named him Clovis. We were both having a fabulous time.

When sunset drew near, I said, "Jean, I'm sad to leave, but I promised Bob I'd meet him for dinner. He's probably waiting at the restaurant and on his second beer by now."

She looked at me with deep fondness and total acceptance. I returned the look, raised a hand, and we slapped our hands together, saying in unison, "Damn we're good!"

I started packing up my Mac.

She reached over, touched my arm and said, "You be my Boswell."

Thinking she was showing off her Jeopardy prowess again, I scanned my memory but came up empty. "Who's Boswell?"

She looked at me in that disparaging way of hers and said: "You really are ignorant, aren't you?"

"Ouch." My response was immediate, uncensored. I had no idea James Boswell was a Scottish biographer who'd written *The Life of Samuel Johnson,* one of the most celebrated biographies in the English language.

In the past, Jean's comment would've caused me to collapse into myself, or put a sock in my mouth, or leave the room—sometimes without even excusing myself. Or I'd go up to the kitchen for some milk and cookies. But this time I stayed with her, and with myself.

With my "ouch" still hanging in the air, I took a breath and settled in deeper. For the first time in our long association, I stayed present rather than vanish in the face of one of Jean's insults. That was her blind spot talking, not the woman I loved.

I knew immediately that I had to be stronger and clearer than ever before. I had identified my own blind spot and pulled the blinders off, whereas Jean had not. That made me the responsible party, "the adult" in this situation. How could she be responsible for a dynamic she had no idea she put in motion? Her corrosive pattern of tossing a rude, off-handed remark my way had always held sway over our relationship in such moments. Not this time. Without any drama, without adding extra emotion to what was happening in the moment, I'd simply said, "Ouch."

And she got it. For the first time in our long friendship, she apologized. "Pussycat, I'm sorry. I didn't mean . . ." her voice trailed off.

I could almost see the pieces fall into place. I looked in her eyes with no judgment and nodded. "That's it," I said in a quiet voice. "That's the thing you do to push people away."

She looked deep into my eyes. I saw the tears rise up in hers. Then, in a softer-than-soft voice, she said, "Where's Gloria." It wasn't a question; it was an observation. The look on her face was reflective. Startled. Proud. Ashamed. Amazed. A myriad of subtle expressions and complex feelings kaleidoscoped across her face. We sat in silence for several long minutes.

The next day I was moved to fill the gap in our exploration about the blind spot by sharing my hot seat experience. "Would you like to hear it?" I asked.

"Yeah," she said.

"I'll get us some tea first."

"Good idea. I'll have Earl Grey."

Five minutes later, I returned with two steaming cups of tea. I arranged her pillows so she could sit up a bit and dragged my chair a little closer. Tulip jumped up on the bed and made herself comfortable as if she, too, wanted to hear the story.

"So . . ." I began. "I took the hot seat and started talking about what I did know of my pattern. For years, I'd been aware that I was a skilled escape artist. When things got rough, I simply disappeared."

"I've seen you do it many times," she said.

I nodded. "I'm sure. The thing is it could get pretty ugly. When I got pissed off or frustrated, I would turn my back in disgust and say, 'Screw this. I'm outta here.' I quit a number of jobs that way. I abruptly ended relationships, often over relatively minor slights, and walked out, saying, 'I'm through.

We're done.' If I was in a seminar or a class and got antsy or bored, I'd head out to the restroom, go out for a walk, or simply ditch class and never go back. I would leave work early over some fabricated excuse. Or I'd simply disappear with no explanation whatsoever."

"That's an interesting way of keeping people away," she said, reaching for Tulip. "Come, pussy." The cat did not move.

"No kidding," I said. "I told the group about this incredibly painful incident of my disappearing act that happened when I was sixteen. John Hershey had asked me to the Christmas dance. He was a handsome guy, a doctor's son and football player who didn't have a jock attitude."

"Washed behind the ears," Jean said with a smile.

I smiled back and reached for her arm, giving it a gentle squeeze. "Yes. Washed behind the ears. John had never had a girlfriend, and I had never had a boyfriend. That was a big deal in the 10th grade. Most of our friends had already coupled up at least once. But we were both shy. I was a cheerleader on the JV pep squad, but horribly insecure and self-conscious. I always felt out of place, like I just didn't belong.

"John's friends had prodded him to ask me to the dance. I felt elated. My mom took me to the mall in Woodland Hills to find a dress. The day before the dance, I bought John a white rose boutonnière. As the day approached, I grew more and more anxious. This was my first real date, and I was a hot mess. When five thirty rolled around the day of the dance, my mom got after me to get ready, but I couldn't pull myself together. At six o'clock, I still hadn't showered or done my hair. John had a 7:00 reservation at the Hungry Hunter. I just couldn't do it. I told Mom I was sick and plopped down on my bed. She could see I wouldn't be able to go. But John was already on his way to pick me up so she sat in the living room and waited. When he arrived, she did the talking. I didn't even go to the door. John gave her the corsage he'd bought me and left. I felt simultaneously relieved and utterly miserable."

Jean looked at me, her eyes full of compassion. She understood how this experience could become a bruise that wouldn't fully heal, casting a greenish-yellow hue over my high school years. John had been "stood up," and the guys in my class would never forgive me.

"The same sort of thing happened to me," Jean said. "Many times. Whatever I do to push people away must be unforgivable because people go away for good."

I nodded.

"Then what happened?" she asked.

I continued to share my hot seat experience.

"So with Tullah directing me, I could go inside and look around, see if an image appeared. I got nothing. She asked me to go back to my earliest memory. That was easy. I'd often wondered why I remembered this specific event so clearly. I couldn't have been more than four years old. My family lived in Pasadena. This was long before whole neighborhoods were torn down to build a web of freeways. We had a smallish one-story, three-bedroom house. It was tucked back away from the road a bit. The yard was small, but lush.

"I remember very clearly standing on a cement walk that went around the side of the house; I was maybe four years old. There was a bank of ivy next to the walkway that covered the ground out to the street. I can still see the broad, shiny leaves of the ivy.

"Tullah led me into the memory, tapping into feelings, sensations, and sounds. My mind scrambled to connect the dots, took a stab at an explanation, hazarded a guess as to what happened on that walkway. Did some random passerby molest me? Was there an earthquake? A snake?

"But my emotional state wasn't at all agitated. In fact, I felt a certain exuberance and curiosity. Tullah told me to just hang out there for a while. I walked up and down the walkway in my mind's eye. I could see a large glass window on the side of the house that looked into the dining area. Tullah asked, 'What's happening inside the house?'

"I felt a sense of anticipation, but nothing came. Then Tullah asked, 'Can you hear anything?' I said, 'Yes, sort of . . . Mommy is there. And a couple kids from the neighborhood. I can hear them giggling.' She led me further into the memory, encouraging me to keep looking, feeling, listening. Minutes passed. The room was silent. Then, BOOM! I am back on the walkway. I look through the window and see a birthday cake on the table. It has two candles on it. My memory opens up as I say, 'It's my little brother's birthday.'

"Tullah encouraged me. She said, 'Go ahead and hang out there a little longer.' I started to overthink it; I was still wondering what horrible thing might have occurred on that cement path. Tullah spoke softly, guiding me gently. She must've sensed that whatever happened wasn't traumatic because she said something to that effect."

Jean was right there with me as I told my story. I looked at her. Her eyes told me that she was tracking the whole process, which wasn't all that different from the childhood regression work she did with her clients—up to a point. She pulled Tulip into her lap.

I continued, "Tullah kept nudging me to explore the sensory elements of my experience. She urged me to get out of my head and just allow whatever was there to arise. I continued to watch and wait and breathe. I no longer felt the group around me. I even forgot Tullah was there. Then, somehow, I was right there in the experience, as if I'd been transported back in time. The entire event flooded back. My mother was inside the house. She was busy with the party, the birthday cake, the children. She didn't know I'd gone out into the yard. Completely absorbed in the party, her all-seeing eye had lost track of me. That powerful mother-protecting-her-cubs instinct watching my every move was on pause. Sweet freedom! My mom wasn't a helicopter mom; she was a fleet of helicopters. I always felt like I was under surveillance. She was that overprotective. So, when the surveillance cameras were not on me, I could feel it. Big time. 'Ha! I've escaped!' was the feeling. An unknown, otherworldly feeling of joy flooded my body. It was just me, the ivy, and the natural world. I giggled and skipped up and down the path. I loved feeling the soft breeze on my skin and in my hair. I felt utterly and completely free in a way I did not know was possible.

"Then, in a small childlike voice, three triumphant words spilled out of my mouth: 'I can disappear.'"

Jean's eyes met mine and we locked in on each other. I saw colors in her eyes I'd never seen before. I sensed she could see how my blind spot had formed, but her words said otherwise.

"I'm not sure I understand," she said.

"I didn't really get it at first either," I said. "Compared to others in the group, my experience wasn't dramatic. There was no trauma involved. But the experience stuck, which meant something entirely new had happened that was fundamentally different from anything I'd ever experienced before."

Jean nodded, "Like the fish thrown up in the air."

"Right." I said, then continued, "My mom was very over-protective. She watched us like a hawk. I wasn't aware of it, because I'd never known anything else. But to suddenly escape that pressure . . . it was pure freedom."

"I can imagine," Jean said. "My experience was the opposite. My mother couldn't care less what I was doing."

"Right. So, you had too much freedom."

"And not enough love," she replied, her voice sounding like that of a lost child.

I reached to comfort her, but she snapped her arm away. Then she looked at me, her face empty of all expression, and said, "Go on."

It felt awkward to skip over the moment, to ignore the child that had always been ignored, expected to be ignored. But I didn't know what to do other than reach out and touch her, so I continued. "You weren't getting enough love, whereas I was being smothered. I didn't even know it until that day when I made my escape and stayed out in the yard. And here's the rub, that response became a template for how I lived my life. And the template still exists—persists, really. It's always there, ready to protect me the moment it perceives a threat. But it does this from way beneath my everyday awareness."

"In your unconscious," she said. "Shoo, pussy." Tulip jumped off the bed.

"Right. 'I can disappear' became my default response to any kind of pressure or expectation from others. And let's face it: life is full of pressure and times when we're expected to be a certain way. I cannot tell you how intense my impulse to disappear becomes in those moments."

She nodded. "I've seen you do it. Just suddenly get up and announce that you have to leave. I always thought you were just rude."

"I just can't help myself. At a certain point, I get so antsy, I have to bolt."

"Interesting. I push people away, and you get up and leave."

"Yes. And even though part of me knows it's impolite or just plain the wrong thing to do, once I'm gone, I feel liberated, as if disappearing allows me to be who I really am, rather than who people want me to be. That day, on the sidewalk, was the first time I slipped out of my mom's world and touched down in my own world—outside, among the plants, feeling the breeze. And the birds. The way they were singing . . . it was as if I'd never heard them before."

"Birdsongs," Jean said.

I smiled and nodded. "That experience planted a seed in me that grew into my great love for nature, a bit like your experience in the Glade."

"Yes, I can see that," she said.

Our eyes met in a moment of complete stillness. Then she smiled, and said, "So. When do I get on this hot seat?"

34.

The Bird Girl

Over the next two weeks, Jean surprised us all. She became less demanding and rarely complained. She was more patient than usual. A deep calm seemed to pervade her room. She was uncomfortable, but not at all hungry. Meanwhile, her bones seemed to stick out more and more every day. She would ask for some chicken broth or a diet root beer. She'd point to the window and ask me to open it, then tell me to close it two minutes later. One foggy day, when a chill breeze prompted me to reach for the window, she said, "Leave it open, pussycat. I like to listen to the seagulls." She patted the bed beside her. "Come. Sit. Did you know that seagulls are highly intelligent? Almost as smart as crows."

"Crows? Intelligent? They nest in our backyard. Their squawking annoys the hell out of me. Especially when they wake me up in the morning."

"I know," she said. "They used to irritate me, too. But now I can hear it. They're just talking to each other."

I nodded, curious, then remembered Jean's great love for the book *Green Mansions: a Romance of the Tropical Forest*. She'd read it half a dozen times in her girlhood and always envied the demigoddess, Rima, who could speak the language of the birds.

"So those seagulls are talking to each other? What are they saying?"

"Mostly they talk about air currents and where the fish are. You know. Seagull stuff."

"That makes sense," I said.

Jean looked at Tulip as if for confirmation and stroked her under her chin. "Pussy knows," she said. Since she'd come home from the hospital, Tulip was always close by her side, holding a vigil. "The last authority is Pussy."

Every visitor that stopped by would hear her latest Tulip pun: "Pussy went out into the meadow with her cell phone and said, 'Can you hear meow?'"

Then she would hold Tulip up to her face for a nose-rub and say, "I don't like to be kissed by quadrupeds. Pussy was willing to overcome her natural way of kissing and go nose-to-nose like an Eskimo."

In the world according to Jean, humans possessed only one divine attribute: Humor. And her sense of humor was truly divine.

One day, a nurse walked into her room and said, "I'd like to take your blood pressure."

Without missing a beat, Jean replied: "Okay, but only if you don't give it back."

If a visitor became overly sad or, God forbid, morbid about her decision to die, she would flip her head and say: "Don't wane on my parade. I'll wax until I wane."

It didn't matter how many times I heard one of her puns; they were always funny. It was her deadpan delivery. And her charming giggle when she made someone smile or laugh.

We continued to talk at length about the blind spot phenomenon when we had time alone. We toyed with a theory or two. I challenged some of Tullah's basic assumptions, most notably the idea that the blind spot comes into play as a result of an early "decision." Jean thought my thesis worthy of further inquiry. I wanted to know if a child's brain actually has decision-making functions that early in life. When I suggested that it seemed to me they were acting more from instinctive intelligence than choice, she said, "Now you're splitting semantic hairs."

"Maybe. But let me ask you this: at what point in a child's development does choice come into play? Choice implies making a decision, right? And a decision implies the person has multiple options and takes those options into consideration. Do you really think a child of two would be capable of weighing options? I'm just curious: at what age can a child hold two different possibilities in mind and make a choice between the two? I know I'm splicing hairs, but you're the one who taught me to be precise with words. I'm just saying, it seems to me, it's not so much a decision as a declaration. Werner used to call it *a declaration of being.*[52]

"So you're looking at it ontologically."

"Exactly! That's it," I said. "From an ontological perspective that pivotal moment in time forces a person to invent a way of being in the world that shapes their character."

"Makes sense," she said.

"The declaration then becomes 'the way it is.' It's an inner command, sort of like a mandate."

"Not sort of," she said. "At that deep level of consciousness, it is literally a mandate."

"Right. And once the mandate is declared, it slips into the unconscious and goes on automatic pilot. And that becomes a person's blind spot."

She looked at me with a soft smile on her face. "So, that's why it's vital to see the point where it all began: once the unconscious mandate becomes conscious, you're no longer controlled by it."

"That's been my experience," I said. "But it's not a quick fix. The real work is learning to see when my blind spot kicks in, and that takes time."

"I don't have time," she said. "But like I always say: anything you set out to do expands or contracts to fit the time

---

[52] I first heard this phrase in the early 80s while working at a company called "Hermenet" that Werner Erhard founded along with Fernando Flores. A Chilean engineer and former cabinet minister of Salvador Allende, Flores obtained his PhD at UC Berkeley where his study of Heidegger and other philosophers influenced his work on workflow. I held a staff position at that company for a few months, and took part in their "Entrepreneurial Tools" course, which examined the ways we humans live from ontological declarations of being, largely unaware we are doing so. I often referred back that insight when reflecting on the blind spot phenomenon.

allotted. Sounds like I'll finally get that instant enlightenment I was promised at EST."

"I vote for that," I replied.

"So, what's it been like for you since you had this grand revelation? Are you still disappearing all the time?"

"Not so much," I replied. "Now I notice when the pattern kicks in. Most of the time, anyway. In the past, that impulse to disappear was always in my blind spot. Because I can see it now, I have the option to do something differently. I still get the urge to bolt or slip away when I feel uncomfortable, but more and more I can choose to stay with whatever is going on. And when I do, remarkable things happen. I might meet someone interesting and fall into a great conversation that I would've missed entirely if I'd disappeared."

The discussion about the blind spot became our primary focus during our daily visits. The more we talked about it, the more Jean wanted to uncover and re-experience what we started to call the *inception point* of the blind spot. But we were just talking about it rather than diving in. Again, and again, she asked me to take her through the process.

I felt wary, didn't trust myself to lead her into her unconscious. I feared that her pattern, and what Tullah called the negative ego, would slay me. I'd seen it happen during the intensive. When a person was on the hot seat, their defense mechanism would grow stronger and stronger each time it was about to be revealed. Tullah had explained it this way: "When the negative ego perceives a threat and realizes the jig is up, it will fight to the death rather than be exposed."

I'd been mulling this over for days, feared that I was too close to Jean, would lose my center should she attack. I told her I couldn't do the process alone, that success depended on the group dynamic. "It's not like therapy where you get reflections and feedback from one person," I said. "Working in a group, you have several people reflecting back to you what they see. That sorta fills in the blind spot somehow."

She looked at me, puzzled.

I explained it further with a metaphor: "It's a bit like buying new jeans. I don't know about you, but when I try on a pair of jeans, I want to see how they look from behind. Looking at the pants straight on doesn't give me a full view. That's why I like dressing rooms that have three-way mirrors. I need to see from multiple angles and get the full view from all sides. It's the same with the blind spot work. Rather than have someone telling you what you're unable to see, you get to show yourself, to catch yourself in the act, so to speak. But that takes multiple mirrors."

"Can you ask that woman to come and help? What was her name?"

"Tullah. I'm afraid she's out of the country" I said.

Her eyes were pleading. In all the years of our friendship, I'd never seen that much emotion on Jean's face.

Struggling to hold back her tears, Jean's voice cracked as she whimpered, "Why can I never find someone who can help me?" It was an understandable lament. After all, hadn't she helped countless clients around the world understand and forgive the wounds of their childhood? Was it so much to ask that someone do the same for her?

Over the years, she had guided many people through their inner terrain, into the emotional body where the hurts of childhood lived and festered. Like Tullah, her knowledge was uniquely informed. The Yequana don't suffer the mind; they don't even have a negative ego or false self. Nor do they have a defensive structure or blind spot. They are people whose bodies and psyches are shaped by a fully enriched infancy and childhood. The Yequana children did not grow up and become wounded, neurotic adults. They did not need inner child work. They did not get tangled up in low self-esteem or lack of confidence. In fact, they had no concept of self-esteem. Their worth was firmly established since birth. Young and old alike were comfortable in their own skin. No anxiety disorders. No depression. No suicides, no sociopaths or psychopathic killers.

Jean had witnessed and been steeped in all of this during her time in the jungle. Her point of view was informed by a culture that had not veered from the continuum. The field of psychology lacks this perspective. Like New Yorkers who talk about the concrete jungle never having seen a real jungle, psychologists work to build their clients' self-esteem, never having seen people who are simply, elegantly, joyously alive.

I felt powerless to grant Jean's final wish. Tullah's warning about how the ego "fights to the death" kept looping through my mind. I thought about my father, how his defenses had crumbled in the days before his death, how the real, unguarded man had come to the fore. It occurred to me that Jean's defenses were already crumbling. Maybe her ego would not put up such a fierce fight. I decided there was nothing to lose. I would do all I could to give her this gift. Beatrice and I would put Jean on the hot seat and help her see her blind spot.

"Tell you what, I'll call Beatrice. She's the woman who introduced me to Tullah, has actually been apprenticing with her. She's quite skilled. And she's one of my best friends, so I'm sure she'll be happy to drive up from Santa Barbara."

Jean sing-songed, "Oh, pussycat that would be sooooo very lovely. Will you do that for me?"

"But of course!" I said.

I called Beatrice an hour later and asked her to come to Sausalito.

"She wants to get in the hot seat," I said.

"I'd be honored," Beatrice enthused. She knew that Jean was very important to me and, moreover, she'd been deeply influenced by Jean's book in her parenting style. "She's the reason I carried mine around in a sling. I credit her with the incredible people my children are growing into."

By now, Jean was sleeping much of the day. Her speech had slowed. She spoke very softly. Her words were hard to understand. She would often fall asleep mid-sentence. But when she was awake, her mind was still sharp.

She hadn't eaten in 40 days. I asked Beatrice to come as soon as possible. She got up early the next morning and drove up from her place in Santa Barbara. Bob met her on the driveway when she arrived at our house.

"Thanks for coming," he said. "It means more to G than you know."

"Oh, I know," Beatrice said. "I couldn't say no."

The three of us sat down for coffee while I did my best to fill Beatrice in on Jean's defensive structure, the effect it had on her relationships, and the frustration she lived with about the mysterious pattern. There was no point in speculating on the nature of her blind spot. The whole point of the process was to guide the person into the deep recesses of memory, where they could "see" the moment they became blind.

"It's funny, B," I said. "Jean's work with people isn't all that different. She just goes at it from a different perspective. There are some key differences. For one thing, it's just her and the client, but she totally gets what we're after. We even came up with a new term for the moment the blind spot forms: the inception point."

"Oh, that's good," Beatrice said. "I'll definitely use that one. So, it sounds like we don't need to give her an overview."

"No need," I said. "She's ready."

The four-day intensive with Tullah typically started on a Thursday afternoon. Participants would settle in, have a light dinner, then gather for the first session. The facilitators would spend the evening giving an overview to lay the groundwork, doing their best to explain how the hot seat process works. One of her apprentices would then tell the story of his or her hot seat experience, then everyone would go off to their rooms and get a good night's sleep. The following morning, they were primed and ready.

"Okay, then," Beatrice stood up and said, "Let's do this."

I said goodbye to Bob and told him I'd call him later. "Maybe the three of us will go out to dinner."

"I'd like that," he said. "And G . . . I'm so proud of you for pulling this together."

When we arrived at the houseboat, the front door was open. Jean's housekeepers were busily tidying upstairs. I asked them to take the day off, telling them my friend and I wanted some time alone with Jean. They were happy for the break in routine.

Jean was as bright eyed as I'd seen her in weeks. She must've thanked Beatrice six times in the half hour we spent talking while the two of them got acquainted. Finally, it was time to dive in. When I asked, "What's your earliest memory, Jean?" she smiled and said, "I thought you'd never ask."

I looked at her, rolled my eyes, and said, "You."

Beatrice took the lead. "Relax, okay, Jean? We'll go slow. You just breathe. Let it all go and, when you're ready, tell us about your earliest memory."

Jean took a breath, blinked several times, then half-groaned, half whispered. "Sitting in my high chair . . . in . . . the kitchen," she said. "But. . . I don't know. . . have never been able to figure out its significance."

I knew this for a fact; she had mentioned the memory several times before. "Tell me what you see," I said.

"Shouldn't . . . you . . . regress me first?"

Leave it to Jean to direct her own process.

"No regression," Beatrice said. "Just say what you see."

"I . . . see. . . a dirty window. And . . . mother is there." Her voice was halting and hoarse.

"Okay, what else?" Beatrice prompted.

Silence.

"Just look around," I said. "What do you see?"

Again silence. We allowed her to rest there for several minutes.

"My mother . . . is moving around. I think she's . . . she's making some food."

"Can you smell anything?" I asked.

She nodded. "It's sweet."

We continued like this for another twenty minutes. With each shard of memory, Jean moved deeper into her emotional body where time does not exist. Beatrice and I continued to track her, to gently urge her forward if her senses shut down or reflect what we noticed when her defenses reared up. Jean's ego put up very little resistance. I could see that she was busy at work behind her closed eyelids. Her face was in repose.

After another long silence I asked, "What do you hear?"

"Nothing," she said.

Another long pause. Then, "Oh, wait."

"Just listen for a moment," I said. "There's no hurry. Let the sound come to you, don't go after it."

"I . . . I . . . I hear a noise," she said. "It's Mother . . . she's chewing."

"What else?"

"She's chewing. I'm hungry. Why isn't she feeding me? That noise, the sound of her chewing, it makes me sick."

That sounds familiar, I thought. No wonder she got so angry about the tortilla chips.

"She should be . . ."her voice trailed off. Clearly, she was reaching for something.

The room was still. A gentle breeze from the bay drifted through the window. Seagulls chattered away on the docks nearby. Beatrice sat motionless, her full attention on Jean. It was as if she were there in that kitchen, sitting to the side, witnessing everything that was happening. "Take your time, Jean," she said. "We're right here with you."

Jean's eyelids were closed, but I could see that her eyes were moving around beneath the skin. After several long moments, she said the phrase, "She should be ..." again. Another long pause. She repeated "She should be ..." two more times, then managed to complete the sentence. "She should ..." pause, "be feeding ME!" Her tone had an insistent quality, like she was speaking from the voice of authority. And, of course, she was right. In a world where mothers had not strayed from the continuum, a hungry baby's mom would be tuned in enough to know exactly what her infant needs.

"That's right. She should," I said.

Beatrice asked, "What are you going to do about it?"

A wave of anger rolled over Jean's face. Her arms were too weak to lift off the bed, but she flailed them as best she could.

"Are you signaling Mother?" I asked.

Jean nodded, her face was full of wanting. "She won't look at me ... She's eating ... I'm the baby. Me. Me. I'm the baby. She should be feeding me—I'm the baby!" Her voice took on even more authority. Her longing was tangible.

"Me hungry. Me." Her statement was a demand.

"Jean. We know you're hungry," I said. "But Mother isn't paying attention. She doesn't see you."

Jean closed her eyes. Turned away.

"Seems you want to move away from Mother," I said.

Jean nodded.

"We know you cannot speak yet," Beatrice said. "But you're feeling something inside. If you did have words what would you be saying?"

Silence.

"It looks like you are angry," I said. "Jean, are you angry?"

"No," she said. Her affect was completely flat.

Beatrice asked, "Can you still feel what baby is feeling?"

"Yes."

"What would she say if she could talk?"

Jean jerked her head back. The words she spoke were familiar to me. I'd heard her speak them any number of times. But the way she said them now was almost spooky. In the voice of an innocent little girl, she said, "You're an idiot."

Immediately, her eyes flew open. She looked at me and held my gaze for several long seconds. Then she eyed Beatrice and smiled a smile I will never forget. Her face was splashed with color. The expression of love and repose on her face told me all I needed to know: she had seen what she had not been able to see, what she'd been totally blind to up until that moment. No one had told her what she does, what her blind spot hides from view. She had shown herself.

When I walked into her room the following day, Jean was asleep. I sat at her bedside reading *The New Yorker* while waiting for her to wake up. She smiled when she opened her eyes and reached for my hand. "Darling. Come. Sit." These would be her last words to me. She looked in my eyes. Her face, so smooth, seemed to be that of a young girl. She slipped off to sleep. Half a minute later, her eyelids fluttered, and her eyes opened again, as wide as the sky. Not a word was said, and yet the sparkle in her eyes spoke the language of forever.

Epilogue

From Gloria's perspective

I started working on this book a few years after Jean's death and quickly realized the importance of her connection with Gloria Steinem. The psychological insights the story wanted to unfold seemed to hinge on that relationship. In addition, on a more personal level, I wanted to clear up the mystery surrounding their friendship.

In May of 2016, I had occasion to speak with Ms. Steinem on the phone. I told her of Jean's concern, certainty really, that her own behavior had caused the friendship to end. "She blamed herself," I explained, "felt certain she'd offended you and, in her words, 'pushed you away.'"

"That's ridiculous," Gloria replied, "It was a question of geography."

She went on to tell me that she had once visited Jean on her houseboat in Sausalito and held her in the highest regard. She had no memory of any slight or offensive behavior on

Jean's part, nor did she recall having ignored phone calls or letters from Jean.

The highlight of my 20-minute phone conversation with Gloria was hearing her say, "I still give Jean's book [*The Continuum Concept*] to anyone I know who's having a baby."

I also felt quite touched by the significance Ms. Steinem assigns to Jean's account of life among the original peoples of the Amazon. She told me she'd been reflecting on Jean's stories of living with the Yequana in the context of a book she had hope to co-author with Wilma Mankiller, Chief of the Cherokee Nation, "about the way of life, the lifeway of original cultures—which, of course, is what Jean had seen up the Amazon—and taking features from them we could learn from. I've been looking for direct descriptions from the people themselves, but so far I haven't found anything as complete as what Jean wrote." Sadly, Wilma Mankiller died in 2015, and the book was never written.

Ongoing Legacy

Jean Liedloff's insights continue to influence several important areas of interest, including evolutionary psychology, psychotherapy, attachment theory, and cultural anthropology, as well as the homeschooling, unschooling, and natural parenting movements. Pediatrician William Sears and his wife Martha, a registered nurse, were inspired by *The Continuum Concept* when they developed *attachment parenting*. Sears took some some of the most important continuum principles and practices, and made them more appealing to mainstream parents. Thanks to the influence Jean's book had on parents, childbirth educators, midwives, doulas, doctors, and holistic health practitioners, "babywearing" is now commonplace and co-sleeping is gaining broad acceptance. Authors such as Gloria Steinem, John Holt, Christian de Quincy, and others have written of Jean's work and helped spread her message of hope for families and society.

Although decades have passed since *The Continuum Concept* was first published, the book continues to sell thousands of copies every year with no promotion other than word-of-mouth. It is widely considered a "classic" in Child Development and is included on the recommended reading lists of countless websites. Likewise, countless parents have proclaimed Jean's book the most important parenting book they've read. The book continues to sell in German, Italian, Dutch, French, Hebrew, Hungarian, Japanese, Polish, Russian, Spanish, Swedish, and Serbo-Croatian. Liedloff's work is as relevant today as it was when *The Continuum Concept* came out in 1975. The significance of Jean's work is evidenced by hundreds of letters she received from parents the world over.

First- and second-generation "continuum kids" (individuals who were brought up by parents who did their best to follow the principles Jean identified) are now grown up and having children of their own. These testimonials often described incredible transformations: chronically stressed mother-baby dyads becoming relaxed and happy for the first time since birth; tantruming toddlers becoming cheerful and cooperative under the influence of newly confident, centered parents; teenagers having no need to rebel when their parents chucked conventional, adversarial attitudes; and parents themselves coming to terms with their own "broken continuum"—finding ways to heal the trauma and reconnect with the feeling of "rightness" Jean found in the jungle and brought home to the pages of her book.

I have met and had occasion to speak at length with many now-adult continuum kids. In my estimation, they have a core sense of self that is not hindered by a shaky psychological foundation full of self-doubt and fear. These clear-eyed young people seem to move through life undeterred by the kind of anti-self feelings that proclaim, "I'm not enough" or, "There's something wrong with me," that plague so many Baby Boomers. Nor do they display the type of low self-esteem and identity confusion that rattles many Gen X-ers and Millennials who have been brought up in a manner far-flung from the requirements of the continuum.

Those reared with even a measure of respect for their continua will have a more solid psychological foundation. Individuals whose upbringing is more consistent with what we are biologically programmed to expect can grow into strong, capable adults. Any measure of respect and degree of alignment can begin to steer us back toward the evolutionary continuum of our antecedents, the lineage to which we all belong.

Acknowledgments

My heart is so full of love for all those who showed up to support me and, when necessary, push me to bring this project to fruition. I want to thank a number of people individually, foremost among them my mother, Carol Gendron. Where would I be if it wasn't for your strength of heart, Mom? Second, my deepest gratitude to Scott Noelle who gave so much of his time and precious energy to ensure this book would be true to the potent message that is *The Continuum Concept.* Special thanks to Anna Ariel for her support and devotion to Jean's legacy.

Deep appreciation to my agent, Terrie Wolf whose foreign rights know-how makes it easy for me to say "Yes!" when publishers from around the world—individuals who share a passion for Jean's insights—ask my permission to translate *Jungle Jean* into their language. Epic gratitude to Brooks Cole for his friendship and amazing work on junglejean.com. Many thanks to Byron Belistos for his publishing expertise, and to Susan Shankin, my indie pub mentor and book designer extraordinaire.

Thank you to my readers who offered valuable feedback: Orion Hawthorn, Bonnie Lee, Arielle Ford, Cheryl Haley, Alexandra Burt, Mark Solomons, Ashley Fincher Franz, and to my sister-in-law Jan Gendron for her bookworm expertise. I am especially grateful to Robert Stryker for his storytelling magic and for having the wherewithal to keep pushing me until I got it right. To Jessica Hadari and the FEM Talks community, I am blessed to be in your company. Thank you for showing me what it is to be part of a heart-centered girl tribe.

Lastly, to my three brothers—Greg, Robert, and Paul— for being there through it all and for spawning our beautiful extended family.

About the Author

 **Geralyn Gendreau** is a California licensed psychotherapist since 1995. She is a playful, soul-provoking, life coach who believes that one of the keys to happiness is being able to laugh at yourself. Her work with clients is grounded in the theories and insights of her mentor, Jean Liedloff, author of *The Continuum Concept*. Her greatest passion is spreading the word on the naturally good-humored child rearing approach of our tribal ancestors, and assisting those who did not have a fully enriched infancy and childhood to understand the impact of "missing experiences" so they can heal that hidden trauma and be free to live the truth of who they really are. https://www.geralyngendreau.com

Made in the USA
Las Vegas, NV
20 June 2021

25106521R00210